Convict Words

Language in Early Colonial Australia

AMANDA LAUGESEN

OXFORD

UNIVERSITY PRESS

OXFORD

UNIVERSITY PRESS

253 Normanby Road, South Melbourne, Victoria 3205, Australia

Oxford University Press is a department of the University of Oxford.
It furthers the University's objective of excellence in research, scholarship,
and education by publishing worldwide in

Oxford New York

Auckland Bangkok Buenos Aires Cape Town Chennai
Dar es Salaam Delhi Hong Kong Istanbul Karachi Kolkata
Kuala Lumpur Madrid Melbourne Mexico City Mumbai Nairobi
São Paulo Shanghai Taipei Tokyo Toronto

OXFORD is a trade mark of Oxford University Press
in the UK and in certain other countries

Laugesen, Amanda.

Convict words: language in early colonial Australia.

Bibliography.
ISBN 0 19 551655 9.

1. English language—Australia—History.
2. English language—Social aspects—Australia.
3. Convicts—Australia. I. Title.

427.994

Edited by Elaine Cochrane
Text and cover designed by Racheal Stines
Typeset by Desktop Concepts P/L, Melbourne
Printed through the Bookmaker Pty Ltd, Australia

Contents

Acknowledgments

Material for this book was gathered from the database of Australian English at the Australian National Dictionary Centre, and from the *Australian National Dictionary*, ed. W.S. Ramson, Oxford University Press, Melbourne, 1988. The collections of the National Library of Australia and the Australian National University libraries provided further important material.

I would like to thank Bruce Moore for reading through drafts and for providing invaluable assistance on the etymologies. The support of other members of the Australian National Dictionary Centre was also much appreciated. Thanks to Elaine Cochrane who undertook the copy-editing.

Publication of this book has been supported by the Publications Committee of the Australian National University.

Introduction

David Collins, one of the first recorders and observers of the new Antipodean colonies, in his *Account of the English Colony in New South Wales* (1798), observed that the term **Botany Bay** was already a 'term of reproach that was indiscriminately cast on every one who resided in New South Wales'.[1] 'Botany Bay' captured the British imagination, seemingly summing up all the evil and immorality of the convict colonies on the other side of the world. Even today, the Australian convict story is popularly seen as the story of this mythic Botany Bay, a depraved or, depending on your point of view, heroic group of criminals banished from their place of birth to a strange and sometimes hostile land where they were subject to a harsh and often arbitrary system of punishment.

Historians have done much to dispel the 'mythic' story of convict Australia, but the popular associations of **flogging, iron-gangs, treadmills**, and brutal **overseers** remain. The scholarly corrective to this rewrites convict history as a complicated story of an evolving system of reform, labour, punishment and discipline, and a colonial society increasingly fraught with tensions produced by an emerging independent society no longer willing to be the dumping ground for Britain's unwanted criminals. It is also a story of the convicts themselves, some undoubtedly **incorrigibles**, but many more aspiring to make something of their lives and this second chance. After gaining their freedom, these **emancipists** formed an essential foundation for the future prosperity of the colonies.

The story of the vocabulary of Australian convictism is shaped by the nature of the society it described and from which it emerged. It reflects the evolution of the convict system. It also reflects the politics of the society as it matured and as **free settlers** arrived. Ultimately, Australian convict society sought to shrug off its image as Botany Bay marked with the convict **birthstain**.

The language of Australian convictism thus reveals the complex nature of this fundamental period in Australian history. It illustrates the importance of words in shaping understandings and perceptions of a society, especially one still in its formative years. Most of these words were, of course, already used in British English—but many came to have new meanings and were more significant to the emerging Australian English. For the most part, many of these terms remain historically specific, but some endured in the lexicon of Australian English.

It is important to note the nature of the evidence for many of these words. Sources are largely either official, or the records of writers who published memoirs, travel writings, or political tracts about colonial society. Freedom of the press in Australia was not secured until 1820, and prior to this, newspapers tended to be the official mouthpiece of government. In particular, the *Sydney Gazette* was used as a means of distributing government orders to the general populace.[2] Official government letters, orders, and messages have been collected in the multi-volume *Historical Records of Australia*. These documents provide insight into the language of administration and bureaucracy. Early publications of private citizens or government officials were published in Britain and, it should be remembered, were aimed primarily at a British and European audience. Nevertheless, such observations of the convict system are invaluable. Other writers sought to promote Australia as a place to emigrate to, such as Edward Curr, who published an *Account of the Colony of Van Diemen's Land, principally designed for the use of emigrants* in 1824.

As the years passed and the convict system evolved, many opponents and reformers published tracts on conditions in the colonies, often with very particular agendas that coloured their language. A good example is William Ullathorne, a Catholic priest, who published his observations on the convict system as he had experienced it in the 1830s in *The Horrors of Transportation briefly unfolded to the People* (1838). Ullathorne also gave testimony at commissions investigating the system—his testimony and pamphlets were part of a large literature that condemned the convict system and sought either to reform or to end it. This literature also reflected the politics of the emancipist and free emigrant struggles. Lurid and sensational accounts of convict life were all part of a political rhetoric, and must be approached as such. When the **anti-transportation** movement began to build in the 1840s, the power of language became central to its politics.

Newspapers and periodicals throughout the convict period built up a record of the language of the colonies, but again reflected, at the very least, the preoccupation of settlers to make the colonies 'respectable' and to downplay the impact of the convict system on the nature of Australian society and culture. The language of the convicts themselves remains fairly hard to find. Some evidence of it has crept in through some of the observers such as Peter Cunningham who had an interest in the more colourful aspects of colonial language. For example, he recorded the term **canary** in reference to convicts in 1827: 'Convicts of but recent migration are facetiously known by the name of *canaries*, by reason of the yellow plumage in which they are fledged at the period of landing.'[3] James Hardy Vaux was the principal source for the **flash** language brought to Australia from the London criminal underworld. His 1812 *New and Comprehensive Vocabulary of the Flash Language* included many words that convicts would have brought with them.

The slang of the convicts therefore is somewhat elusive, although not completely absent from the written record. It is clear, however, that the written records generally reflect the official language of convict administration on the one hand,

and the observations and views of the literate middle and upper classes, often writing for a British audience, on the other.

1788–1820

In 1788 Arthur Phillip led the **first fleet** into Port Jackson where he would establish the first **penal settlement** for Britain. Between 1788 and 1852, 150,000 convicts were to be transported to the eastern half of Australia, with about 25,000 of these women.[4] New South Wales and Van Diemen's Land were established as **convict colonies** and became the destination of English and Irish convicts for whom there was no longer adequate space in the prisons and hulks of the United Kingdom.

A vocabulary of convictism that would remain until the end of the convict period was quickly put into place, with many terms becoming common currency in the new society. Both **hard labour** and **iron collars** were used, as were **absolute emancipation** (1799) or **absolute pardon** (1802), **indulgence** (1794), **conditional pardon** or **emancipation** (1794 and 1792), and **certificate of freedom** (1810; the shortened form **certificate** dates from 1796). These terms reveal the nature of the convict colonies as a place where punishment might be severe, but rewards were also offered as an incentive for reform and good behaviour. As historians have noted, both were essential in an 'open' system of punishment[5]— convicts were not kept in prisons in the early years, but worked during the day and would be housed either in **barracks** (which they built) or in private houses. The need for adequate supervision and discipline in the colonies was shown in the use of terms such as **night-watch** (1793), **overseer** (1788), and **constable** (1794)—all terms that had been in use in Britain for centuries.

The idea of 'public' as applied to aspects of the convict system was present early: **public gang** (1796), **public labour** (1792), **public servant** (1797), and **public store** (1802). 'Public' dates to the fifteenth century in Britain, in the sense 'pertaining to the people as a whole; that belongs to, affects, or concerns the community or nation'. In Australia, the use of 'public' to denote aspects of the convict system reveals the early nature of New South Wales as a penal settlement: it was a 'public' settlement, rather than a place where people came as free settlers and lived 'privately'. **Government** was also used, similarly to 'public', from the earliest period: the convicts were **government workmen** (1803) or **government labourers** (1807), and worked in **government gangs** (1808) on **government labour** (1807). The presence of the **broad arrow** (1803) on government stores, also known as **King's stores** (1801), and convict uniforms was a powerful reminder of the pervasive presence of the British government. The broad arrow was the 'monarch's mark', used to mark government property from the seventeenth century.

The early period of the convict era was one in which convicts were transported to places that at first had no infrastructure, and for which they would be the labour force to build it. They worked in **gangs** (1789) on such tasks as building roads, bridges, and government buildings. Gangs detailed to perform particular kinds of work had particular names describing the kind of work they did, such as **battery gang** (1801) or **road gang** (1819). Gangs were also named according to where they worked, for example, **town gang** (1796).

Convicts were **assigned** (1806) to a **master** (1796) or **mistress** (1813) to work in private homes as servants or to rural properties as labourers. Good behaviour might mean early remission of their sentence through some form of pardon. Once pardoned, they were free to take up land and settle, and the term **convict settler** dates from 1792. Along with the **free settlers** who in the early years arrived only in small numbers, they were dependent on the government for survival. The government stores often provided the only means of survival when times were difficult. The phrases **on the stores** (1801) and **off the stores** (1792) were therefore frequently used in the colonies. It took a number of years before the colonies were self-sufficient.

Subversion of the system, though, also quickly became apparent. Collins noted in 1798 how a convict **absconded** into the **woods** (1788), or (as would become a more frequent Australian phrase from 1804) 'took to the **bush**'. These **absconders** or **runaways** (1790) often became **bushrangers**. The term 'bushranger', now thought of as quite distinctively Australian, was first used in the United States in 1758 in a neutral sense and was used in Australia from 1805. By 1814, a pejorative meaning had become attached to it with numerous government declarations against 'these Banditti, Commonly Called "*Bush Rangers*", Who in the present State of the Country are beyond All Control'.[6] Absconders generally were attempting to escape permanently—few could survive in the bush, and if they tried, they were often forced to turn to **bushranging**. Otherwise, they eventually turned themselves in, or, in some cases, perished in the bush. Punishment might be severe—being **re-transported** ('a sentence they dread more than death', recorded Hunter in 1799),[7] that is, the sentencing of a convict in the colonies to a term at a penal settlement (also known as a **colonial sentence** from 1811) such as **Norfolk Island**, was a frequent response to these crimes, or, in some cases, execution. **Absentees** (1805) on the other hand tended to be convicts who disappeared from work for short periods of time and returned.

The **flash** language, brought from the British criminal underworld, was another form of subversion of authority. Watkin Tench commented on the flash language in 1791, linking it to the continuing immorality of the convicts:

> I have ever been of the opinion, that an abolition of this unnatural jargon would open the path to reformation. And my observations on these people have constantly instructed me, that indulgence in this infatuating cant, is more deeply associated with depravity, and continuance in vice, than is gener-

ally supposed. I recollect hardly one instance of a return to honest pursuits, and habits of industry, where this miserable perversion of our noblest and peculiar faculty was not previously conquered.[8]

The flash terms did contribute, however, to the new colonial lexicon as Cunningham more charitably observed: 'A number of the slang phrases current in St. Gile's *Greek* bid fair to become legitimatized in the dictionary of this colony.'[9] Some examples of flash terms that took on a general currency in the colonies include: **bellowser** (from West Yorkshire and coming to mean one sentenced to life), **lag** (another term for a convict), **gammon** (meaning deceit or nonsense), and **trap** (a police officer).

Thus the early decades of the British presence in Australia, as revealed by its language, were dominated by the language of government and administration, and revealed the overwhelming pervasiveness of that government. This vocabulary also reveals a system of discipline based on rewards and punishment, and the essential role convict labour played in establishing the infrastructure and basis for the future self-governing colonies. It is also clear, however, that the early colonial system and its language were shaped equally by the convicts and their actions. Thus terms such as 'absconding' illustrated the need for the administration to shape itself around convicts as much as it sought to control convict lives. Language reveals the attempt to create an ordered society, but also reveals a society where disorder always threatened—a careful balance of power; a process of negotiation and accommodation.

Lags and Government Men—Terms for Convicts

While 'convicts' is by far the most recognised term used today to refer to those who were transported to Australia, one of the most fascinating aspects of the vocabulary of the convict system is the variety of terms for the convicts that developed. Some of them have already been mentioned: **canary** (1827), adopted because of the yellow uniform (yellow being the traditional European colour of disgrace) and because of the idea of being jailed like a caged canary bird; **government man** (1797) and **government labourer** (1807), along with **crown servant** (1815), **crown labourer** (1824), and **crown prisoner** (1819), all illustrated the convict's status as the property and worker of the British government and Crown. Indeed, **servant of the Crown** dates to the first year of settlement, 1788. The standard **prisoner** dates to 1800. A few slang words applying to convicts also developed: **old lag** and **new chum** were recorded by Vaux in 1812, **new hand** (1817) and **old hand** (1826) have both passed into broader currency subsequently.

Over time, terms were adopted that were more specific to particular groups of convicts, or, like 'canary', were descriptive of them in some way. **Educated convict** and **gentleman convict**, referring to a convict with some education and possibly a trade or profession, both date from 1830, although such convicts would already have arrived in Australia. Clearly, distinctions in status existed within the convicts as a group, as well as between convicts and the rest of colonial society. Educated convicts saw themselves as distinct and above the rest of the convicts. Some of those who arrived in Australia were political prisoners, a group of which were known as **croppies** (1800). These were Irish rebels of 1798, who had their hair cropped short in sympathy with the French Revolution. The term was extended to Irish convicts generally, and later applied to any convict, especially one who was at large. **Magpie** (1841) was, like 'canary', a reference to the convicts' appearance, and referred to those who wore uniforms of yellow and black.

Terms for convicts also referred to places from which they came or were located. **Cockatoos** (1846) were those men (generally **incorrigibles**) sent to Cockatoo Island in Sydney Harbour to work from 1839 to cut sandstone for use in building wharves on the Sydney foreshore and Circular Quay. **Pentonvillain** (1844) and **Vandemonian** (1847) both played on the place of origin of convicts and their bad reputation—Pentonville plus villain; Van Diemen's Land plus demon. 'Pentonvillains' was used by free settlers to condemn the sending of **exiles**—prisoners who had served part of their sentence in British prisons (often the famous Pentonville)—who were sent to the colonies on tickets of leave to work. 'Vandemonians' was also used by free settlers who condemned the convict presence in Van Diemen's Land society, and more particularly, by those on the mainland who resented Vandemonians arriving there.

Surprisingly, given its subsequent prominence, the use of the term **convict** (1787) as a noun was not very common. While perhaps at first fairly neutral, it clearly became more pejorative, especially as convicts were emancipated and sought to rise above their former status. A citation for **servant of the crown** reveals their concern that they be given a title more fitting their perception of themselves:

> Those sent into private families are without any mark of disgrace, but are apparently the same as hired servants in England; they are fed and clothed, but receive no wages. It is said they never forgive a person who accidentally calls them 'convicts;' they denominate themselves 'servants of the crown,' and settlers invariably do the same.[10]

'Convict' was, however, frequently used in some compounds, for example **convict department** (1842), **convict mechanic** (1837), **convict police** (1838) and **convict system** (1834).

The *Sydney Monitor* noted in 1826 that '[t]he decent term of *Prisoner*, had been substituted by [Governor] Macquarie, for the degrading one of *Convict*, as the latter designation had in its turn taken place of the old British appellation of

Felon'.[11] The more pejorative than descriptive term **felon** was, despite this observation, of some popularity in the colonies, given a boost by the inflammatory writing of James Mudie, who coined the term **felonry** in 1837 to describe the convicts, and used it to condemn convicts and ex-convicts. The *Sydney Monitor*'s observation suggests that 'felon' was revived by writers such as Mudie who had a distinct political agenda.

The terms for convicts show both the complexity of the convict system as well as its evolution over the years. They suggest also the increasing tensions and disputes over the convict presence and the status of ex-convicts in colonial society and the continuation of transportation. Examining the vocabulary that evolved as colonial society developed and transportation became contentious reveals much about arguments over the convicts themselves—their punishment and reform; the presence of **emancipists** and **expirees** in convict society and free settler resentment towards them; and the arguments over continuing transportation and the convict system in the colonies. In other words, language reveals much about colonial politics.

1820–60

By the 1820s colonial society was beginning to develop its own identity and voice. In 1823 the New South Wales Act gave New South Wales its own Legislative Council, and the courts were given independence. In June of 1825, Van Diemen's Land became a colony separate from New South Wales. This new voice expressed the concerns of colonial society. A distinct generation of the native-born had come into being—the first recording of 'currency', referring to those born in the colonies, and derived from the colonial money which was discounted against the British sterling, dates from 1824. A term also used for these new Australians was 'cornstalk' (derived from the vigorous growth and health of the native-born), which dates from 1827. Generally, the terms were pejorative in intent, implying that those born in Australia were of lesser value and status than those born in Britain.[12] Cunningham, who recorded both in 1827, reveals: 'We have, as I said before, first, the *sterling* and *currency*, or English and Colonial born, the latter bearing the name of *corn stalks* (Indian corn), from the way in which they shoot up.'[13] Cunningham turns the pejorative nature of the terms around and mocks the 'sterling' and their pretensions thus:

> It is most laughable to see the capers some of our drunken old Sterling madonnas will occasionally cut over their Currency adversaries in a quarrel. It is then, 'You saucy baggage, how dare you set up your *Currency* crest at me? I am *Sterling*, and that I'll let you know!'[14]

While it is clear that one colonial identity derived from those born in the colonies, there were still clear distinctions between the convicts, ex-convicts and the free emigrants/settlers that had a large role in shaping colonial politics. The Macquarie governorship (1810–21) had seen numerous privileges and rights being granted to **emancipists** (1822), appointing them to important roles including the magistracy, giving out extensive land grants, and demanding that they should be treated as equal to the free. However, his policies alarmed the British government and the Bigge reports of 1822–23 on the state of the colonies condemned the lenient treatment of convicts and emancipists.[15] Bigge was a judge, appointed in 1819 as a commissioner of inquiry into New South Wales. He was instructed to investigate the laws and operation of the colony. His report urged more supervision and stricter punishment to ensure that transportation remained a deterrent punishment in Britain. 'To it [Britain],' writes A.G.L. Shaw, 'New South Wales was still primarily a place of punishment; to Macquarie it was a growing colony.'[16] Shaw sums up the new view colonial society was beginning to have of itself; nevertheless Bigge's report was influential and led to changes in colonial policy and the convict system that would see less lenient treatment of convicts.

Condemning Macquarie, the Bigge Report first recorded the term **convict colony** to label New South Wales, arguing that Macquarie had given too much status to the emancipated convicts. By seeing New South Wales as a convict colony, it inferred that the colony was 'established for their [the convicts'] benefit … [and] that it was brought to its present state (meaning, of course, a state of prosperity) by their means'.[17] Ideally Bigge hoped for free emigrants to be the privileged class of colonial society and to be the employers, while convicts and emancipists would only be labourers.[18]

The conflict between emancipists and free settlers accelerated in the 1830s as free settlers, especially those of the wealthy pastoral gentry, sought to limit the rights and privileges of the emancipists, which led to deep resentment between the two groups. The term **exclusive** was in use by 1836, to refer to those who wished to maintain their exclusive privileges and position in society. The exclusives saw it as essential to bolster their own status (especially in relation to Britain) by denigrating the ex-convicts. Their theory of 'moral ascendancy'—that they were morally superior to the ex-convict—provided the basis for the social hierarchy they were trying to create. At the most extreme end of the anti-emancipist sentiment was James Mudie who, as has already been noted, coined the term **felonry** to refer to convicts and sought to paint all ex-convicts with the same brush:

> The author has ventured to coin the word *felonry*, as the appellative of an *order* or class of persons in New South Wales,—an order which happily exists in no other country in the world. The major part of the inhabitants of the colony are felons now undergoing or felons who have already undergone their sentences. … Hitherto there was no single term that could be employed to designate these various descriptions of persons, who now bear the denomina-

tions of 'convicts' and 'ticket-of-leave-men'; as also, 'emancipists', (as they are absurdly enough called), who again are subdivided into 'conditionally pardoned convicts', 'fully pardoned convicts', and 'expirees', or transported felons whose sentences have expired; together with 'runaway convicts', subdivided into 'absentees', (a name foolish for its mildness), and 'bushrangers'. The single term, the *felonry* (which comprehends all these descriptions of the criminal population), though new, is evidently a legitimate member of the tribe of appellatives distinguished by the same termination, as *peasantry, tenantry, yeomanry, gentry, cavalry, chivalry, &c.*[19]

Mudie was hoping to gloss over the many distinctions and complexities of colonial society, and make a political point at the same time. Nevertheless, it should be noted that the free settlers, emigrants, and emancipists had little choice but to work together—practicality demanded that the rhetoric often exaggerated the tensions within colonial society.

Many of these issues are illuminated by looking at the complicated meanings and usages of **free**. 'Free' assumed two meanings in the colonies and these meanings suggest tensions within colonial society. **Free** meaning those who had served their sentence or been given a pardon and reassumed their free status was in use from 1792 in the colonies. These convicts were restored to all the rights of a British citizen, yet as people came to the colonies as free people, a second usage of 'free' as pertaining to them (that is, one who had never been a convict) came into currency in 1795, and as the years passed this status was of increasing importance. Thus the distinction between the **freed** (1829) and free became crucial. Even though convicts had gained their freedom and served their sentences they were not given the full status of being free. As the *Colonial Times* observed in 1844, 'the community is composed of three classes, the *free*, the *freed*, and the *bond*.'[20] James Mudie, although opposed to giving equal status to the freed, observed, probably fairly accurately, 'that the admission of freed convicts, whether by pardon or expiry of their sentences, to the same social and legal rights as the emigrants, is not only a subject of discussion, but of bitter and well-grounded complaint'.[21]

The tenuous status of the **free emigrant** (1827) could only be reinforced by creating this distinction from the freed. Something needed to distinguish the free from the freed, so that the free would not be tainted by the alleged questionable morality of the ex-convicts. Many of these working-class immigrants came to Australia under government-assisted migration schemes from the early 1830s, and sought both work and land in the colonies. The increasing number of free immigrants were determined to prevent emancipists from owning land—land they saw as the basis for their future prosperity, the promise of which had brought them to Australia. Their own status depended on the subordination of the emancipists.[22] This resentment would manifest itself most strongly in the emerging protest against transportation and the convict system (although, of course, emancipists too had similar reason and desire to end the transportation system). Free immigrants resented the convict labour system—an important part of the ideology of this emerging urban capitalist working-class, as Connell and Irving argue, was the notion of 'free labour' and a free market linked to a free society. This ideology would feed into the anti-transportation movement of the 1840s.[23]

By the late 1830s there was enough criticism in the colonies to prompt another investigation into the system. The Molesworth Commission of 1837 signalled the beginning of the end for transportation. 'The evidence and report of the Molesworth committee was the official, public indictment of the convict system in New South Wales,' John Hirst has written.[24] It was a document in which language played a large part in the understanding and subsequent condemnation of the convict system. Most pointedly, Molesworth equated the convict system with slavery:

> Transportation, though chiefly dreaded as exile, undoubtedly is much more than exile; it is slavery as well; and the condition of the convict slave is frequently a very miserable one; but that condition is unknown, and cannot be made known; for the physical condition of a convict is generally better than that of an agricultural labourer; the former is in most cases better fed and better clothed than the latter; it is the restraint on the freedom of action, the degradation of slavery, and the other moral evils, which chiefly constitute the pains of transportation, and of which no description can convey an adequate idea to that class in whom Transportation ought to inspire terror.[25]

The use of the powerful and emotive term 'slavery', within a report that saw the colonies as places that were degraded, immoral, and evil, had a powerful effect on the British. While many in the colonies were angry at having their home condemned thus, the rhetoric of Molesworth continued to echo through the rhetoric of the anti-transportation movement. Equating the convict system with slavery infused the anti-transportationist rhetoric with particular power, but it also led to a biased and exaggerated view of the system that would shape perceptions of the convict system then and later. It was to long condemn the convict system in the popular and historical imagination.

The system itself was also condemned as ultimately being horrific rather than beneficial to the convict. Molesworth saw transportation as an 'inefficient, cruel, and demoralizing' punishment.[26] But even worse, the convict system corrupted all in the colonies: it essentially turned colonists into 'cruel and hard-hearted slave-owners'.[27] The language of slavery already echoed through the language of convictism: the term **bond** (first used in Australia in 1800) originated as meaning 'in a state of serfdom and slavery' although it had acquired a wider meaning by the nineteenth century; **indent** (1802) and **indenture** (1804) echoed the methods of the Atlantic slave trade; and **overseer** (1788), while generally meaning one who supervised workers, had strong slavery connotations. **Emancipation** itself was a term that in the British and American context developed strong slavery connections, although it was not particularly loaded in the Australian context.

The anti-transportation movement was keen to use slavery as a means of describing the convict system, for by the mid-nineteenth century nothing to most British (and increasingly to many Americans) was more odious than the system of slavery. It corrupted master and slave, it was also inefficient and not in keeping with the 'enlightened' nature of Western society. Certainly, for the 'currency' seeking to show that they were indeed a 'civilised' and respectable society it was essential to rid themselves of this hideous and essentially pre-modern institution. Beyond that, practical considerations were at work: few free immigrants wanted more labour competition and the colonies had yet to establish stable economies independent of Britain, so economic depressions were common.

The term **abolitionist** dates from 1847 in Australia and was a revival of the anti-slavery movement terminology of Britain (first recorded 1790) and still common in the United States (1836). **Anti-transportationist** and **anti-transportation** also became current in 1847, as colonists sought to organise their opposition. The first anti-transportation league was formed in Launceston in January 1849; in September 1850 colonists in New South Wales, concerned about the revival of transportation, formed a New South Wales Association for Preventing the Revival of Transportation. **Anti-convict** (1852), although used in the same way as **anti-transportation**, nevertheless suggested the more general antipathy towards the convicts that was developing in this period. The anti-transportationists' opposition were known simply as **transportationists** (1847), or as they preferred to label them, more pejoratively, **pollutionists** (1850).

The result of agitation by people such as Molesworth, Ullathorne, and Mudie in New South Wales led to the end of transportation to that colony in 1840. However, transportation continued to Van Diemen's Land, and transportation and convictism would continue to be discussed both there and in New South Wales over the next decade. Additionally, in the 1820s and 1830s, Britain's penal system was undergoing reformation, and new ideas of discipline and punishment were being developed.[28] From the late 1820s and until the middle of the 1830s, British reformers, in particular the Society for the Improvement of Prison Discipline, pushed for reforms. In the second half of the 1830s, therefore, the newly appointed Inspectors of Prisons in Britain evolved a modified **separate** system designed on the American model. Primarily this type of system, which would be adopted in some measure in the Australian colonies, 'worked on the principles of solitude, silence, anonymity and moral reflection',[29] and was based on keeping convicts in separate cells in a prison designed along these principles. The emphasis was on surveillance, and discipline aimed at moral reformation (the 'soul') rather than physical punishment.

Developments from the 1830s onwards in penal and convict discipline thus added new terms to the colonial lexicon. The **separate** system was experimented with in building a prison at Port Arthur, based on the British prison of Pentonville. Mundy commented in 1852 on his visit to the prison: 'an admirable edifice nearly finished at vast expense for the prosecution of the solitary and silent system'.[30] The idea of a **separate** or **model** prison was borrowed from the new language of penal discipline being developed in Britain. The idea of penal establishments for the punishment of **double-convicted** convicts—that is, convicts who committed offences in the colonies—dated back to early in the convict system but after Bigge was taken to be an integral part of making transportation a more serious and deterrent punishment. **Norfolk Island**, which was notorious for its appalling conditions, was reopened in 1825 after having been abandoned in 1813. It was to take in the **incorrigibles** (1827), recalcitrant convicts who were believed to pose a significant threat to the community.

It was the very problem of the incorrigibles that posed a dilemma for those administering the convict system. The advocates of the separate system believed that their system could lead to repentance and the reformation of even the most hardened of criminals; yet, for the Australian colonies, the threat (or at least the threat perceived by the free settlers) to 'respectable' society, for example from bushrangers, was real. Penal establishments far from the settled areas did not acknowledge that these prisoners could be redeemed, rather it was a case of exiling for a second time the convict already once exiled.

Thus for Australia, debates over the best method of dealing with convicts continued. The model prison was built in Port Arthur, following the British system. Other prisons were built, gradually transforming the system to a more modern prison system for those still under sentence, and reoffenders. In Van Diemen's Land more generally a new system took the place of the old assignment system after the Molesworth report. This was the **probation** system. It was introduced slowly from 1839, and aimed at organising convicts into stages of servitude: they began with serving a period labouring in a **probation gang** (1841) (often assigned to **probation stations** (1842) in unsettled areas; the system was also meant to aid the clearing of bush in Van Diemen's Land) and could then progress on to working for themselves after being granted a **probation pass** (1843). The main reason why this system proved to be less than successful was that there was little employment for the former **probationer** (1840), who often turned to crime out of idleness and for material gain. This, of course, only increased resentment towards the system and led to the **anti-transportation** movement.

Another experiment tried at this time was the 'social system' proposed by Alexander Maconochie (1787–1860). Maconochie went to Van Diemen's Land as the private secretary of Sir John Franklin, but was asked by the British Society for the Improvement of Prison Discipline to report on the state of the convict system.

His attack on the assignment system was to influence the Molesworth Committee; he suggested a **social system** (1839) of punishment as an alternative. Under this system, prisoners received **marks** (1839) for their work and behaviour—the accumulation of an adequate number of good marks might lead to remission of a sentence; bad marks might lengthen the time served. Maconochie was appointed commandant of Norfolk Island in 1840, partly as an effort to put his proposals into practice. His system was seen as a failure and after four years he was removed. It failed partly because he was not given an adequate amount of time to implement his system; he was also thwarted by a number of uprisings and attempted escapes during his time there.

The cessation of transportation to New South Wales and the increasing opposition in Van Diemen's Land posed a dilemma for the British government. Despite the shift to the separate prison system and the building of several new prisons in Britain in the early nineteenth century, they still wanted to send some of their great numbers of criminals out of the country (thereby also ensuring that they would not return). This led to the proposition of the exile system. These **exiles** (1840) were prisoners who had served part of their sentence in prisons in Britain and were then sent to the colonies with a ticket of leave (they were initially given conditional pardons but this was replaced by tickets of leave as they were thought to provide more control over the convicts, because they could be revoked for bad behaviour). This system was supposed to help supply labour when needed, and the exiles were, ideally, to be partially reformed. They were also known as **Pentons** (1847) and **Pentonvillains** (1844) because many had served their sentences at Pentonville prison in Britain. Another part of this scheme was to send out juveniles to the colonies under an apprenticeship scheme—these boys had served their sentence at Parkhurst prison and were known as **Parkhurst boys** and **Parkhurst lads**.

Opposition to this scheme was strong—most exiles ended up in Van Diemen's Land, although some went to the Port Phillip district. Concern over the criminal influence of these Pentons, along with **Vandemonians** who were leaving Van Diemen's Land, led to anger and resentment among the free settlers. When many headed to Victoria in the 1850s after gold was discovered (most were conditionally pardoned, but some were escapees), the settlers' anger led to the 1852 Convicts Prevention Act, which excluded from Victoria all holders of conditional pardons from Van Diemen's Land; the Act was never rigorously enforced but represented, however, the strong anti-convict sentiment present among free settlers.

The Parkhurst boys as well as the exiles were welcomed in one colony, however—Western Australia. Transportation, begun in 1850, continued there until 1868, but few words seem to have originated that were particular to the convict system there. One exception is **imperial convict**, which suggested the nature of transportation and the role of convict labour in Western Australian history.

Convict labour was seen as being essential to establishing a successful colony on the western coast of Australia and had to be paid for largely by the British government, and indeed this was what an imperial convict was—one paid for by the British rather than the colonial government.

Legacies

The convict era had almost passed into history by the middle of the nineteenth century, and colonial society had begun to erase their convict origins as best they could. The convict 'stain' or 'birthstain' became a mark on those of convict ancestry that had to be overcome—a sign of inferiority and even disgrace. Not only did it mark those who had convict ancestry, it also stigmatised the Australian colonies when they most sought to place themselves on an equal footing with the mother country. The *Truth* in 1909 wrote 'John Bull's tainted legacy has somehow come to stay. The "birthstains" on the blanket they will *never* wash away.'[31] The relationship of Australian society to its convict past continued to be ambivalent through the early twentieth century. However, by the end of the twentieth century, Australians embraced their convict ancestry, tourism played up places significant to the convict system, and houses were sold with the added attraction of being built with 'convict bricks'.

Some terms continued to be important to Australian English, some with transferred meanings. **New chum**, which had referred to a convict new to the system, was used extensively from 1828 to refer to a newly arrived immigrant in the colonies and continued to be used well into the twentieth century. It was transferred into a more general use to refer to any person new to a particular activity or occupation from 1851. The flash term **swag**, meaning the booty of a criminal, became an important Australian term referring to the collection of possessions carried by a traveller (or swagman) and was widely used in the second half of the nineteenth century and first half of the twentieth century.

The term **station**, which was first used in 1816 to refer to places of employment for convicts, was transferred to refer to a reserve or mission for Aboriginals (from 1833) and therefore links the government's attempts to control convicts as well as Aboriginals. It was also used in a broadened sense to refer to a rural residence and its lands. **Station** was thus a key term in the language of Australian settlement. **Muster** was similarly transferred to the language of rural Australia: originally it referred to the gathering of livestock in one place for the purpose of counting, branding, and so forth from 1841.

Public servant, which today refers to those who work in the Australian public administration and a viable, and even attractive, career option, is a descendant of the original 'public servants', the convicts working less willingly for the government. The essential meaning of the term remains, however—public servants then and now work for the benefit of the public. Another interesting term transferred to a more general use after the convict period was **government stroke**, which originally meant a deliberately slow way of working adopted by convict workers as a mild form of resistance to the system. It passed into wider currency largely as a derogatory reference to the public service. The *Truth* noted in 1901: 'The "Government stroke" … is having a fair run. … Men with their coats and vests off, and their sleeves rolled up, were standing about doing—what think you? Nothing',[32] and Mercier observed in 1943: 'There appear to be two occasions when the Government stroke is not noticeable in a Government department—when it is hounding a private citizen for money, and when it is trying to pass a liability on to another department.'[33]

Several terms that developed within the Australian convict system were to be adopted and commonly used within the British and American penal system as well as in Australia. Three examples of these are **probation**, **hard labour**, and **life**. Probation was adopted as a central concept within criminal reform in the second half of the nineteenth century—indeed, as Britain introduced long-term incarceration after the end of transportation, it adopted a model of early release of prisoners on tickets of leave and this evolved into the probation system. Probation was used first in Britain in 1897, but had already been used in parts of the United States from 1878. Hard labour, first used in Australia as early as 1803, was incorporated into British sentences after 1853 (along with the introduction of the legal term 'penal servitude'), and meant that long-term prisoners were made to work as part of their sentence of imprisonment. The introduction of these two terms reveals the changing nature of British prison methods after the end of transportation, as well as the lessons learnt from the Australian experiences translated into the British system. **Life**, referring to a life sentence, was used much earlier in Australia than anywhere else; as was **lifer**—both terms were to be adopted in Britain and the United States.

In general, many terms of the convict era remain historically specific, but have continued in historical novels and more generally in the popular imagination. Marcus Clarke, for example, in *For the Term of His Natural Life* (1884 edition) included a number of convict terms. He also popularised a few terms for which little contemporary historical evidence can be found. He refers to 'the Ring', a criminal conspiracy on Norfolk Island: 'A sub-overseer, a man named Hankey, has been talking to me. He says that there are some forty of the oldest and worst prisoners who form what he calls the "Ring," and that the members of this Ring are bound by an oath to support each other, and to avenge the punishment of any of their number.'[34] He also used the term 'old dogs' for experienced convicts.[35] This dictionary has included terms that have at least two contemporary citations to provide adequate evidence of its usage. Nevertheless, some of these other terms with limited evidence are worth briefly mentioning.

David Collins in 1802 noted that the convicts called a loaf of bread consisting of 'more chaff and bran than flour' a 'scrubbing brush'.[36] Cunningham, a perceptive recorder of the new colonial idiom, noted a number of colourful terms including 'pure Merinos' for those 'who pride themselves on being of the purest blood in the Colony' and 'legitimate exquisites' for the ex-convicts.[37] 'Felonswells' was also used in a similar sense to 'legitimate exquisites' to refer to those ex-convicts and gentlemen convicts who thought themselves superior to the rest of the convicts.[38] Another interesting term was noted in the Bigge Report of 1822–23, referring to 'Captain Cox's liberty' in mentioning a number of passes given out by a certain magistrate.[39]

The convict period of Australian history thus contributed a number of colourful and, in some cases, enduring words to Australian English. The language of the convict system reveals much about the workings of the system and the nature of early colonial settlement and society. The British government created colonies to which they could banish the unwanted of their own society, but almost immediately a new and distinct community came into being, with its own emerging vocabulary. This vocabulary provides an essential and valuable insight into this new society.

Notes

1   D. Collins, *An Account of the English Colony in New South Wales*, T. Cadell & W. Davies, London, 1798, vol. 2, p. 502.

2   W. Kirsop, *Books for Colonial Readers: The nineteenth-century Australian experience*, Bibliographical Society of Australia and New Zealand in association with the Centre for Bibliographical and Textual Studies, Monash University, Melbourne, 1994, pp. 7–8.

3   P. Cunningham, *Two Years in New South Wales*, Henry Colburn, London, 1827, vol. 2, p. 116.

4   M. Quartly, 'Convicts', in G. Davison et al., *The Oxford Companion to Australian History*, Oxford University Press, Melbourne, 2001, p. 156.

5   A.G.L. Shaw, *Convicts and the Colonies*, Melbourne University Press, Melbourne 1966, p. 229. J. Hirst provides an excellent discussion of convict society and its system of discipline in *Convict Society and Its Enemies*, George Allen & Unwin, Sydney, 1983.

6   Governor Macquarie to Earl Bathurst, *Historical Records of Australia*, Library Committee of the Commonwealth Parliament, Sydney, 1916, series one, vol. VIII, p. 307.

7   Hunter, *Historical Records of Australia*, Library Committee of the Commonwealth Parliament, Sydney, 1914, series one, vol. II, p. 352.

8   W. Tench, *Sydney's First Four Years, being a reprint of A Narrative of the Expedition to Botany Bay and A Complete Account of the Settlement at Port Jackson* (L.F.

Fitzhardinge, ed.), Angus Robertson, Sydney, 1961, p. 297. Paul Carter in his *The Road to Botany Bay: An Exploration of Landscape and History*, Knopf, New York, 1988, has an interesting discussion on the importance of language and imagination in the convicts' subversion of power and also notes Tench's observation. See especially pp. 317–18.

9 Cunningham, *Two Years*, vol. 2, p. 59.
10 J. Roberts, *Two Years at Sea*, R. Bentley, London, 1834, pp. 125–6.
11 *Sydney Monitor*, 19 May 1826.
12 J. Moloney deals with the first generation of the Australian-born in detail in his *Native Born: The First White Australians*, Melbourne University Press, Melbourne, 2000, but, although he mentions the distinction between those born of convicts and those born of free settlers, his main concern is with the distinctions between the first colonial generation and the British-born.
13 Cunningham, *Two Years*, vol. 2, p. 116.
14 Cunningham, *Two Years*, vol. 2, pp. 53–4.
15 For detailed study of the Bigge report, see J. Ritchie, *Punishment and Profit: The Reports of Commissioner John Bigge on the Colonies of New South Wales and Van Diemen's Land, 1822–1823; their origins, nature and significance*, Heinemann, Melbourne, 1970; for an edited version of the Bigge Reports, see J. Ritchie (ed.), *The Evidence to the Bigge Reports*, Heinemann, Melbourne, 1971, vols 1 and 2.
16 Shaw, *Convicts and the Colonies*, p. 106.
17 J.T. Bigge, *Report of the Commissioner of inquiry into the state of the colony of New South Wales*, London, 1822, pp. 147–8.
18 Hirst, *Convict Society*, p. 88.
19 J. Mudie, *The Felonry of New South Wales*, Whaley and Company, London, 1837, p. vi.
20 *Colonial Times*, Hobart, 10 July 1844, p. 2.
21 Mudie, *Felonry*, p. 220.
22 Moloney, *Native Born*, p. 44.
23 R.W. Connell and T.H. Irving, *Class Structure in Australian History: Poverty and Progress* (2nd edn), Longman Cheshire, Melbourne, 1992, p. 96.
24 Hirst, *Convict Society*, p. 27.
25 W. Molesworth, *Report from the Select Committee of the House of Commons on Transportation*, Henry Hooper, London, 1838, p. 21.
26 ibid., p. iv.
27 ibid., p. 31.
28 This was a period of significant and complicated change in British penal thought. It was clear that an alternative to transportation had to be developed; this was to be long-term imprisonment in British prisons, but how best to design and run these new prisons was debated. This was also a period in which the number of convicted criminals was rising, causing much agitation to the

British people, and making the topic even more important. For further reading on this, see W.J. Forsythe, *The Reforms of Prisoners 1830–1900*, Croom Helm, London, 1987; M. Ignatieff, *A Just Measure of Pain: The Penitentiary in the Industrial Revolution 1750–1850*, Columbia University Press, New York, 1978; N. Morris and D.J. Rothman (eds), *The Oxford History of the Prison: The Practice of Punishment in Western Society*, Oxford University Press, New York, 1995.

29   J. Frow, 'In the Penal Colony', *Australian Humanities Review*, April–June 1999, <http://www.lib.latrobe.edu.au/AHR/archive/Issue-April-1999/frow3a.html>

30   G.C. Mundy, *Our Antipodes*, Richard Bentley, London, 1853, vol. 3, p. 215.

31   *Truth*, Sydney, 20 June 1909.

32   *Truth*, Sydney, 8 September 1901, p. 5.

33   E. Mercier, *Giggles*, Sydney, p. 13.

34   M. Clarke, *For the Term of His Natural Life* (1884 edn) in *Marcus Clarke* (Michael Wilding, ed.), University of Queensland Press, St. Lucia, 1976, p. 386.

35   Cited in S. Baker, *The Australian Language* (revised edn), Sun Books, Melbourne, 1966, p. 28.

36   Collins, *An Account of the English Colony*, vol. 2, p. 271.

37   Cunningham, *Two Years*, vol. 2, p. 116; p. 123.

38   J. Ward, *Perils, Pastimes, and Pleasures of An Emigrant in Australia, Vancouver's Island and California*, Thomas Cautley Newby, London, 1849, p. 66.

39   Bigge, *Report*, p. 125.

Select Bibliography

Bateson, C., *The Convict Ships 1787–1868*, A.H. & A.W. Reed, Sydney, 1974.

Bogle, M., *Convicts*, Historic Houses Trust, Sydney, 1999.

Brand, I., *Port Arthur 1830–1877*, Regal Publications, Launceston, n.d.

Connell, R.W. and T.H. Irving, *Class Structure in Australian History: Poverty and Progress* (2nd edn), Longman Cheshire, Melbourne, 1992.

Damousi, J., *Depraved and Disorderly: Female Convicts, Sexuality and Gender in Colonial Australia*, Cambridge University Press, Cambridge, 1997.

Daniels, K., *Convict Women*, Allen & Unwin, Sydney, 1998.

Graeme-Evans, A.L., *Tasmanian Rogues and Absconders 1803–1875*, Regal Publications, Launceston, 1994.

Hirst, J.B., *Convict Society and Its Enemies: A History of Early New South Wales*, Allen & Unwin, Sydney, 1983.

Kerr, J.S., *Design for Convicts: An Account of Design for Convict Establishments in the Australian Colonies During the Transportation Era*, Library of Australian History, Sydney, 1984.

Maynard, M., *Fashioned from Penury: Dress as Cultural Practice in Colonial Australia*, Cambridge University Press, Cambridge, 1994.

Morris, N. and D.J. Rothman (eds), *The Oxford History of the Prison: The Practice of Punishment in Western Society*, Oxford University Press, New York, 1995.

Ritchie, J., *Punishment and Profit: The Reports of Commissioner John Bigge on the Colonies of New South Wales and Van Diemen's Land, 1822–1823; their origins, nature and significance*, Heinemann, Melbourne, 1970.

Robinson, P., *The Hatch and Brood of Time*, Oxford University Press, Melbourne, 1985.

Salt, A., *These Outcast Women: The Parramatta Female Factory 1821–1848*, Hale & Iremonger, Sydney, 1984.

Shaw, A.G.L., *Convicts and the Colonies: A Study of Penal Transportation from Great Britain and Ireland to Australia and Other Parts of the British Empire*, Melbourne University Press, Melbourne, 1966.

Guide to Using the Dictionary

For each entry, there is a headword, given in bold, followed by a short definition. In some cases for synonyms, there is no definition, but rather the reader is directed to another entry (given in small capitals) where a definition and further information about the word is located. In general, the word used most frequently has been selected as the main entry. The information in square brackets provides the etymology, or word-history, of each term, and gives the date of the first recording in Australia. In most cases, further information follows; generally this is historical information that helps to explain the context in which the word was relevant. Cross-references are given in small capitals and direct the reader to other terms for further explanation and information. Citation evidence (excerpts from contemporary sources) follows this. Citations have been chosen to illustrate the contemporary meaning and usage of the terms, as well as for the interesting insights they provide into the convict era. All original spellings in the citations have been retained throughout.

A

abolitionist a person who advocated the ending of the TRANSPORTATION of convicts to Australia. [*Abolitionist* in the sense 'one who aims at or advocates the abolition of any institution or custom' was used first in standard English with reference to the abolition of African slavery (1790). In Australia its application to the convict system was first recorded in 1847.]

Transportation to New South Wales ended in 1840 but convicts continued to be transported to Van Diemen's Land, thus raising strident opposition from abolitionists, who were also known as ANTI-TRANSPORTATIONISTS. The term appears to be used mainly from the late 1840s onwards, chiefly in Tasmania. The first anti-transportation league was formed in 1849 in Van Diemen's Land. Abolitionists were mainly free emigrant settlers. Some resented the use of penal labour as it undermined the value of free labour. There were also strong moral objections to the convict system, which was seen to corrupt colonial society. Convicts were seen to degrade their MASTERS and MISTRESSES who might be tempted to abuse their power; also, the very presence of convicts with their (perceived) lack of morals and criminal tendencies posed a threat to making a more civilised and ordered society in the Antipodes. The strong views of such people ensured that the 'stain' of CONVICTISM was suppressed for many decades after its end.

1852 Opulent settlers who visited Europe found it convenient to conceal their home, and some less prudent were repelled with unconquerable distrust. In a small community the public reputation is of personal importance, and it was alleged that to neglect the offer of social freedom would be infamy unexampled. To this feeling the **abolitionists** appealed. 'Parents of Van Diemen's Land,' said the author of a pamphlet called *Common Sense*, 'can you hesitate? … That land which they tell you will become a desert when the clank of chains, the cries of torture, the noise of riot, and the groans of despair shall be heard no longer, will *not* become a desert; "it will blossom abundantly, and rejoice with joy and singing," when your sons and daughters shall go forth, the free among the free.' J. WEST *The History of Tasmania* vol. 1 p. 282

abscond (of a convict) to escape from custody. [*Abscond* in the sense 'to hide oneself; to retire from the public view; generally used of persons in debt, or criminals eluding the law', has existed in standard English since the late sixteenth century. It was used in Australia with some intensity during the convict era, and was first recorded in a convict context in 1788.]

One of the principal convict crimes was to abscond, or escape from custody. This was sometimes a response to harsh treatment and poor conditions, or simply a bid for freedom. Convicts might escape from ASSIGNMENT to private households, from GOVERNMENT GANGS, or from places of SECONDARY punishment such as Port Arthur and Norfolk Island. Newspapers frequently announced the names of those who absconded. They often fled into the unsettled areas and the phrase ABSCOND INTO THE WOODS (or BUSH) was frequently used. See also ABSCONDER.

> **1798** Some of the worst among the convicts availed themselves of the opportunity that was given them in the evening, by the absence of several of the officers and people from their tents and huts, to commit depredations. One officer on going to his tent found a man in it, whom with some difficulty he secured, after wounding him with his sword. The tent of another was broken into, and several articles of wearing apparel stolen out of it; and many smaller thefts of provisions and clothing were committed among the convicts. Several people were taken into custody, and two were afterwards tried and executed. One of these had **absconded**, and lived in the woods for nineteen days, existing by what he was able to procure by nocturnal depredations among the huts and stock of individuals. His visits for this purpose were so frequent and daring, that it became absolutely necessary to proclaim him an outlaw, as well as to declare that no person must harbour him after such proclamation. D. COLLINS *An Account of the English Colony in New South Wales* vol. 1 p. 32

> **1848** The term *bushranger*, it will be recollected, applies to runaway felons, generally men of the most desperate character, who, hopeless of receiving any other liberty or indulgence, or perhaps, as has often been the case, driven to a state of desperation by the heartless tyranny and oppression of their masters, are tempted to **abscond** and *take to the bush*, where, cut off from the pale of forgiveness by the step they have adopted, and with a price set on their heads, they defy all laws both moral and divine. Conscious that their case is hopeless, and that all men's hands are against them, they retaliate on all men, and procuring fire-arms at the first hut or station that they come to, rob, plunder, and

murder all that come in their way, or offer the slightest resistance. C. COZENS *Adventures of a Guardsman* p. 148

absconder a convict who escaped from custody. See ABSCOND. [The term is first recorded in an Australian convict context in 1840.]

Escapees, when captured, were subjected to numerous punishments, such as FLOGGING or being put on the TREADMILL. Those who gained a reputation as absconders (also known as ABSENTEES or BOLTERS) were often put into leg IRONS to prevent future escapes. Absconders in Van Diemen's Land found it difficult to escape the island and some tried to stow away on departing vessels—few were successful. Alternatively, like absconders on mainland Australia, they took to the BUSH. Most either gave themselves up or took to BUSHRANGING to survive.

1852 With these men was executed Alexander Pearce, whose confessions to the priest were, by his consent, published at his death. He formed one of the second party who absconded from Macquarie Harbour (1822). They had planned their escape with considerable skill: one was a sailor, and able to direct their course: they possessed themselves of a boat, and proposed to capture the vessel of the pilot, then laden for town. It was the custom, when a prisoner was missing, thus giving notice to the sentinels: to prevent such information, the **absconders** poured water on the embers kept in readiness. This was not effectually done: and thus, when they had proceeded half-a-mile, they saw the smoke rising, and their passage cut off; they therefore landed, destroyed the boat, and entered the bush. J. WEST *The History of Tasmania* vol. 2 p. 196

1855 They reached Mount Harris, and learned that two Irish **absconders** had there been killed and eaten by the blacks. J. BONWICK *Geography of Australia and New Zealand* p. 27

absconding the act of escaping from custody. See ABSCOND, ABSCONDER. [First recorded in an Australian convict context in 1804.]

1805 One of the prisoners belonging to the out-gangs, being sent into camp on Saturday, to draw the weekly allowance of provision for his mess, fell unfortunately into the company of a party of convicts, who were playing cards for their allowance, a thing very frequent amongst them. With as little resolution as his superiors in similar situations, after being a while a looker-on, he at length suffered himself to be persuaded to take a hand; and in the event, lost not only his own portion, but that of the whole mess. Being a man of a timid nature, his misfortune overcame his reason, and conceiving his situation amongst his messmates as insupportable, he formed and executed the extravagant resolution of **absconding** into the glens. J. TURNBULL *Voyage Around the World* vol. 1 p. 113

1834 Town-bred prisoners are found to abscond in great numbers. *Absconding*, is a term given to the first act of departure from an assignee. When the convicts have been absent a short time, they cease to be called *absentees*; they are then termed *bushrangers*. When Sydney was a mere village, absentees did not harbour there; they took up their abode in the bush—that is, the wild forests of the Colony. They were there harboured by their friends, such as convict stockmen in lonely and remote parts, and settlers of bad characters. J. MUDIE *Vindication of James Mudie and John Larnach* p. xxiii

abscond into the woods (or **bush**) (of a convict) to escape from custody into unsettled areas. See ABSCOND. [First recorded 1790.]

1801 William Crozier Cook, having rendered himself obnoxious to the law, had **absconded into the woods**, where not being able to grind the wheat he had stolen from the store he ate it unground, which upon drinking a quantity of water fermented in his bowels, and caused a mortification, and notwithstanding, (on his being obliged from the excessive torments he endured to crawl into the town) the most efficacious medicines were administered he soon after expired. G. BARRINGTON *A Sequel to Barrington's Voyage to New South Wales* pp. 29–30

1827 The Lieutenant Governor has much Pleasure to announce the Capture of the three remaining Convicts, who after attempting to surprise the Emma Kemp cutter, **absconded into the Bush**. *Colonial Times* (Hobart) 27 July p. 1

absent (onself) (of a convict) to remove (oneself) from custody. [This reflexive use of *absent* meaning 'to keep or withdraw (oneself) away' has existed in English since the fifteenth century (as in Hamlet's 'Absent thee from felicitie awhile'), but the legal sense is Australian and belongs to the convict era. It is first recorded in this sense in 1806.]

This is one of the many terms used to describe the escape of convicts from custody, although it also referred to convicts who might go off without permission for a short while but return. Notices such as the one cited below from the *Sydney Gazette* informed people about absentees and warned them against providing any aid to them. However, settlers were often sympathetic to these ABSENTEES and sometimes assisted them.

1810 Notice is hereby given, that the following Prisoners have **absented themselves** from Public Labour in the Town and other Gangs at Sydney;— Whereupon all Persons are hereby cautioned against harbouring, concealing, employing, or maintaining the said Absentees on pain of the Penalties provided by General Orders in that behalf against persons who shall so offend, being strictly enforced; And all Constables and others are hereby enjoined to do their utmost in apprehending the said Runaways, and to lodge them in safe Custody:—Viz.

> James Marton, from Lane Cove
> George McCurr, from Mr Guise's farm at George's River
> John Osborn *alias* Sullivan

Thomas Kelso	James Stewart
Michael Connaugh	Richard Woollaghen
Robert Dawson	Edmund Smith
John Tifford	Thomas Coin
Samuel Harris	James McKay.

Sydney Gazette 28 Jan. p. 2

absentee a convict who escaped from custody and remained at large. See also ABSCONDER. [*Absentee* in the sense 'one who is absent, or away, on any occasion' has existed in English since the sixteenth century, but the legal sense is Australian and belongs to the convict era. It is first recorded in this sense in 1805.]

> **1805**   The gardener's house of His Honor Lieut. Governor PATERSON was broke into and plundered of every thing that could possibly be removed, comprising his whole wearing apparel, bedding, tea, sugar, and provisions; and such part of which as could not be taken away wantonly and shamefully spoiled. A hat was found in the place, which is supposed to have been worn by *Wm. Page*, an **absentee** into the woods; from which and other circumstances the offence is considered to have been committed by him and his accomplices. *Sydney Gazette* 29 Dec. p. 2

absentee from public labour a convict who escaped from government work. [First recorded 1805.]

If a convict went missing from, or did not present himself for, a government work project, he was specifically seen as an absentee from public labour. Convicts were often used as PUBLIC LABOUR to construct buildings and other works for the benefit of the colony and the government.

> **1805**   *Lee*, one of the **absentees from public labor**, was seen last night at a late hour behind Back Row East.—If he has a friend to communicate with, we trust he will be advised to surrender himself—that being the only avenue to hope. *Sydney Gazette* 3 Nov. p. 1

absolute emancipation = ABSOLUTE PARDON. [The term is first recorded in 1799. See EMANCIPATE for the history of the term *emancipation*.]

> **1799**   When the Hillsborough was searched, not less than thirty convicts were found to have been received on board, against the orders and without the

knowledge of the officers, and secreted by the seamen. This ship and the Hunter, shortly after these transactions, failed on their respective voyages. But although, by the measures which had been adopted, it was supposed that none of these people had escaped in the ships, yet many were still lurking in the woods. About this time a young ox was missing from the government stock-yard at Toongabbe, and there was every reason to suppose had been driven away and slaughtered by some of those wretches. In the hope of discovering the offender, a notice was published, holding out a conditional emancipation, and permission to become a settler, to any convict for life, who would come forward with the information necessary to convict the persons concerned in this destructive kind of robbery; and an **absolute emancipation**, with permission to quit the colony, to any one transported only for a limited time; but nothing was ever adduced that could lead to a discovery. D. COLLINS *An Account of the English Colony of New South Wales* vol. 2 p. 268

absolute pardon a complete remission of a convict's sentence, including restitution of the right to return to the British Isles. [First recorded 1802.]

An absolute pardon, or ABSOLUTE EMANCIPATION, was an incentive for convicts to behave well, in the hope that they would be restored to the status of a free person. Absolute pardons remitted a convict's entire sentence, restored all citizenship rights, and meant a person could leave the colonies if they wanted. The first was given in 1790 to John Irving. Absolute pardons could be home pardons (issued for offences not committed in the colony and granted by the authorities in London) or colonial pardons (issued for offences committed in the colony and these were granted by the Governor, although the Governor's ability to do this was limited after the New South Wales Act of 1823). Convicts granted absolute pardons or emancipations were given a CERTIFICATE OF FREEDOM to prove their free status. See also CONDITIONAL PARDON.

1811 On Monday the 25th, and Tuesday the 26th, the whole of the Free Men on and off the Stores, including such as came free into the Colony, such as have become free from their Sentence of Transportation being expired, and such as are free by **Absolute Pardon** or Conditional Emancipation, residing at Sydney, or any of the Districts adjacent thereto, at which time if any of the above Descriptions of Persons are Settlers or Landholders; they are to give in an Account of their Land in Cultivation, &c. together with the Stock and Grain in their Possession. *Sydney Gazette* 19 Jan. p. 1

1822 Absolute pardons were not to be applied for by convicts for life, until they had been 15 years in the colony; nor by convicts for limited terms, until they had resided at least two-thirds of their original sentences. ... An absolute pardon of the governor of New South Wales contains a declaration under his hand, and the seal of the territory, that the unexpired term of transportation of the convict is absolutely remitted to him. It is registered in the secretary's office, and a fee of 5 *s.* is paid there to the principal clerk, and 6 *d.* to the government printer. J.T. BIGGE *Report of the Commissioner of Inquiry into the State of the Colony of New South Wales* pp. 119–20

anti-convict league = ANTI-TRANSPORTATION LEAGUE. [First recorded 1852.]

> **1852** Nearly in the words of Mr. Sidney, to whose information on various points we are much indebted, amongst other events which occurred between 1846 and 1850 were the attempt to re-introduce convicts into Australia, the consequent formation of the **anti-convict league**, the long struggle to obtain steam communication, and the passing of the Act of Parliament which separates Port Phillip, under the name of Victoria, from New South Wales, and gave representative assemblies to the three colonies of New South Wales, Victoria, and South Australia. On the transportation question, the Home Government was defeated, and suffered to retain only Van Diemen's Land as a settlement to which felons might be transported. *The Four Colonies of Australia* p. 16

anti-transportation a term used to describe an association, proposal, etc., opposed to the continuance of the convict system. [First recorded 1847.]

Opposition to the TRANSPORTATION SYSTEM existed from its inception as a system of punishment. It was first strongly expressed by William Molesworth, whose 1837 Select Committee into Transportation questioned the problems of transportation as an effective system of punishment and also highlighted many problems within the penal settlements. However, it was not until the late 1840s that free settlers formed strong opposition to TRANSPORTATION and organised associations to achieve their purpose of ending the system permanently. Their opposition was to the continued transportation of convicts to Van Diemen's Land and the resumption of transportation to New South Wales through the EXILE system. They wanted colonial society to be free of the 'taint' of the convict system. Anti-transportation leagues were formed to organise the protest and to exert political pressure. Transportation to Van Diemen's Land was abolished by 1852.

> **1848** We have no idea of *signing* one way and *voting* another, in reference to this question as many have done, who, after appending their names to **anti-transportation** petitions, did all in their power to neutralise the effect of such petitions, by assisting with their votes and interest to send ultra-transportationists into the Council. *Maitland Mercury* 6 Sept. p. 2

anti-transportationist a person who opposed the continuance of the convict system. [First recorded 1847.]

Those who participated in ANTI-TRANSPORTATION activities were known as anti-transportationists. They mostly consisted of free emigrant settlers who resented the cheap labour that convicts provided and also worried about the effect of convicts on the nature and morals of colonial society.

> **1847** Mr. M'Combie addressed the meeting, and was followed by Mr. Camp-bell, of the firm of Campbell and M'Knight, in a few telling remarks, in which he attempted to charge the **anti-transportationists** with inconsistency, and endeavouring to prevent the importation of convicts and Pentonvilles, and employ them after. It is perfectly analogous says he, to the case of a person who does all in his power to suppress a disorderly house, and because his efforts fail, he then patronizes the establishment. (Roars of laughter.) *Port Phillip Herald* 23 Sept. p. 2

Anti-transportation League an association formed to end transportation (in any form) to the Australian colonies. See ANTI-TRANSPORTATION. [First recorded 1851.]

> **1852** Van Diemen's Land is, in fact, neither more nor less than a huge gaol, more than half of its male population consisting of convicts. The free settlers there protest loudly against this, and strenuous efforts have recently been made to procure an exemption from the further influx of convicts, a great '**Anti-transportation League**', which includes delegates both from that island and the neighbouring colonies, having been formed for the purpose. But, after all, convict-labour appears to be by no means a drug in the market, even in that (in the opinion of the Anti-transportationists) much-abused settle-ment,—some even of those who exclaim most loudly against the system being themselves among the ready employers of convict servants. W. HUGHES *The Australian Colonies* p. 113

assign to make over the services of a convict to a private individual. [This is a specialised Australian use of *assign* in the sense 'to allot or appoint to a person (those that shall perform certain functions in relation to him)'. First recorded in the Australian sense in 1789.]

Convicts were put into the services of, or assigned to, private households or properties to work in such occupations as servants or shepherds. This was seen to put convicts into useful employment, and despite punishments that might be suf-fered at the hands of particular MASTERS, convicts generally benefited, through gaining skills and being better clothed and fed. It was also hoped that this would encourage convicts' reform and moral improvement, although this again depended on individual masters. The system benefited the colony in providing necessary labour and services and saved the government money while providing a system for managing the convicts. Convict women were frequently assigned as domestic servants. Upon their arrival in the colonies, they were taken to the FEMALE FACTORY while they awaited ASSIGNMENT. If they behaved badly or committed any crimes while assigned they might be sent back to the factory. The uncertainty of the ASSIGNMENT SYSTEM (that it was so reliant on the master or mistress) was used by critics to condemn the entire convict system. The Bigge commission (1822–23) saw assignment as a 'lottery' and argued that it provided inadequate punishment and would not deter criminal activity in Britain; the 1838 Molesworth committee report was so critical of assignment and the convict system that the system was brought to an end in New South Wales soon thereafter.

> **1789** And whereas many of the non-commission officers and men of the marine detachment, or other persons who may become settlers upon Our said continent of New South Wales, or the said islands dependant thereupon, may be desirous of availing themselves of the labour of part of the convicts now under your orders: It is Our Will and Pleasure, that in case there should be a prospect of their employing any of the said convicts to advantage, that you **assign** to each grantee the service of any number of them that you may judge sufficient to answer their purpose, on condition of their maintaining, feeding, and clothing such convicts in such manner as shall appear satisfactory to You, or to Our Governor of New South Wales for the time being. *Historical Records of New South Wales* vol. 1 part 2 p. 258

> **1826** [Governor Darling to Under Secretary Hay] No convict will be **assigned** to any person, who shall be known to treat his servants with inhumanity, or who does not supply them with proper Food and Clothing. … No convict will be assigned on arrival to his or her wife or husband, or to his or her relation, or to any person applying for a particular individual. The ends of Justice would be defeated by such assignment, and evil consequences could hardly fail to result from it. *Historical Records of Australia* 1st series XII pp. 252–3

assignable (of a convict) eligible to be assigned to a private individual. [First recorded 1829.]

Once convicts were ready to be ASSIGNED or reassigned to work in private service, they were deemed to be assignable. Their status as being assignable might depend on the nature of the crimes of which they had been found guilty, the length of their sentence, their behaviour on board the CONVICT SHIP or on arrival, or their particular skills.

> **1834** Convicts returned to Government, without complaint, and otherwise unobjectionable, may be immediately re-assigned. But those returned by their respective masters with complaints touching their conduct, are to be considered as 'probationary,' and not **assignable** to any other individual for six months. They are therefore to be sent to the Surveyor of roads and bridges,

and the Principal Superintendent of Convicts to be apprised accordingly. *Australian Almanack and Sydney Directory* p. 140

1840 On looking at the report of the Female Factory in Parramatta, as published in the *Government Gazette*, for three months past, we find that the number **assignable** averages about four hundred women, and yet the scarcity of female servants is one of the greatest wants that hundreds of respectable families complain of. *South Australian Record* 25 July p. 53

assigned (of a convict) made over into the service of an individual. See ASSIGN. [First recorded 1806.]

1806 Any **assigned** Prisoner off the Stores with Individuals, who do not appear as above will on conviction before a Bench of Magistrates be sentenced to Three Years hard Labour in the Gaol Gang, and such other punishments as the case may deserve. *Sydney Gazette* 16 Mar. p. 1

assigned convict a convict made over into the service of a private individual. See ASSIGN. [First recorded 1827.]

1838 An **assigned convict** is entitled to a fixed amount of food and clothing, consisting, in New South Wales, of 12lbs. of wheat, or of an equivalent in flour and maize meal, 7lbs. of mutton or beef, or 4½ lbs. of salt pork, 2oz. of salt, and 2oz. of soap weekly; two frocks or jackets, three shirts, two pair of trousers, three pair of shoes, and a hat and cap, annually. Each man is likewise supplied with one good blanket, and a palliasse or wool mattress, which are considered the property of the master. W. MOLESWORTH *Report from the Select Committee of the House of Commons on Transportation* p. 9

assigned convict servant = ASSIGNED CONVICT. [First recorded 1824.]

1824 And his Excellency the Governor is pleased further to order, that, in addition to all the existing colonial regulations touching the summary jurisdiction of magistrates over the relation of master and **assigned convict servants**, the said magistrates shall have the power of transmitting a copy of the depositions taken before them to the Solicitor of the Crown for the time being, for the purpose of sueing the master and his surety or sureties in the Civil Court, upon their bonds for the maintenance and keeping of convicts assigned with grants of land. E.M. CURR *An Account of the Colony of Van Diemen's Land, principally designed for the use of emigrants* pp. 161–2

assigned servant = ASSIGNED CONVICT. [First recorded 1817.]

1819 It appearing that of three Men who lately absented themselves from Hobart Town, and who gave themselves up on Monday, one was an **assigned Servant** and another a Government Man; the LIEUTENANT GOVERNOR finds it necessary once more to require of the Settlers to give Notice within twenty-four Hours at the Police Office, or in the Country to the nearest Magistrate or District Constable, of the Absence of any of their assigned Servants. Any Settler who shall be found to have allowed assigned Servants to absent themselves without such Notice will be excluded from that Indulgence in future. *Hobart Town Gazette* 1 May

1839 It has been found in several instances that the wives of emigrant farm labourers, are not proof against the seductive arts of the **assigned** and emancipated **servants**, when living on the same establishments. The women are naturally objects of the regard and attention of the labouring convicts, and of unmarried fencers, splitters, bullock drivers, carpenters, &c. Indeed, the women, too, learn too often to drink, and infidelity to their husbands is the consequence—while they connive at the dishonesty of the convict servants. *Port Phillip Patriot* 20 May p. 7

assigned service = SERVICE. [First recorded 1818.]

1818 The Female Prisoners in **Assigned Service** having misbehaved in many Instances, and there being at present no Factory or Public Establishment in this Settlement for placing such Women under regular Restraint and Labour; His Honor the Lieutenant Governor makes known his Intention of sending up to Port Jackson, to be placed in the Factory there, such Female Prisoners as from their bad Conduct cannot be continued in Assigned Service, or allowed the Indulgence of a Ticket of Leave. *Hobart Town Gazette* 28 Mar.

assignee a person to whom the services of a convict are made over. [First recorded 1825.]

Assignees were sometimes free settlers, local officials, or even EMANCIPATED convicts. Assignees varied in how they dealt with their convict servants, and some were notorious for treating their servants very badly. The government had the right to withdraw the assignment if abuse occurred.

1838 MORAL QUALIFICATION OF **ASSIGNEE.**—The Sessions, or Magistrate, as the case may be, shall not recommend as assignee for Convict servants of any description, any person who is not free, of good character, capable of maintaining the servants applied for, and to whose care and management they may not in their, or his opinion, be safely entrusted. The strictest attention is particularly enjoined to this rule, as the moral improvement of the convict population so much depends on its careful observance. *Tegg's New South Wales Pocket Almanack* p. 85

assignment the making over to a private individual of the services of a convict; the state of being so placed. [First recorded 1822.]

The assignment system was integral to the convict system as a whole. It began in August 1789 and ended in July 1841. It greatly reduced the cost of the convict system. However, from the 1830s onwards, critics of the system were unhappy with leaving convicts subject to the whims of private masters. After the Molesworth Committee investigated and highlighted the problems of the system, publishing its findings in 1838, the assignment system did not continue for long. Molesworth felt that convicts did not receive adequate moral and religious instruction for their reformation, and condemned colonial society as a whole as immoral and corrupt. Critics also felt that assignment did not provide an adequate deterrent to potential criminals back in England.

1822 The Superintendent of convicts is thus perfectly apprized of every thing requisite for directing a just and satisfactory **assignment** of the prisoners; and as, when once they are placed in his hands, no other authority interposes, much good or evil is to be expected from his management. Mr. Hutchinson, the person now exercising that office at Sydney, was himself formerly a convict; and from his various means of obtaining intelligence, well may he be supposed,—so far as the ample jurisdiction he exercises can extend,—to possess information universally correct regarding the circumstances of every family: he is therefore fully competent to determine what description of convict is best suited for any particular service: too often, however, does caprice, if not motives more unworthy, appear to influence him in the performance of this important duty. T. REID *Two Voyages to New South Wales and Van Diemen's Land* p. 252

1843 Assignment, whether for good or for evil, exists no longer, and the convict after having gone through an ordeal of probation, first either in a penitentiary in England, or at Norfolk Island, afterwards in Van Diemen's Land, under the superintendence of Government, must be hired, if hired at all, at wages to be fixed upon by the parties and the Government, the payment of which wages the Government will enforce partly by payment to the convicts themselves, partly by lodgments in the Savings' Bank, for the benefit of the convict when he shall have regained that stage in society when by law he will be entitled to hold property for himself. *Sydney Morning Herald* 15 Sept. p. 2

assignment system the system whereby convicts were made over into the service of a private individual. [First recorded 1838.]

1838 The only other authority, with regard to the effects of the **assignment system**, which Your Committee deem it necessary to quote, is Captain Maconochie, secretary to Sir John Franklin, the present Governor of Van Diemen's Land. In a report to the Government on the state of convict discipline in Van Diemen's Land, Captain Maconochie has stated that: 'The practice of assigning convicts to masters is cruel, uncertain, prodigal, ineffectual either for reform or example. ... It defeats, in consequence, its own most important objects; instead of reforming, it degrades humanity.' W. MOLESWORH *Report from the Select Committee of the House of Commons on Transportation* p. 11

B

bad a term used by convicts to describe another convict who dissociated himself from his fellows and cooperated with police and officials—while in the eyes of the officials such a convict had become 'good', to his fellows convicts he had turned 'bad'. [Ironic use of *bad* 'wicked'. First recorded 1835.]

> **1838** While in prison, on this occasion, he became privy to a plot, for rescuing some men, sentenced to death, which he was not comfortable till he had disclosed. His comrades suspected that he had communicated their plans, they marked also his altered conduct, for he could no longer join in many of the evil practices in which they indulged, and he became in their estimation and language, 'A **bad** fellow.' Before, when he ran with them into the depths of iniquity, he passed among them as a 'good fellow'; for thus, among this depraved portion of our race, is good too generally called evil, and evil good! and a man, who in any measure becomes reformed, is liable to much persecution. J. BACKHOUSE *A Narrative of a Visit to the Australian Colonies* pp. 277–8

> **1838** Dr Ullathorne likewise said: 'I was very much struck with the peculiar language used by the convicts at Norfolk Island. When a prisoner has been conversing with me respecting another individual, he has designated him as a good man. I suspected that he did not mean what he said, and on asking an explanation, he has apologised, and said, that it was the habitual language of the place, and that a **bad** man was called a good man; and that a man who was ready to perform his duty was generally called a bad man. There is quite a vocabulary of terms of that kind, which seems to have been invented to adapt themselves to the complete subversion of the human heart which I found subsisting.' W. MOLESWORTH *Report from the Select Committee of the House of Commons on Transportation* pp. 17–18

barrack (often in plural **barracks**) a building or set of buildings for the temporary accommodation of convicts. [In standard English the term refers to 'a set of buildings erected or used as a place of lodgement or residence for troops'. The Australian sense is first recorded in 1822.]

Convicts who were not ASSIGNED to private service and who worked on public works projects in and around the towns usually lived in barracks. This was the case from 1819 when, during Macquarie's governorship, the Hyde Park barracks designed by Francis Greenway were completed. This was part of Macquarie's plan to implement a more systematic convict system. Prior to that, convicts generally paid for lodgings in private houses or hotels, using the wages earned for extra work performed in their own time. Housing in barracks was believed to be more effective for discipline and reform as it allowed for much closer supervision and control of convicts. It also meant the convicts would work for the government for the entire day, making them more productive.

1822 It has already been observed, that in consequence of there being no **barrack** at Hobart Town for the confinement of convicts, their control, after the hours of government work, is more difficult than it is at present at Sydney. J.T. BIGGE *Report of the Commissioner of Inquiry into the State of the Colony of New South Wales* p. 34

1838 The Hyde Park **Barrack** is the principal depôt of prisoners, in the Colony. It is a substantial, brick building, rather handsome, and of three stories, enclosed in an open area, formed by buildings of one story, with sloping roofs resting against the outside walls, at the angles of which there are circular, domed, small buildings. … The lower story of the central building is chiefly devoted to the offices of the Assignment-board, &c. The second and third stories are divided into large wards, in which the prisoners sleep in hammocks, in single tiers. Those who arrive by one ship, occupy one ward, till taken away by the masters to whom they are assigned. This is a good regulation; it keeps them in some measure, from the contamination of the 'old hands'. The mechanics, retained in the employment of the government, and some others, are also lodged in separate wards. One ward, in a side-building, has a barrack-bedstead, or platform, on which the prisoners sleep side by side, without any separation. There are only ten solitary cells in this prison, in which, flagellation is the usual punishment. J. BACKHOUSE *A Narrative of a Visit to the Australian Colonies* p. 45

battery gang a party of convicts assigned to labour in the construction of a gun battery. [First recorded 1801.]

Convicts who worked on PUBLIC WORKS were generally placed in working parties known as gangs. A battery gang worked to build batteries, that is, they worked to construct fortified emplacements for heavy guns.

1801 [Government and General Orders] Any person not appearing at these musters will be taken up as vagrants and punished to the utmost extent of the law, if free; if a prisoner, they will be sentenced [to] twelve months confinement in the **battery gang**. *Historical Records of Australia* 1st series III p. 257

Bay (usually as **the Bay**) = BOTANY BAY. [First recorded 1841.]

A common short form of BOTANY BAY was Bay or 'the Bay'. 'Botany Bay' came to be a popular term referring to Sydney or New South Wales as a general destination of transportation for British and Irish prisoners.

1852 The ordinary of Newgate, Mr. Cotton, a well-known name, in his evidence before the Commons in 1818, has left nothing to conjecture. The prisoners of his day 'looked on transportation as a party of pleasure:' they departed from the prison with huzzas, and bade glad adieu to their less happy companions and keepers, exclaiming, 'what a glorious kangaroo hunt we will have at the **Bay**.' J. WEST *The History of Tasmania* vol. 2 p. 150

bay ship a ship carrying convicts from Britain to New South Wales. [First recorded 1825.]

Bay ships (see also CONVICT SHIPS) transported convicts under a variety of conditions. The transports were contracted out to private firms that provided the ships, and early journeys—the second and third fleets in particular—had a high death and illness rate. After these tragedies, the firms were made to sign contracts that specified conditions had to be improved and that a surgeon had to be on board. Over time, conditions on board the ships improved significantly.

1830 Here I am at last embarked in a '**Bay Ship**', as the Convicts call those bound to Botany Bay, and very uncomfortable it has hitherto been; but, now I am settled on board, by far the worst part of it is over. H.W. BUNBURY *Early Days in Western Australia* p. 2

1865 On the evening of the 11th of August, we learned that a '**bay ship**' (vessels for New South Wales being so-called) had anchored at Spithead; and on the following morning a draft from the two hulks, York and Leviathan, was taken out to her. J.F. MORTLOCK *Experiences of a Convict* p. 54

bellowser a sentence or term of transportation for life; a person who serves such a sentence. [*Bellowser* is recorded in the dialect of West Yorkshire meaning 'a violent blow or hard task which takes away one's breath'. The *English Dialect Dictionary* gives some quotations from *The Dialect of Leeds, and its Neighbourhood* (1861), indicating how the term could be used figuratively: 'A crowner in the way of argument, a "decided hit"; "a good say," knocking the wind out of your antagonist'. Transportation for life was a punishment that would knock the wind out of a prisoner. The sense is first recorded in Australia in 1812. See also FLASH LANGUAGE.]

1812 WIND, a man transported for his natural life, is said to be *lag'd for his wind*, or to have *knap'd a winder*, or *a **bellowser***, according to the humour of the speaker. J.H. VAUX *Memoirs* (1964) vol. 2 p. 225

1844 *Henry Garland*, a ticket-of-leave holder in the employ of the Revd. Mr. Woodward, of Parramatta, was charged by the Chief Constable, with having, on the previous evening, answered his enquiry, as to his condition in the scale of the population of New South Wales, by asserting that he was a free man. Subsequent reference to those long thin volumes which the Principal Superintendent of Convicts considerately favors the Police Office with, yclept 'The Indents,' proved Garland to be what is termed in colonial phraseology a '**Bellowser**' vulgo, a transport for life. Garland endeavoured to explain away the *lapsus linguae* he had made, by stating that he considered holding a ticket to be freedom; but this was out of the frying-pan into the fire, as his indulgence being for Bathurst, he had no right to be in Parramatta without the authority of a pass, which necessary document he had forgot to provide himself with. The Bench considering it was proper that Garland should arrive at the correct meaning of the words 'free' and ticket-of-leave, and understand their relative difference, adjudged translation to the cells for seven days. *Parramatta Chronicle* 29 June p. 2

birthstain the stigma attached to the convict period or to convict ancestry.

Rudyard Kipling first referred to a convict 'birthstain'—that the Australian colonies had been born as a place for criminals—in his 1892 poem 'The Song of the Cities'. In 1899 William Lygon, Seventh Earl Beauchamp, upon his arrival as Governor of New South Wales, reiterated the idea of a birthstain, to the disgust of the colonial population (see 1899 citation). Free emigrant settlers and emancipists, from the 1840s ANTI-TRANSPORTATION agitation through the rest of the nineteenth century, worked hard to erase the memory of the colonies' convict heritage and ancestry, seen negatively as a 'birthstain'. Shame and silence over the convict origins of Australia [lingered on into the] early part of the twentieth century and only recently has convict heritage been rediscovered and embraced by many Australians.

1899 When requested to grant an interview Lord Beauchamp informed your representative that he intended refraining from being interviewed, and had decided to have all communications made through his private secretary. Under these circumstances no interview could take place. Lord Beauchamp said that at present he was not in a position to express his views regarding federation. Mr. Corcoran, private secretary, handed the press the following message from

Lord Beauchamp to the people of New South Wales. It is in verse, being an adaptation of a verse of Rudyard Kipling's "The Song of the Cities":—

> Greeting,—Your **birthstain** have you turned to good,
> Forcing strong wills perverse to steadfastness.
> The first flush of the tropics in your blood,
> And at your feet success.—Beauchamp.

Sydney Morning Herald 11 May

1910 The district was spotted with '**birth stain**.' The 'old hands' formed almost a community of themselves. Horse and cattle-duffing was not looked upon as a crime, but rather as a legitimate means of livelihood. Wheat was grown, but only in sufficient quantity to provide flour for the usually large family of more than half-wild youngsters. *Bulletin* 17 Mar. p. 14

birthstained tainted with the stigma of convict ancestry or BIRTHSTAIN. [First recorded 1904.]

1904 From this it would appear as if an invitation to Government House, in the first quarter of the nineteenth century, was in the nature of a command, or was it that the 'exclusives' were toadies enough to go to Government House, knowing well Macquarie's partiality for the '**birthstained**?' *Truth* (Sydney) 29 May p. 7

black book (in Tasmania) a register that held the names and particulars of identification of every prisoner in the colony, together with a summary of the offender's career, typically noting offences and punishments.

According to Reverend John West, Lieutenant-Governor Arthur in Van Diemen's Land instituted this system to improve the supervision and punishment of convicts. The moral index was compiled in the office of the principal superintendent of convicts by a convict clerk, Edward Cook, beginning in 1827—he wrote up the careers of 12,305 convicts. Arthur also kept 'white books' in which good deeds and behaviour on the part of convicts were recorded. Arthur's system became a fundamental part of the sentencing and treatment of convicts in Van Diemen's Land.

1852 Arthur watched with great diligence the operation of his system. The character of most masters was known: they were bound to make annual returns of the number and conduct of their men. Their recommendation was required to procure the prisoner's indulgence: his police character was drawn out in form—the parliamentary papers shew into what minute particulars those documents entered; even an admonition of the magistrates was noted, and made part of the case. **Black** and *white* **books** were kept, in which meritorious actions and the reverse were recorded. J. WEST *The History of Tasmania* vol. 2 p. 229

bolt *verb* (of a convict) to escape from custody. [*Bolt* in the sense 'to take flight, escape; to rush suddenly off or away' has existed in standard English since the sixteenth century. In Australia there developed two specialised senses. First, 'to abscond, either abandoning one's debts or in possession of illicit gains' (first recorded in 1829). Second, it described the actions of a convict in escaping from custody (first recorded 1832).]

Like ABSCONDING, bolting was often an attempt to escape harsh employers, to escape working on CHAIN GANGS, or to escape places of SECONDARY punishment. Lack of adequate surveillance often encouraged bolting—for example, CONVICT SHEPHERDS used their relative freedom to make their escape. While many were recaptured and punished, some made new and successful lives for themselves, as is clear from the Mortlock citation below.

> **1865** He [a friend of the author] '**bolted**,' as it is termed, from Van Diemen's Land, in 1849, and wrote to say that he was rapidly amassing a fortune at the American gold fields, should probably return in disguise to England, and had thoughts of entering Parliament by the purchase of an Irish borough. Should he ever become Home Secretary, it is to be hoped he will not forget his shipmate, who, being then labouring under his old complaint, 'an attack of the heart;' could not make up his mind to accompany him. J.F. MORTLOCK *Experiences of a Convict* p. 58

bolt *noun* the act of escaping from custody.

> **1848** I repeat, if these inexcusable felons, who are in no want of any *one necessary* of life, were *invariably* subjected to a uniform and unalterable punishment, the alarm and inconvenience and distraction and loss of the valuable settler would be greatly lessened, if not wholly prevented; but it is in Van Diemen's Land, as it is in the Old Bailey, the greatest rogues get off best, and so it is with many of these culpable and deliberate and determined offenders; for one has this excuse, and the next has another equally false, fallacious, and groundless; and there being, I believe, instructions from the higher authorities to deal leniently with these incorrigible men, they are too often let off with light punishment, such as seven, fourteen, or twenty-one days' solitary confinement, which is, in truth, no punishment at all, for the sentenced man is well supplied with other additions, while he enjoys the much-prized luxury of ease and idleness, at the sametime very possibly forming the plan of his next '**bolt**'. J. SYME *Nine Years in Van Diemen's Land* pp. 194–5

bolter = ABSCONDER [First recorded 1832.]

> **1832** *Margaret Champion*, assigned to Mr. Wood of George street, was brought in by a constable, who said; he had just *grabbed* her, and knowing her to be a ***bolter***, took her under his *protection*. It appeared, that the prisoner, who was bedizened out in bridal attire, having an unconquerable penchant for

a husband, left her master's house with a gay Lothario some ten or twelve days back, and was not heard of till within this day or two, when it came to her master's knowledge, that she had applied to a priest, to unite her fate to the swain aforesaid; and she was accordingly seized by the rude grasp of the *Charley* at the very moment when 'her blushing honors stuck upon her,' and when she was about to submit to the softer hands of matrimonial rule. *Hill's Life in New South Wales* 17 Aug. p. 2

1833 John Jones, was charged as a **bolter** from the house of his master; when found, he was singing lustily—

> 'From rocks and sands,
> And barren lands,
> Kind fortune set me free;
> From great guns,
> And woman's tongues,
> Oh! Lord, deliver me.'

Having a character called pretty good, he escaped with only seven days to the spring board. *Sydney Herald* 19 Sept. p. 2

bond of convict status; not free.

[*Bond* in the sense 'in a state of serfdom or slavery; not free' arose in the fourteenth century. It derives from Old English *bonda* which meant 'householder, freeholder'. After the Norman Conquest the status of the *bonda* was reduced, as he sank from the position of a free man tilling his own land to that of a tenant bound to certain services to a lord. As with the words *churl* and *villain*, as the social status of the *bonda* was reduced, the term itself attracted negative connotations. At a later date the word was probably associated with the other word *bond* meaning 'anything with which one's body or limbs are bound in restraint of personal liberty'. The Australian convict sense is first recorded in 1800.]

People were generally thought of in the Australian colonies as being of the status 'bond' or 'free'. 'Bond' was a less pejorative term than 'convict'.

1829 We would advise Mr. Patrick to be less insulting to persons who may be placed beneath him, and not to tell any one that—'you are only a Prisoner, and Government does not mean that Prisoners should get money!' As Mr. Gordon very properly remarked, Government likes to see every man, free or **bond**, do well, and every man who is sworn in as Constable, is, by virtue of his office raised above the disabilities of a Prisoner. *Launceston Advertiser* 16 Nov. p. 3

bondage the state or condition of being a convict. See BOND. [First recorded 1831.]

1837 The number of criminals annually transported is above 6,000. In 1835, the last year of which I have a full account, there were transported, to New South Wales, 3,006 males, and 179 females; to Van Dieman's Land, 2,054 males, and 922 females; making a total of 6,161 criminals. The entire number in actual **bondage** is, in New South Wales, nearly 30,000, whilst in Van Dieman's Land there are nearly 20,000, to which must be added 3,000 for the penal settlements of Norfolk Island, Moreton Bay, and Port Arthur. It is to be further considered, that the great proportion of free inhabitants of these colonies consist of emancipists from a similar condition of bondage. W.B. ULLATHORNE *The Catholic Mission in Australasia* pp. 14–15

1849 The labour of the convict is of course unpaid; and in this and in banishment from his country, his punishment *within the colony* consists. But whilst thus labouring without wages, he is learning much that will ultimately be of advantage to him; he is taught how to maintain himself in a new country; and when, as he terms it, his '**bondage**' is over, he generally comes from the hand of his master an useful man. The settlers prefer men so tutored to emigrants; who, on their first arrival are, comparatively, but 'babes in the wood.' The settler inquires, not what a man has been, but what he can do. J.P. TOWNSEND *Rambles and Observations in New South Wales* p. 220

bond labour = CONVICT LABOUR [First recorded 1847.]

1852 The public works performed by convict labor, though sometimes extensive and important, will appear inconsiderable, if compared with the imperial or colonial cost. The deep cuts and massive bridges, which please the eye, are yet disproportionate to the traffic, and produce no adequate return. The proportion between free and bond labor, is as 2 and 3 to 1. Task labor has been commonly found incompatible with discipline, or liable to favoritism and official dishonesty: the overseer 'approximates' or guesses, when not inclined to reckon. Day work is still less satisfactory: the pick is slowly uplifted, and descends without effect. The body bends and goes through hours of ineffectual motion; or if the rigour of discipline renders evasion penal, the triangles disgrace a civilised nation, and the colony is filled with violence and vengeance. Yet convict labor has, generally, been deemed important to an infant settlement; to secure a combination, without which preliminary stages of colonisation are slowly passed. Such has been its undoubted use; but who, with the prodigies of modern enterprise before him, will assign to **bond labor** a peculiar efficiency, or doubt that well directed capital can ensure all that force can effect. J. WEST *The History of Tasmania* vol. 2 p. 330

bond list a list of all those who were BOND in a locality (including those on TICKETS OF LEAVE). [First recorded 1845.]

1845 Saturday's police list exhibited the same gratifying of Boxing day as that day's list did of Christmas day. Not a single free case of drunkenness, and only three charges for such offence on the **bond list**, all ticket holders, and who were discharged, one of them stating by the way that he had taken 'a spell' from drink for five years until the previous day; the bench advised him to go and take another spell for another five years. *Sydney Morning Herald* 30 Dec. p. 2

bond man = CONVICT MAN. [First recorded 1830.]

1845 The **bond-man** frequently saves his few shillings, received as indulgences for good conduct, in order that when he becomes free he may buy a horse to carry him. Rich and poor, young and old, male and female, bond and free, all equally 'put their trust in horses.' D. MACKENZIE *The Emigrant's Guide* p. 77

bond servant = ASSIGNED CONVICT. [First recorded 1848.]

1848 The course generally adopted in such cases was the following:—When an assigned servant, say a lifer (that is, one sentenced for life), after the usual probationary period of eight years had expired, had become eligible, from good conduct and servitude, for the indulgence of a ticket of leave, (which ticket exempts him from Government employ, and enables him to work in any one chosen district for his own particular benefit,) his master, conscious that when he left him he could not obtain another **bond servant**, and that, if he retained his services after he obtained his ticket, he would be compelled to pay him a free man's wages, generally contrived, on some frivolous, and often *false* charge, to get him punished prior to the time allotted. This punishment, according to the convict regulations, would defer and prevent his liberty for two years longer, during which period, of course, he would serve as before; and in the course of that time his master would again contrive to take him to court, and add a still further probation. C. COZENS *Adventures of a Guardsman* pp. 159–60

bondsman = CONVICT MAN. [First recorded 1839.]

1850 We understand the rules which it has been determined shall govern the [Tasmanian] 'UNION,' will be based upon the broadest principles of civil and religious freedom,—and that a spirit of concord and generous sentiment will be scrupulously disseminated by this new political body. No exclusiveness whatever will characterize the union—all will be eligible to come within the extended line traced out as its boundary—that is, all persons of good character—the man who has fallen, but repented and atoned for his errors—as well as those to whom crime has never been legally imputed. This is new ground, and the only ground which a people inhabiting a great and rising colony, like this, aspiring to independence, should condescend to occupy. The man of wealth and influence, the employer and the employed, the **bondsman** and the free, can once for all co-operate for the common good. We gladly hail this new movement, as shadowing forth bright hopes for the future independence of this fine island—independence in the true and fullest sense; and with independence a concurrent improvement in the social, moral and religious habits of the people. Political independence and a cordial union of classes must generate virtue amongst any people, whilst political degradation, social oppression and class tyranny are sure to beget vices and enormities, and to degenerate, corrupt and produce licentiousness in the most virtuously disposed community. *Irish Exile* (Hobart) 19 Oct. p. 2

bond stockman = CONVICT STOCK-KEEPER. [First recorded 1835.]

1835 Cattle stealing generally commences with stockmen in charge of herds in remote stations; they receive and herd for each other a portion of the young and unbranded stock of their masters, and by the time they are free, or obtain tickets-of-leave, many have considerable herds of stolen cattle. The records of the Supreme Court or Quarter Sessions will prove that four out of five of the persons convicted of cattle stealing were originally **bond** or freed **stockmen**. They very frequently follow up their successful game of stealing or receiving stolen cattle, which they usually herd in concealed recesses, and dispose of to butchers at a low rate, to the great loss of those from whom they were stolen, and to the injury of all graziers. *Colonist* (Sydney) 30 July p. 243

bond woman = CONVICT WOMAN. [First recorded 1827.]

1827 We shall make a little Eden of this place by and by—our cultivation proceeds rapidly, and in another year we shall have no occasion to buy wheat—my maid Agatha, is then to be married to my brother's freeman, who will have 100 acres in fee and a small portion of stock; my **bond-woman** is offered as a prize to the best deserver or truest lover, and 30 acres in fee. *Sydney Monitor* 30 Mar. p. 363

Botany Bay a generic term for a penal colony in Australia. [First recorded in this sense in 1789.]
Botany Bay was the name given to the site where Captain James Cook first landed in 1770, and derived from the many botanical specimens collected by Joseph Banks while there. It did not become a place of settlement as it was deemed unsuitable by Captain Arthur Phillip due to a lack of fresh water and being an unsafe harbour. Port Jackson at Sydney Cove became the place of the first British settlement. 'Botany Bay' became a generic term for the destination to which convicts were transported, although they were actually taken to Port Jackson. 'Botany

Bay' was used as a general term for the penal colonies. It was also often used in a derogatory sense in relation to the perceived degradation and criminal notoriety of the colonies. It was sometimes shortened to simply the BAY.

1796 From the disposition to crimes and the incorrigible characters of the major part of the colonists, an odium was, from the first, illiberally thrown upon the settlement; and the word '**Botany Bay**' became a term of reproach that was indiscriminately cast on every one who resided in New South Wales. D. COLLINS *An Account of the English Colony in New South Wales* vol. 2 p. 502

1852 A person may now, however, confess to a temporary sojourn in the Australian colonies, and to a personal acquaintance with the shores of '**Botany Bay**', without the fear of being supposed a member of that numerous class who have 'left their country for their country's good'. W. HUGHES *The Australian Colonies* p. 110

Botany Bay aristocracy a derogatory term for the social pretentions of those who sought to place themselves above others.

From the 1820s, when large numbers of free settlers came to the colonies, the social tension between ex-convicts or EMANCIPISTS and those free settlers who saw themselves as superior was clear. Often this was exacerbated by the fact that some convicts might be of a superior British status (see GENTLEMAN CONVICTS) while settlers might be of lower status. 'Botany Bay aristocracy' probably first was used of free settlers who, acquiring wealth and property, saw themselves as superior. It then appears to have become a term also referring to emancipists who, having improved themselves, sought to erase their convict past and present themselves as part of respectable society.

1838 If convicts were given into the servitude of a virtuous and industrious peasantry or tenantry, say in the proportion of three, four, or even, in some .cases, as many as ten in a family—these free people would have an interest in, and would be *able* to reform them, and make them useful members of society. But if our readers come to know, that some, (we must say many) of the **Botany Bay aristocracy** possess fifty, seventy, one hundred, and three hundred convicts (gratuitously given away white slaves)—talk then of improving them, reforming them!—they have to produce carriages and carpets and silver chandeliers for the rich, and if seven at once get hanged, the so-and-so Esquire, or so-and-so Venerable or Honorable, can get as many more without any trouble. A.L.F. *History of Samuel Terry* p. 16

1872 Mr. de Beausant's grandfather was a desperate ruffian, a sailor who nearly murdered his captain, and who was 'lagged' to Australia, where-in remembrance of his former calling, he was known to his mates in the chain-gang by the *sobriquet* of 'Bo'sun.' Mr. 'Bo'sun' became an expiree, took up land, married an industrious young lady of the 'Jenny Diver' class (sent out 'filching,') and became the sire of Mr. 'Bo'sun' the second, who, in the fitness of time, happening to read Scott's 'Ivanhoe,' hit upon the happy thought of changing his name to 'Beausant.' *His* son added a *de*, and it is generally expected the next of the breed will make it 'de la Beausant,' and brag about his ancestors' estates in Normandy. A man is not answerable for the faults or crimes of his relatives or progenitors; but when we find 'The Block' thronged with this **Botany Bay aristocracy**, whose insufferable pretentions would be unbearable in the bluest blood to be found in 'Debrett,' one cannot help reminding these gaudy tulips that they spring from very dirty roots. G. BUNSTER & R. THATCHER *It Runs in the Blood* p. 61

box a moveable box-like shelter in which convicts were confined at night. [First recorded 1836.]

When convicts worked on ROAD GANGS and other public works in undeveloped areas, they were housed in such boxes. The boxes varied in size and standard. This system was instituted under the governorship of Sir Richard Bourke, probably from around 1836, in an attempt to establish stricter control over the convicts and to prevent escapes. See also CARAVAN.

1838 The prisoners on Goat Island also amount to about 200, most of them are in irons; they are employed in erecting a powder-magazine, which is nearly completed, and is of sandstone. … The prisoners are lodged in twelve wooden '**boxes**,' which are whitewashed inside and out, and are very clean. Each of these boxes is furnished with a few Bibles, Testaments, and Prayer Books. J. BACKHOUSE *A Narrative of a Visit to the Australian Colonies* p. 457

1838 Sir R. Bourke stated 'that the condition of the convicts in the chain-gangs was one of great privation and unhappiness.' They are locked up from sunset to sunrise in the caravans or **boxes** used for this description of persons, which hold from 20 to 28 men, but in which the whole number can neither stand upright nor sit down at the same time (except with their legs at right angles to their bodies), and which, in some instances, do not allow more than 18 inches in width for each individual to lie down upon on the bare boards. W. MOLESWORTH *Report from the Select Committee of the House of Commons on Transportation* p. 16

broad arrow the arrow-shaped mark placed upon government stores, convict uniforms, etc. [A shortening of *broad arrow-head*. From the seventeenth century this mark was used by the British Board of Ordnance on all government stores, and was regarded as the monarch's mark. Although the term is not specifically

Australian, it appears commonly in the literature of the convict era. First recorded in Australia in 1803.]

> **1803** J. Harding, charged with having taken a piece of iron from the Government Wharf, marked with the **broad arrow**, was ordered to work for Government 12 months. *Sydney Gazette* 20 Mar. p. 2

> **1851** On first arriving at Sydney … you soon become aware that you are in a country very different from England. The government gangs of convicts marching to and fro in single military file, as they go or return from their work, and the solitary ones straggling here and there, with their light woollen Parramatta frocks and trousers, or grey and yellow jackets, all daubed over with **broad arrows**, P.B's or C.B's, these initials denoting the Prisoners or Carters Barracks, and various numerals in black, white, and red; with perhaps the jail-gang straddling sulkily by in their jingling leg-chains, tell a tale too plain to be misunderstood. A. MAJORIBANKS *Travels in New South Wales* p. 15

bull seventy-five strokes of the lash. [As explained in the citation below, slang terms for coins were applied to numbers of lashes. The value of the coins increases as the number of lashes increases: *tester* or sixpence (25 lashes), *bob* or a shilling (50 lashes), *bull* or five shillings (75 lashes), *canary* or a sovereign (100 lashes). See also FLOGGING and LASH. First recorded 1859.]

> **1859** I might, by speaking to the magistrate, have had the culprit put upon the treadmill for a month, or placed in a road-gang, to work in irons, for three, six, nine, or twelve months, or flogged to the extent of one hundred lashes, twenty-five being the minimum. (By the way, there were slang terms applied to these doses of the lash: twenty-five was called a 'tester;' fifty, a 'bob;' seventy-five, a '**bull**;' and a hundred a 'canary.') J. LANG *Botany Bay* p. 40

bush used in phrases with various verbs of motion, especially **to take (to) the bush**, where (of convicts) it means 'to escape from custody'. [First recorded in this sense in 1804.]

'The bush' was a generic term for the destination of escaped convicts who fled from custody into the unsettled areas of the colonies. Usually those who took to the bush adopted a life of crime and came to be known as BUSHRANGERS.

> **1813** [Governor Macquarie to Lieutenant-Governor Davey] A number of Male Convicts having, at different times within the last few years, absconded from the Settlements of the Derwent and Port Dalrymple, and **betaken themselves to the** Woods, *or **Bush***, where they continually molest the Natives of the Country, and from whence they carry on Predatory incursions on European Settlers and other Inhabitants of the Country, to the danger of their lives and great injury and destruction of their Cattle and other Property, you are hereby

directed to endeavour to ascertain the number and Names of these Runaways and Depredators … in order that the necessary measures may be adopted for apprehending or destroying them. *Historical Records of Australia* 3rd series II pp. 20–1

1838 MEN MISSING.—These are convicts who have **taken to the bush**. These unfortunate creatures are driven to this dreadful alternative through the cruel usage of the settlers and overseers of the different road parties and chain-gangs. … I have seen these men *executed*, and heard them declare in their dying moments, the horrid and disgusting particulars of how they have murdered their mates one after the other, and lived upon their dead bodies, until the whole party, originally consisting of perhaps ten individuals, had been butchered, leaving the narrator and another only alive, and how he and his companion were afraid to fall asleep, lest the other should knock his brains out; and how at last nature became exhausted in his comrade; and then, how he deprived him of life, and immediately satisfied his hunger on his flesh, tearing the remaining portion from off his body and skin, started for the inhabited districts, to end his suffering in an ignominious death. G.C. INGLETON *True Patriots All: or news from Early Australia—as told in a collection of broadsides* (1952) p. 194

bushranger an escaped convict subsisting in the bush, often by resort to robbery. [The earliest evidence for the term *bushranger* is in the United States, where it appears to be a translation of Dutch *boschloper* 'woods runner'. Earlier forms *bossloper* and *bushloper* are recorded in the United States in 1687 and 1694 respectively. The form *bushranger* is first recorded in American English in 1758 referring to 'one who ranges in the bush', a 'frontiersman', a 'woodsman'. The word appears to have been borrowed into Australian English with this sense. Thus in the Banks Papers, 19 July 1805: 'If the Bush rangers will always bring plants from the remote parts of their tours, I can form a good idea of what distance they have been'. Many of the people who 'ranged in the bush' were of course escaped convicts, and it is through this association that the term acquired its pejorative associations. The 1814 citation provides clear evidence of the establishment of the pejorative meaning.]

Escaped convicts were often desperate and there was little option but to turn to criminal acts such as stock theft and armed robbery if they wanted to avoid recapture and survive. These escaped convicts made up the first generation of Australian bushrangers.

1814 [Governor Macquarie to Earl Bathurst] Indeed the protection of the Settlers in the Interior, and of the persons passing from one Settlement to the other, Who are now Numerous, on the Necessary Intercourse of Trade Against the Attacks and Depredations of the lawless Banditti of Runaway Convicts, who Infest the intermediate Country, Cannot be otherwise effected than by Means of Military Stations. The principal part of the Shipping touching only at the Derwent, the Articles of Trade required at Port Dalrymple are consequently sent thither over Land. All which, together with the Herds, Flocks and Grain of the Settlers are now Subjected to the plunder of these Banditti, Commonly Called '**Bush Rangers**', Who in the present State of the Country are beyond All Control. The proposed Military Stations Would soon disperse these Depredators, and finally bring them to Justice. *Historical Records of Australia* 1st series VIII pp. 306–7

1822   The convicts assigned to the military officers, according to the custom and necessities of that day, were obliged to furnish to their masters, and to procure for themselves, a certain quantity of kangaroo flesh; and having first gone into the woods for these temporary supplies of food, they gradually acquired a knowledge of the country, and of the means of supporting themselves in it. To this at length they were driven; and the predatory habits of these men, who have since received the common appellation of **bush-rangers**, have continued from the year 1805, more or less of violence and rapacity, until the month of October in the year 1818.   J.T. BIGGE *Report of the Commissioner of Inquiry into the State of the Colony of New South Wales* p. 108

1851   The years 1829, 1830, and 1831, are the years in the history of that colony, when bushranging may be said to have been at its greatest height; as, during these three years, there were nearly 500 escapes from iron gangs. During these three years also, the notorious **bushrangers** Walmsley, Webber and Donohoe, spread consternation throughout the whole colony; whilst Macnamara, the celebrated murderer, with his associate Dalton, carried terror into the very heart of Parramatta, situate about fifteen miles from Sydney, and the second largest town in the colony. ... During these three years, about 150 were executed, fifty-two in 1829, and the rest in 1830 and 1831, which thinned their ranks very much, as they were never a very numerous body, and bushranging has declined ever since.   A. MAJORIBANKS *Travels in New South Wales* p. 158

bushranging the practice of the bushranger; the committing of armed robbery and other crimes by one who escapes into the bush or who lives as a fugitive in the bush.

1813 [Instructions for Major Geils, Commandant at Port Dalrymple, by Thomas Davey, Lieutenant-Governor of the Settlements on Van Diemen's Land] You are on no account to make purchases of Gunpowder or Stationary from private Merchants or Traders; but, on your wanting a Supply, a regular demand must be made through me, which I will forward to Head Quarters. As

I have Reason to apprehend that some Sales of Gun Powder have lately taken place in this Island, contrary to the 7th Article of the Port Regulations, I beg leave to call your very particular attention thereto, and to request you will not on any Account suffer any such proceedings to take place, and at the same time to prohibit its being sold by any private Merchant or Trader, or any other Person whatsoever, without a special permission from yourself. I am certain there are no means which can be devised that will so effectually destroy the System of **Bush-ranging**, as a rigid observance of this order. Deprive those Depredators of the Means of procuring Ammunition, and they can no longer live in the bush. *Historical Records of Australia* 3rd series II p. 441

1829 *Government Order of the 9th Instant*, requires all occupants of lands on which Government has any lien, and all persons who value the right of being allowed the services of new convict servants, to fix on their farms a commodity which is unattainable, namely, *free men*, AND OF GOOD CHARACTER as Overseers and Bailiffs. The object of this is to prevent ***bush-ranging***. And for the like reason, other laws are being proposed; equally expensive and oppressive to a poor people. But the only way and the cheapest way to prevent bush-ranging, is to give the iron-gangs better food and more of it, and to cover their nakedness, and to treat them with humanity. The absence of this policy in our iron and road-gangs, is the canker of this Colony. Iron-gangs are the seed-bed of bushrangers. *Sydney Monitor* 24 Oct. p. 4

C

camp gang a convict working party. [First recorded 1808.]

There were many GANGS or working parties in which convicts worked. Camp gangs worked solely for the government on public works, such as clearing away the bush for building and settlement.

> **1822** At the early periods of this establishment, and when there were few convicts in the settlements near Launceston, small parties of government convicts were sent from George Town to assist the settlers in the harvest; but this mode of employing them has ceased for the present, and those whose services are not useful in the buildings are employed in what is called the **camp gang**, in clearing stumps of trees, and preparing the ground for building. J.T. BIGGE *Report of the Commissioner of Inquiry into the State of the Colony of New South Wales* p. 47

canary a convict. [Both *canary* and *canary bird* (see CANARY BIRD) are attested in British criminal slang in the sense 'a prisoner' from the end of the seventeenth century. The basic metaphor is of the bird in the prison cage (cf. *jail bird*). In Australia the term was no doubt enforced by the colour of the convicts' clothing, which was yellow like the canary bird. Those who were dressed in uniforms of yellow and black were dubbed MAGPIES. In Europe, yellow was the traditional 'colour of disgrace' and worn as a form of punishment and humiliation in the eighteenth century. Wearing yellow was probably also important in making the convicts highly visible and easy to supervise. See MAGPIE for more information on convict clothing. First recorded 1827.]

> **1827** Convicts of but recent migration are facetiously known by the name of *canaries*, by reason of the yellow plumage in which they are fledged at the period of landing; but when fairly domiciliated, they are more respectfully spoken of under the loyal designation of *government-men*, the term *convict*

being erased by a sort of general tacit compact from our Botany dictionary, as a word too ticklish to be pronounced in these sensitive latitudes. P. CUNNING-HAM *Two Years in New South Wales* vol. 2 p. 117

canary bird = CANARY. [First recorded 1839.]

1839 I left the scene early in the afternoon, joined the steamer, and at six I was just in time to see what are called the '**canary birds**,' returning from labour. These were the convicts dubbed canaries, from their yellow-and-brown dress. They were marched into their barracks by a guard of soldiers, who also reside there; and as they passed the steamer, they cast a melancholy look towards the happy faces which presented so striking a contrast to their own. I wish the thieves and vagabonds at home could see such scenes as these; it would have a better effect than the exhibition of a poor wretch on the scaffold, and is assuredly a worse punishment. W.H. LEIGH *Reconnoitering Voyages* p. 201

capital convict a prisoner sentenced to capital punishment (execution, usually by hanging). See also COLONIAL CONVICT. [First recorded 1838.]

Executions were public events in Sydney and were reported and debated widely in the press. Sometimes such a sentence might be commuted to a sentence of time at a place of SECONDARY punishment, such as Port Arthur or NORFOLK ISLAND. The FLASH or convict slang term for hanging was SCRAGGING.

1852 Two classes of prisoners were sent to Norfolk Island under the new system. The doubly-convicted colonial prisoners, and persons sentenced in England to transportation for fifteen years or life: the accumulation of both was rapid. Many bushrangers and other **capital convicts**, were transmitted to that settlement, to whom the arts of a prison were fully known; who were celebrated as 'flash' robbers; and who bore down by their tyrannical wickedness all the weaker or better men within their influence. J. WEST *The History of Tasmania* vol. 2 p. 296

caravan = BOX. [*Caravan* in the sense 'a covered carriage or cart' has been in use in standard English since the late seventeenth century. First recorded in the convict context in 1835.]

1862 The prisoners lodge in small **caravans**, capable of containing sixteen at a time, which are moved from one place to another upon small wooden wheels. Here they are locked in, at six in the evening, after having partaken of their principal meal: there is just room for them to lie down side by side. From hence they are not liberated until sunrise, when they are turned out to breakfast. This close confinement often proves prejudicial to the health of the men. BACKHOUSE & TYLOR, *Life and Labours of George Washington Walker* pp. 219–20

carrying gang (chiefly in Tasmania) a party of convicts assigned to hard labour at carrying. [First recorded 1835.]

These were convict working parties whose specific task was to carry materials for public works, such as bricks, timber, and so forth. They were especially engaged in the carrying of timber from where it was felled to where it was to be used. In Port Arthur, carrying gangs were also known as 'centipedes' as they had to carry long pieces of felled timber which were used for masts or yards for large sailing vessels. Up to sixty convicts might carry one length, thus resembling a centipede.

> **1846** He conducted us to a saw-pit, where there was a large quantity of lumber of various descriptions. ... Although seventy pounds was a *legal load*, according to the settlement rules, some of these sticks weighed from 200 to 300 lbs. I selected as light a one as I could, shouldered it with the greatest difficulty, and staggered away. Several men swore they could not carry them, to which Sawyer replied, 'Go along without them, then; and I will take you to the office. But perhaps you don't know what the office is? It is where you heard that d—d long code of laws read to-day. So sure as I take you there, you will be flogged and sent to bring the very loads you now refuse, when if you don't carry them, you will be flogged until you do. There's no such word as *can't* at Port Arthur.' When we got half way to the settlement, we were allowed to rest for five minutes, at the expiration of which, 'pick them up!' was shouted, and we carried them in, a distance of half a mile, the overseer walking as fast as he could without any load, and continually singing out, 'Come on, you bloody crawlers; keep up or go to the triangles.' The moment the loads were deposited in the lumber yard, 'come on,' was again shouted, and back we went for another load. This time four poor fellows were unable to carry their loads. One of them got his stick about two-thirds of the distance, and fell under it, close by my side. 'Pick it up,' said Sawyer, 'or be flogged.' 'Flog and be d—d!' said the other, 'for I *can't* carry it another inch.' Three of the four were flogged in less than an hour. They were covered with blood when they returned and carried their loads. ... I knew that I could not long endure the horrors of the **'carrying gang,'** as it was called, for I was sadly emaciated, and worn out already. L.W. MILLER *Notes of an Exile to Van Diemen's Land* pp. 328–9

cat the cat-o'-nine-tails. [*Cat* as a shortened form of *cat-o'-nine-tails*, a whip with nine knotted lashes used as an authorised instrument of punishment in the British navy and army, is attested in standard English from the late eighteenth century. The term cat-o'-nine-tails, as the OED suggests, 'was originally one of grim humour, in reference to it "scratching" the back'. Although not a specifically Australian term, it is commonly mentioned (and used) in the convict era outside its usual context of navy and army discipline. See also FLOGGING. First recorded in an Australian convict context in 1830.]

1830 New **cats** were always made every field day. The cords were about the thickness of a tobacco-pipe, and are whipped at the end with wax. Three knots in each lash. Three floggers administered the punishment. *Sydney Monitor* 14 Aug. p. 2

1834 I witnessed the infliction of the punishment of flagellation, in the Penitentiary-yard, upon a prisoner belonging the Hulk Chain-gang, who was a very refractory man. The scars upon his back bore testimony to frequent previous inflictions of this degrading punishment. The Superintendent of Convicts said this man had been more frequently flogged, than almost any other in the Colony: he writhed and cried out greatly under the strokes of a '**cat**' of knotted cords, which raised red wheals, and drew some blood: his sentence was to receive fifty lashes. J. BACKHOUSE *A Narrative of a Visit to the Australian Colonies* p. 200

cell a special place of confinement for a convict.

Cells were places of confinement in some BARRACKS and penitentiaries in which convicts were held. Solitary confinement began as a common form of punishment in the 1820s and 1830s, but moves in England for reform in prison discipline from the late 1830s led to the establishment of the idea of 'model prisons' and the 'SEPARATE system' aimed at dealing with the more serious offender. This system was intended to confine each prisoner separately, allowing them to reflect on their crimes, and to prevent criminal and homosexual activity. The building of the Port Arthur penitentiary, completed in 1852, was the best example of this system being put into practice. Punishment might consist of 'solitary', which was confinement in a DARK CELL with a half ration of bread and water, or 'separate' treatment, which consisted of confinement to a light cell with more food. Bibles were often provided in cells for the moral improvement of the prisoners.

1859 At five o'clock in the morning the bell rings to get up and make the beds. The **cells** are then opened, and a tub of water placed in each passage to wash. Two men then come round with a large tub, and give you seven ounces of bread and a pint and a half of gruel: and the prisoners go into their cells again. The bell rings again at half past six for work. The men fall in two by two, and a watchman at the end of a passage searches them, and looks to see that those who are sentenced to irons have them on. Thence to the muster-ground, and the names are called. The overseers of the different gangs then order the men to fall in, and go to work. J. LEONARD *John Leonard's Narrative: A Convict in Van Diemen's Land* (1987) p. 104

centipede see CARRYING GANG.

certificate = CERTIFICATE OF FREEDOM. [First recorded 1796.]

> **1822** The **certificates** issued by the secretary attest, that after an examination of the indents, so many years have expired since sentence of that term was passed on the party entitled to it, describing the year and ship in which he arrived, and ending with a declaration, that by reason of the expired service, the said party is restored to all the rights of a free subject. J.T. BIGGE *Report of the Commissioner of Inquiry into the State of the Colony of New South Wales* p. 120

certificate of freedom a document issued on the expiry of a convict's term of penal servitude, certifying the recipient's status as a freed person. [First recorded 1810.]

The certificate of freedom was a New South Wales invention, introduced in 1810, and was an official piece of paper issued to convicts who had completed their sentences. It was used as a way of proving one was free as distinct from those still of convict status. Upon expiration of a sentence, a convict declared himself free and applied to a magistrate who would check the convict-ship indents to check the original sentence. If all was in order, a certificate would be issued. It restored all rights and privileges of free subjects, and gave emancipists and emigrants similar legal rights, something that some emigrants resented and tried to change.

> **1810** All Persons whose Term of Transportation to this Colony has expired, and who have not obtained a legal **Certificate of Freedom**, are directed to give into this Office in the course of next week a List of their Names, where tried, their Terms of Transportation, by what Ship conveyed, and their time of Arrival here.—Those whose Applications may be found correct will get their Certificates of Freedom on the first Saturday in February. *Sydney Gazette* 14 Jan. p. 2

> **1834** A **Certificate of Freedom** is granted to all persons who have duly worked at the periods of their sentenced exile, and it expresses that the individual in whose favour it is given is restored to all the rights of a free British subject. Yet in the very teeth of this declaration, a handful of men, the self-constituted guardians of public orality, attempt to arrogate to themselves the power of creating disqualifications of citizenship against this portion of their fellow Colonists, which were never contemplated by the law, much less sanctioned by it. EMIGRANT OF 1821 *Party Politics Exposed* p. 20

chain 1 a bond or fetter. [This is the standard English sense, but of special importance in the convict era.]

Chains or IRONS were used to shackle convicts who worked in CHAIN GANGS. Generally, convicts were fitted with ankle fetters, with a long length of chain tied to the centre of the convict's belt to allow for reasonable freedom of movement. To prevent chafing, some fetters had strips of leather between the ankle and the iron. Those convicts placed in irons were known to be ON THE CHAIN.

> **1851** [Norfolk Island/Port Arthur] What is called the punishment of the '**chain**', consists of a heavy cable, to which, at certain distances, the leg chains of the men are riveted, consequently whatever one man does must be participated in by the others. There is something truly brutal and disgusting in this novel species of torture, and he that introduced it deserves to meet the same fate as did the inventor of the guillotine. 'The chain' is usually composed of gangs from thirty to fifty men, and their ordinary task is, that of rolling a heavy log of wood a certain distance one day, and rolling it back the next. H. MELVILLE *The Present State of Australia* p. 160

2 Also found in the phrase **on (or upon) the chain** (of a convict) secured with a CHAIN. [First recorded 1835.]

> **1838** He [a prisoner] had cherished a strong desire to see his parents again; but now had no hope of ever effecting this, unless he could escape from the settlement: he therefore joined some others in taking off a boat. They were pursued, one of the party shot dead, and another dangerously wounded, and the whole recaptured. He had indulged in infidel principles; but the sight of the dead man had a powerful effect upon him, and he could not help looking upon him as lost for ever. He was committed to gaol in irons, with the rest of his fellows, and they were put **upon the chain** (i.e.) had a chain passed over their irons, and fixed outside of their prison to render them more secure. J. BACKHOUSE *Extracts from Letters* ii p. 74

chain gang a party of convicts assigned to hard labour in chains. [First recorded 1822.]

The chain gang, or convict parties that worked in IRONS, was a common form of organising convict labour on public works. Chain gangs worked up to ten hours a day and often slept in BOXES at night. In New South Wales from 1826 to 1836, nearly 5000 men, or about 18 per cent of men transported, were confined to a chain gang at some time. In penal settlements such as Port Arthur, life on the chain gang was especially difficult as the chain gang was usually for hardened offenders and would often have convict OVERSEERS who were brutal in their treatment of prisoners. Often these prisoners also lived in BARRACKS separate from other prisoners.

> **1838** CHAIN GANGS.—Composed of very incorrigible characters, there are two of them, one employed at a place called Bridgewater, throwing a bridge over the Derwent, about 11 miles from Hobart Town; the other chain-gang is employed making a wharf for the landing of merchandize at Hobart Town, to

induce ships to come alongside and discharge their cargoes. Here the greatest vigilance for the safe keeping of the prisoners is absolutely necessary, as the continual bustle affords frequent opportunity for them to abscond, which they seldom omit to embrace. They are under the military at both places, and wear irons on each leg, and yellow clothing; prisoners are sent to these gangs for what are called serious offences, or for a repetition of minor ones; their lives are truly miserable, being debarred of speaking to any but their unfortunate companions; their sentences in these gangs varies from 6 months to as many years, according to the nature of their crimes. G.C. INGLETON *True Patriots All: or news from Early Australia—as told in a collection of broadsides* (1952) p. 194

1849 Very many convicts in New South Wales were employed in '**chain-gangs**.' In passing through Maitland you might observe a cluster of bark huts. These were the quarters of chain-gang; and at dusk you might observe, guarded by soldiers, a body of convicts (all heavily ironed, and in grey serge dresses) marched along the road, some dragging hand-carts, and their fetters ringing as they moved. These culprits were re-convicted convicts, and were condemned to be worked on the roads. Their discipline was severe, and at night they were packed together in the bark huts aforesaid, where, in the hours of darkness, they committed every kind of wickedness. The wit of man could not have devised a more effectual method of depraving criminals; and many, driven to desperation, continually escaped from such gangs and lived by plunder. J.P. TOWNSEND *Rambles and Observations in New South Wales* pp. 233–4

chain gangsman a convict assigned to hard labour in chains. [First recorded 1846.]

1846 Behold me now a **chain-gangsman** working in chains; the thermometer was often at 120 degrees of heat in the sun, which burned ulcers in the back of my neck, my eyes were sore and running, from the intense heat of the sandy place where we were working. My poor bleeding wrist still carrying the chain, my legs raw from the friction of the leg irons. I would have given five pounds if I had it, for only one yard of calico to have wrapped round the irons and prevented them from rubbing away the raw flesh. The labour in the chain-gangs is very severe, and the discipline very strict; the men are flogged for the most trifling offence. H. EASY *The Horrors of Transportation* p. 7

chief constable the head of a group of constables or policemen. [First recorded in Australia in 1811.]

The chief constable and his constables were responsible for keeping order in colonial Australia. Constables were poorly paid, and were generally convicts or former convicts themselves, thus their effectiveness in preventing crime was not great. A chief constable was responsible to local magistrates in country areas, and in Sydney, to the Police Magistrate. This localised system of police organisation and dependence on magistrates was based on the English model and lasted until the 1850s.

1819 [Testimony of John Evans] Who was Smith, the **Chief Constable**? He was a prisoner I believe for life at Sydney. He made his escape to England, was tried again and came out to Sydney. He was tried there for robbing S. Lord and sentenced to this place for the remainder of his original sentence. J.W. TURNER *Newcastle as a Convict Settlement: The Evidence Before J.T. Bigge in 1819–1821* (1973) p. 92

1827 Sydney is divided into six police districts, with a lock-up house and a night-watch, under the orders of a conductor, attached to each. Constables are also on the alert through the town during the day to pick up the offenders. The whole is under the direction of the **chief constable**, who again acts under the orders of the head magistrate, by whom (with the assistance of two ordinary magistrates) charges are investigated daily at the police office; the offences being either summarily punished, or sent for adjudication before the criminal court, or quarter-sessions,—according to their magnitude, or as committed by convicts or free men. P. CUNNINGHAM *Two Years in New South Wales* pp. 60–1

class any of a number of groupings into which convicts were divided according to the severity of their sentences and their behaviour while in custody. [First recorded 1824.]

The CONVICT POPULATION was separated into a number of such classes. This system aimed to establish a hierarchy of worth and value, with privileges available for good behaviour and punishment for breaking the rules. Arthur in Van Diemen's Land and Darling in New South Wales in their attempts to bring about more 'scientific management' of convicts instituted particular systems of classifying them. In the female FACTORIES a system of three classes was introduced: first class was for assignable women of good character; second class was for those guilty of minor offences; and the third or crime class was for those who committed SECONDARY offences. From the mid-1820s through the 1830s, Governor Arthur's system of classifying prisoners in Van Diemen's Land consisted of seven classes. First class were those allowed TICKETS OF LEAVE for good behaviour; second class were those ASSIGNED; third class were those on public works; fourth class the road gangs; fifth class those in hard labour in CHAINS; sixth class those in hard labour under surveillance in penal settlements; and the seventh class those like the sixth class but serving their sentences in chains.

1833 The other prisoners are divided into a chain-gang, and a first and second **class**, distinguished by the kind of labour allotted them, by their clothing, and by the second class having an allowance of tea and sugar. This classification produces a good effect. Captain Charles O'Hara Booth, the Commandant, has succeeded in establishing a more strict discipline than his predecessors.   J. BACKHOUSE *A Narrative of a Visit to the Australian Colonies* p. 167

1835 The new arrangement is that the convicts shall be formed into three **classes** according to the measure of their crimes. The first class, which is to consist of the most hardened offenders, is to be sent to the penal settlement at Norfolk Island, where they are to be subjected for the remainder of their lives to labour; the second class, consisting of persons convicted of less heavy offences, and of whom there are some hopes of reformation entertained, is to be sent to Van Diemen's Land, or New South Wales, there to be kept to labour in chains upon the high roads, and upon public works; and the third class, consisting of prisoners convicted of minor offences, is to be sent to the colonies for distribution among the settlers. It is thought that this arrangement will better suit justice than the plan at present adopted, has worked wonderfully upon the moral condition of the poor beings, and I see no reason for a change in it.   H.W. PARKER *The Rise, Progess and Present State of Van Diemen's Land* pp. 39–40

clearing gang a detachment of convicts detailed to clear trees, undergrowth, etc., from a settler's land in order to fit it for cultivation or pasturage. [First recorded 1824.]

The clearing of tracts of land and the bush for cultivation and settlement was one of the primary jobs of convict GANGS. Convicts engaged in this activity were known as being in clearing gangs or clearing parties.

1834 This superabundance of convict-labour led, during the earlier part of the administration of Sir Thomas Brisbane, to an arrangement which was highly beneficial to a number of respectable settlers in certain parts of the colony, but of which the continued influx of free settlers prevented the extension to other districts, in which it would doubtless have been equally beneficial, and so led to its entire discontinuance. The arrangement I allude to consisted in the institution of *clearing-gangs*, or parties of convicts in the service of Government—each under the charge of an overseer—who were stationed for certain periods on the lands of private individuals to fell and to burn off the standing timber. This was done at so much per acre, the proprietor who obtained the indulgence engaging to pay the Government in wheat—the produce of the land so cleared by Government-labour.   J.D. LANG *An Historical and Statistical Account of New South Wales* vol. 2 p. 5

clearing party = CLEARING GANG. [First recorded 1824.]

1846 Mr Kentish's Report states—and indeed there can be no doubt of the fact—that at or near to the several sites proposed as bridges for the new road to cross the six large rivers in its course, admirable situations may be selected for future towns … which sooner or later must spring up in those parts; as a first step towards which, as well as to the placing of **clearing-parties** of probation pass-holders, on the rich tracts which may be selected for cultivation, the road should be bridged and made travellable for carts, which therefore, we trust, will be done without losing the present season.   N.L. KENTISH *Work in the Bush of Van Diemen's Land* pp. 17–18

cockatoo 1 A convict who was serving, or had served, a sentence at Cockatoo Island. [First recorded 1846.]

Cockatoo Island (also known at one time as Banks Island), a sandstone island in Sydney Harbour, was first established as a location to send convicts in 1839. They were employed in cutting stone for use in building wharves on the Sydney foreshore and Circular Quay. They also worked to create silos out of the sandstone for storing grain. The island was abandoned as a prison in 1872. Generally INCORRIGIBLE offenders were sent there. The terms COCKATOO MAN and COCKATOO ISLANDER were also used to refer to these convicts.

1851 Those in the Government employ are stationed on a barren rock called Cockatoo Island, distant some few miles from the city towards the Paramatta River. These men must be the very *élite* of unhung rascals, 'masters of arts' and 'professors' of villainy. If there be at the station one convict under punishment that has not received some half dozen sentences in the colony, he is improperly detained there, for all that could be liberated have long since obtained their indulgences of partial freedom. There can only be a few hundred remaining, because there is not room for many more on the island. Malefactors now convicted of crimes in New South Wales are transported to the cesspool of convictism—Van Diemen's Land: so that the **Cockatoos** are, in fact, the old gaol-birds of New South Wales.   H. MELVILLE *The Present State of Australia* p. 88

2 Used as an adjective in combinations to refer to a person who was serving, or had served, a sentence on Cockatoo Island, such as **cockatoo convict**, **cockatoo gentry**, **cockatoo man**, etc. [First recorded 1845.]

1845 COCKATOO MEN.—The total number of prisoners on Cockatoo Island under sentence yesterday was two hundred and fifty-three.   *Sydney Morning Herald* 7 Jan. p. 2

1848 *Convicts from Sydney*—As the Comptroller General left Hobart Town some time since, for Sydney, and as it was generally believed his visit to the great metropolis of the Southern Seas, was in connexion with the removal of these **Cockatoo Gentry**, we have no doubt the *Treaty* is settled, and that within a very few days these men will be landed on our shores. *Hobarton Guardian* 9 Feb. p. 2

Cockatoo Islander = COCKATOO. [First recorded 1841.]

1841 **Cockatoo Islanders**— ... a report was forwarded to the proper authority in Sydney, from Cockatoo Island, that two of the convicts ... had effected their escape. *Sydney Herald* 14 July p. 2

colonial convict a convict serving a sentence for a crime committed in the Australian colonies. [First recorded 1843.]

Convicts who committed crimes in the colonies, the most serious being murder, but which might include offences such as theft, ABSCONDING, or more minor offences such as being drunk and disorderly, or being insolent and disobedient, might be given a COLONIAL SENTENCE. For serious offences, they might be sentenced to be executed. See also CAPITAL CONVICT.

1843 The information was then read and sworn to in the usual form. It set forth that Wickham Mayer Hesketh, being the editor and principal writer for the *Australian* newspaper, the defendant had maliciously printed and published, and procured to be printed and published, of and concerning him, in the *Colonial Observer* of the 4th March, the malicious and defamatory matter following:—'By the way, there are certain parties connected with the *Australian* who are likely to be heard of at Hyde Park Barracks soon. Their principal writer was convicted of forgery yesterday.' The informer on his examination gave substantially the same statement as contained in the information. On being cross-examined, he admitted that he himself understood the paragraph in the sense in which it was written, as relating to a literary forgery in the *Australian* of the previous day. He further stated that he was part proprietor of the *Australian* newspaper, and registered as such in terms of the act. He was not aware whether they were English or **Colonial convicts** who were detained at Hyde Park—all he knew was, that it was a very bad place; and he was annoyed by the injurious impression the paragraph might produce in England, where the paper it appeared in was extensively circulated, and where he was known as the Editor of the *Australian*. *Colonial Observer* (Sydney) 18 Mar. p. 892

colonial offence a crime committed by a transported convict in the Australian colonies. [First recorded 1838.]

1838 There is no society in the world more united than the convict party in our Australian Colonies. It is of no consequence a shade or two of difference in the duration of their sentences, and it is no matter what may be the different grades in their ladder of disgrace—whether they be seven years men—fourteen years—or life; whether they have been re-sentenced since their first arrival, for **colonial offences**, and been on a visit to Norfolk or the Northward (slang terms for Norfolk Island and Moreton Bay) no matter: whether they have obtained their absolute or conditional pardon, their emancipation, ticket-of-leave, or ticket-of-exemption, the special, the scourger, or the scourged, one universal *esprit de corps* animates and pervades the whole convict body, uniting them like Freemasons in one silent, deep-rooted sentiment of hostility to the free settler; or, as they profanely call them, the b— emigrants. T.H. JAMES *Six Months in South Australia* p. 43

colonial prisoner = COLONIAL CONVICT. [First recorded 1843.]

1849 My horse, a fine and high-spirited fellow, had hurt his knee against the manger. I wrote a requisition for the services of George Smith, a **colonial prisoner**, to come and see him. Smith was a skilful farrier. He was on the settlement station. My requisition was disallowed by Mr Price, *because* no 'old hands', i.e., colonial prisoners, were to be permitted to leave the settlement station. A Sunday or two after as I was riding home from church at Longridge, I met an old hand or colonial prisoner *two miles from the settlement.* I asked him how he came to be there; he said Mr Price had given him leave to walk wherever he pleased over the island. *Another colonial prisoner*, who was in company with the man I questioned, confirmed the account. If these two colonial prisoners had not had permission to leave the settlement, they would have been taken into custody and punished. T. ROGERS *Correspondence Relating to the Dismissal* pp. 127–8

colonial sentence the punishment inflicted upon a convict who committed a crime after arrival in the Australian colonies. [First recorded 1811.]

1838 The time spent on Norfolk Island, under a **colonial sentence**, is not reckoned as any part of an original sentence. Thus, a man transported from England, or from Van Diemens Land, to New South Wales, for seven years, committing an offence at the expiration of three years, and being sentenced to Norfolk Island for seven years, will have, at the expiration of that period, to serve the four years remaining of his original sentence, in New South Wales, on being returned thither. J. BACKHOUSE *A Narrative of a Visit to the Australian Colonies* p. 263

commandant an officer appointed to be in control of a penal settlement. [First recorded 1788.]
Commandants were responsible for the day-to-day running of places of secondary punishment, such as Norfolk Island and Newcastle. In New South Wales,

a commandant was responsible to the Governor; in Van Diemen's Land, to the Lieutenant-Governor.

> **1827** Newcastle contains two government houses; a jail; military and convict barracks; a hospital; two tolerable inns; and an episcopal church. It is under the jurisdiction of a half-pay military officer, denominated ***commandant***, but whose functions merely extend to the superintendence of the government works, and the general police of the town, in his capacity of a colonial magistrate, wherein he is aided by the assistant surgeon of the hospital, who has been recently appointed to the magistracy also, in order that a bench may readily be formed when more heinous offences come on for investigation—the power of a single magistrate being now very limited. P. CUNNINGHAM *Two Years in New South Wales* p. 149

conditional emancipation = CONDITIONAL PARDON. This term was used less frequently than conditional pardon. [First recorded 1792.]

> **1798** [Government and General Orders] Any person who shall come forward and lead to such discovery of the above offenders as may serve to convict them before a Court of Criminal Judicature, if a convict, shall receive a **conditional emancipation**, that is, to be made free in this country and have permission to become a settler. *Historical Records of Australia* 1st series II p. 208

conditional pardon a remission of a convict's sentence, subject to varying territorial stipulations, but always precluding return to the British Isles until the expiration of the term of the original sentence. [First recorded 1794.]

In the early years of the colony of New South Wales, many pardons were granted. Men with skills or the ability to develop business were of more value free than not. GENTLEMAN convicts were also likely to be pardoned soon after their arrival in the colony. From 1812, the British government, unhappy with the numbers of pardons being granted, sought to take over the power to grant pardons. The 1823 New South Wales Act limited a governor's powers to recommending only, not granting, pardons. In practice, however, these rules were sometimes broken as necessity dictated—waiting for London to approve pardons was impractical. The system of pardons allowed many convicts to develop businesses and infrastructure necessary to the early success of the Australian colonies. From 1810 to 1820, 1365 conditional pardons were granted in New South Wales. Under the system that involved the TICKET OF LEAVE, a conditional pardon could be applied for after a set number of years on a ticket. They limited a freed convict to staying within the colony of residence. While they were technically free and could work as they wished, they could not leave the colony until the term of their original sentence expired. The conditional emancipation was the next step up from a ticket of leave in terms of the freedom it granted, as it could not be revoked. It was thus also an important incentive to reform in the convict system. From 1842, under a new law, tickets of leave and conditional pardons could be applied for at the same time.

> **1822** A **conditional pardon** contains a declaration of the governor, under his hand and official seal, that the unexpired term of the convict's sentence is conditionally remitted to him; and the condition is expressed to be, that he shall continue to reside within the limits of the government of New South Wales during the space of the original sentence, under pain of incurring all the penalties of re-appearing in Great Britain, for and during the term of his original sentence or order of transportation; or as if the remission had never been granted. J.T. BIGGE *Report of the Commissioner of Inquiry into the State of the Colony of New South Wales* p. 120

> **1853** After remaining the allotted number of years in the ticket-of-leave class, the deserving convicts usually received a '**conditional pardon**,' which permitted them the range of the Australian colonies; and to some was granted a 'free pardon,' which generally found them fully prepared to keep and value the liberty it bestowed. MRS C. MEREDITH *My Home in Tasmania* p. 39

conditonal pardon man a convict who had been granted a CONDITIONAL PARDON. [First recorded 1845.]

> **1859** The eldest girl in the Annesfield Asylum, of which we are here speaking, is engaged to be married in six weeks from this time, (June 17, 1858) to a well conducted, sober, industrious **conditional-pardon man**. She is younger than it is desirable that she should leave the home of her adoption to enter upon the cares and duties of a wife, but it is the second application that has been made for her, the first having also been made by a conditional-pardon man, after a liberation of upwards of two years. ... After due consideration, she asked to be allowed to accept the offer of the one who last proposed. ... If persons opposed to the civilization of the natives could divest themselves of the prejudice against the colour, they would be constrained to acknowledge that now she would bear comparison with any white girl among the most respectable of the labouring population. M. MACKAY *Natives' Institution King George's Sound* pp. 9–10

constable a police officer. [This is the standard English term, but what is unusual is the fact that they were usually convicts or ex-convicts. First recorded in Australia in 1794.]

In the colonies, the police were badly organised, with no central organisation but usually organised locally and controlled by local magistrates. Constables were generally convicts or ex-convicts and were poorly paid; this limited their effectiveness. (See also CHIEF CONSTABLE; CONVICT CONSTABLES.)

1822 The care of the factory, therefore, except during the hours of labour, was committed to a **constable**, who was still a convict, who had continued in that office for 15 years, and received no larger allowance as a reward for his fidelity than a ration and a half. The security for the performance of his duty, depends upon the risk of detection; the same presumptive check that is supposed to provide for the official integrity of many other establishments in New South Wales, aided by the further probability of disclosures, to which the intoxication of the women would lead, if they were permitted by the constable to go out of the factory, when confined there. J.T. BIGGE *Report of the Commissioner of Inquiry into the State of the Colony of New South Wales* p. 69

1839 The pilfering of assigned servants is equal upon the employer, to what his taxes would be in England. He is always apprehending theft, and for this reason is in constant disquietude. He is for ever in communication with **constables** and magistrates—appearing against one servant, and supplicating for another. His liberty, and that of the society is abridged, because these servants are scattered about in it. He submits to the rule of convict constables, because such constables alone are suited for such a society; and he stands in the midst of perplexities, annoyances, and humiliations. J. DIXON *The Conditions and Capabilities of Van Diemen's Land* p. 82

convict 1 a person sentenced in the British Isles to a term of penal servitude in an Australian colony. [From the sixteenth century *convict* was used to describe a person 'convicted in a judicial investigation of a punishable offence'. With the introduction of transportation, however, a narrower sense developed: 'a condemned criminal serving a sentence of penal servitude'. First recorded in an Australian context in 1787.]

The prisoners transported to the Australian colonies were known as convicts. The label 'convict' was not always used—it was seen as carrying the stigma and degradation of being a prisoner, and many ex-convicts attempted to distance themselves from it. A convict might also be known by such terms as GOVERNMENT MAN, PRISONER or ASSIGNED SERVANT. An ex-convict might be referred to as a FREED or FREE MAN, or an EMANCIPIST.

1791 The first settler was a **convict**, whose time being expired, a hut was built and one acre and an half of ground cleared for him at Parramatta. A. PHILLIP *Copies and Extracts of Letters from Governor Phillip* (1792) p. 126

1827 Only a few years indeed have elapsed since an individual transported to Van Dieman's Land for piracy, who had been emancipated for meritorious conduct there, obtained a verdict of 50£. damages against a libeller, who had attempted to malign his character by spitefully spouting the opprobrious epithet of 'd—d **convict**!' in his teeth; and a most just and praiseworthy verdict it certainly was; for, if such language were tolerated here, eternal contentions would reign among us, while it is enough for an individual to bear the *punishment* he may have been sentenced to without *reproach* being superadded; and if his period of punishment has expired, there can be neither propriety nor justice in individuals insulting him with that for which the public has already exacted ample satisfaction. P. CUNNINGHAM *Two Years in New South Wales* vol. 2 p. 118

2 The term 'convict' was also used in an attributive sense—to describe things that were deemed to be of a convict nature, for example, convict clothing, being of convict descent, or even convict poetry. The more common combinations are given separate entries.

1837 In the factory, too, there is a good chance of getting *married*; for the **convict swains** scattered amongst the settlers, when they obtain the consent of their masters, or choose, when they become free, to enter into the connubial state, usually apply for permission to go to the factory in quest of a fair helpmate, with the full knowledge that it is more likely to be for *worse* than for *better* that they make their election. J. MUDIE *Felonry of New South Wales* p. 196

1855 There is another and lower class of ruffians, who prowl about the outskirts of the towns and diggings on foot, singly or in pairs. I once encountered two of them at nightfall, near the Fryer's Creek Diggings. … Two men in blue serge shirts suddenly appeared on the road, walking towards me, and when within a few paces both presented pistols. … As I looked searchingly on the face of the taller man, he swore a deep **convict oath** that he would blow 'my b—y brains out if I looked at him'. G.H. WATHEN *The Golden Colony: or Victoria in 1854* pp. 142–3

convict barrack(s) = BARRACK(S). [First recorded 1819.]

1819 [Governor Macquarie to Earl Bathurst] The New **Convict Barrack** is a Commodious Spacious Building with all the Necessary Offices to render it Convenient and healthy; it is Surrounded by a very high Stone Wall and is Calculated to Contain between Five and Six hundred men. *Historical Records of Australia* 1st series X p. 96

convict boy a transported juvenile offender; the son of a convict. [First recorded 1833.]

A large number of convicts were youths, either coming to the colonies as juvenile offenders or with their mothers; some children were born on the trip. The males were sometimes referred to as 'convict boys'. They were kept in special barracks in Sydney, known as the Carter's Barracks, where under Governor Darling's tenure they were taught a trade and how to read and write. After 1832, young convicts were placed on a semi-apprentice assignment system, which was successful enough that the Carter's Barracks were closed. In Van Diemen's Land, a special establishment existed for boys at Point Puer (established 1834). In 1838, approximately 375 boys were located there; by 1843, there were approximately 800.

> **1822** On the upper side of the second yard [of the carters' barracks] are three rooms, which are constructed purposely for the separate accommodation of the **convict boys**, and in which an attempt has been made to class them; one room is allotted for those who misconduct themselves, and both their diet and their bedding are inferior to that of the first class. ... In the two rooms of the first class 64 boys were lodged and fed in messes, composed of eight: they are allowed mattresses and blankets, have tea for breakfast, and, in addition to their pound of bread and meat, are allowed soup for dinner. The boys of the second class receive a single ration only, consisting of one pound of meat and bread per day, and sleep on boards, with a thin India blanket.   J.T. BIGGE *Report of the Commissioner of Inquiry into the State of the Colony of New South Wales* p. 23

> **1838** An interesting addition has lately been made to this Settlement, in an establishment for **convict boys**, on a point of land, now called Point Puer, access from which to the main land is cut off by a military guard. 157 of these boys, formerly kept on board the hulks, on the Thames, are here placed under restraint and coercive labour, as a punishment. By these means, combined with attention to education, they are acquiring habits, calculated to enable them to maintain themselves honestly.   J. BACKHOUSE *A Narrative of a Visit to the Australian Colonies* pp. 226–7

convict chaplain a clergyman appointed to minister to the spiritual needs of convicts. [First recorded 1844.]

A chaplain or religious minister oversaw the religious instruction and reform of convicts. Religious instruction was seen as a vital part of the rehabilitation of convicts. The Church of England was the official chaplaincy to the convict settlement established in 1788, and the first chaplain was Richard Johnson. The second chaplain to arrive in New South Wales was Samuel Marsden in 1794; and Robert Knopwood arrived with the first settlers in Van Diemen's Land in 1804. By 1821 there were eight chaplains in New South Wales and many churches being built. Protestant ministers and Catholic priests ministered to the convicts and often viewed this as essential missionary work. Catholicism, however, was only encouraged from 1820 when two Irish Catholic chaplains were appointed to minister to Irish Catholic convicts to pacify and improve them. All PENAL SETTLEMENTS had a church or chapel and a chaplain (minister). An exception to this was NORFOLK ISLAND, where conditions were perceived to be so bad that until 1836 no minister would go there except for short visits. Some became involved in colonial politics, denouncing the evils of the convict system—such as John West, a Congregational minister and William Ullathorne, a Catholic priest. Both published treatises on the topic, with Ullathorne's agitation leading to the appointment of the first Catholic bishop, J.B. Polding, in 1835 and the subsequent significant growth of the Catholic church in the colonies.

1844 But to return to Mr. Medland. … He was told in England that the Bishop wished particularly to ordain all the **convict chaplains** himself, that he would probably remain some months in Hobart Town to read, and then be appointed to a station by the Bishop. F.R. NIXON *The Pioneer Bishop in Van Diemen's Land 1843–1863* p. 41

convict class the convicts as a social group. [First recorded 1837.]

The Australian colonies were made up of many different social groups—the army officers and their families, the ordinary soldiers, convicts, and later free emigrant settlers. Convicts as a group within colonial society were sometimes referred to as the convict class, but within this group there were many social distinctions from the EDUCATED or SPECIAL convicts to the hardened criminals.

1837 On returning to our lodgings, last evening, we found the family in a state of alarm. While some of them were at a place of worship, two of the servants had gone out, and got drunk, and on their return, had cruelly beaten a poor, Mauritian Black, who was also a prisoner-servant, in the house: his cries brought in a neighbour, who by the free use of a horse-whip, made the drunkards desist; but they had severely bruised the object of their spleen. Subsequently, the black man preferred a charge against the others, before the Magistrates, and they were sent to prison. Servants of the **convict class**, are amongst the greatest drawbacks upon domestic comfort, in these Colonies; and by their drunkenness, they clearly shew, that the use of intoxicating liquors has been a principal cause of their becoming convicts. J. BACKHOUSE *A Narrative of a Visit to the Australian Colonies* pp. 464–5

1855 [Western Australia] The land was sandy and inferior; the early settlers lost time and means in foolish indulgence; indentured servants left their masters; and a serious famine followed. Numbers left the colony for Van Diemen's Land. The others struggled on with their little farms. In consequence of want of labourers they petitioned the Home Government for convict labour, and have since received about 7,000 prisoners. The population is nearly one-half of the **convict class**. J. BONWICK *Geography of Australia and New Zealand* pp. 62–3

convict clerk a convict assigned to do clerical work within the colonial administration. [First recorded 1827.]

One of the convict occupations in the colonies was that of clerk, that is, a person who kept records and accounts and did paperwork. Generally, those who were clerks had worked at similar occupations in Britain.

> **1837** Many notorious convicts have been barristers or attorneys at home, but have been transported for forgeries, altering of wills, or the commission of other infamous frauds. These ruffians, instead of being sent to Norfolk Island, worked in irons on the roads, or assigned as labourers to settlers, are at once assigned to their brother lawyers in the colony, and generally to such of these as are remarkably deficient in legal knowledge or talent of their own. ... The **convict clerks** are often entrusted by their masters with the entire conducting of their business. The scoundrels have access to the jails, in which they make themselves masters of the cases of the prisoners. They tamper with the witnesses. Where hard swearing is required, it is not difficult in such a place as New South Wales, to find men who will swear to any thing. Instances have even been known, while trials have been going on, of convict clerks going out of court, and making bargains with fellows, perhaps for half a pint of rum, to give prisoners a character, though these rum witnesses, may never even have seen the prisoners, till they behold them in the dock! J. MUDIE *The Felonry of New South Wales* pp. 248–9

convict colony an Australian colony regarded primarily as a place of penal servitude. [First recorded 1822.]

New South Wales was a colony specifically set up for the accommodation of British and Irish prisoners. Subsequently, Van Diemen's Land (Tasmania) became another convict colony. The Swan River Colony (now the Perth/Fremantle area in Western Australia) was established as a free settlement in 1829 but began receiving convicts in 1850, and was the last place to accept convicts before transportation to that colony was ceased in 1868. South Australia, in contrast, was set up as a FREE COLONY.

> **1822** In bestowing upon the emancipated convicts so great a mark as that of introduction to society, he ought to have been aware that the same act which might be consolatory to their feelings, and perhaps to that of their own body, was likely, at the same moment, to be an act of violence to those of the free population. In considering this point, I conceive that the governor has viewed only one of the parties affected by it. He has thought, and often repeated, that New South Wales was a **convict colony**; that it was established for their benefit; and he further has declared an opinion, which I conceive to be a very erroneous one, that it was brought to its present state (meaning, of course, a state of prosperity) by their means. Of the free classes, and of their origin, as well as of their efforts, he has always entertained a very unfavourable estimate.

J.T. BIGGE *Report of the Commissioner of Inquiry into the State of the Colony of New South Wales* pp. 147–8

1827 The idea of Australia being a ***convict*** colony has, I believe, hitherto deterred many worthy individuals from emigrating thereto, fearful of trusting their persons and property among such a dubious community; but a very short residence with us would serve to allay the fears of the most timorous on this head, and bring them to unite in opinion with the older settlers, that the transportation of convicts hither is one of the greatest benefits that could be conferred upon us, inasmuch as it affords (as has been seen) an abundant supply of cheap labour to the settler for the furthering of his agricultural operations; and to the government, also, for the purpose of opening new communications through the country for the settler's accommodation, enabling him to carry his surplus produce to market. P. CUNNINGHAM *Two Years in New South Wales* vol. 1 p. 12

convict constable a convict appointed as an officer of the peace. [First recorded 1834.]

Due to a lack of manpower in the colonies, those appointed as constables, or police, in the colonies were generally convicts themselves. This practice began on the convict ships. Some of those convict constables might obtain their freedom as a reward for good service. See also CONSTABLE, CHIEF CONSTABLE.

1856 [Tasmania] A man was hung for sheep stealing, on a charge supported only by two **convict constables**. One of these worthies was the sole survivor of a notorious band of bushrangers, his comrades being all executed, chiefly through his traitorous information. The other one had been heard to say, that he would hang twenty men to save his punishment in the chain-gang, or anything like it. J. BONWICK *The Bushrangers: Illustrating the early days of Van Diemen's Land* p. 10

convict constabulary the CONVICT CONSTABLES as a group. [First recorded 1835.]

1838 I lately saw a petition from a prisoner, setting forth that he was 'a good hand at shooting, and requested therefore, that he might be employed against the bushrangers, that he might obtain some indulgence.' A prisoner was also taken up some years ago on his way to assassinate a gentleman strongly opposed to the government, 'in order,' as he said, 'to gain his emancipation.' These are not individual anecdotes, but traits of a class. And I believe the **convict constabulary** to be most vexatiously officious, both as regards the free and the bond. I believe this because it is the current opinion, and also because it is consistent with human nature. A. MACONOCHIE *Thoughts on Convict Management* p. 124

convict department the government department responsible for the management of the convict population. [First recorded 1842.]

The convict department oversaw all the workings of the convict system. It was in charge of all the administration involved, and supervised places of SECONDARY punishment. The citation below refers to Colonial Secretary Lord Stanley's attempt to reorganise the convict system in Van Diemen's Land through the introduction of the PROBATION SYSTEM from 1842. This involved the reorganisation of the convict department, not least to try to reduce expenditure for the government.

> **1845** The only specific feature of the new system, as conveyed to me in Lord Stanley's despatch, which I shall here notice, is the appointment which his lordship announced to me of a new officer, to be called the Comptroller-General of Convicts, who was to unite in his own person the powers, if not the labours of various subdivisions of the **convict department**, and was to communicate directly with the Governor, without the intervention of the Colonial Secretary; thus diminishing the labours and the influence of the latter officer, and transferring them to the new official, who would become in fact a second Colonial Secretary. J. FRANKLIN *Narrative History of Van Diemen's Land* p. 54

convict establishment a place designed for the punishment, accommodation, etc., of convicts. [First recorded 1827.]

Any place designed for convicts was referred to as a convict establishment. This might include: places of SECONDARY punishment, such as the penal settlement at Norfolk Island, the female FACTORIES that housed convict women, and barracks such as the Hyde Park Barracks.

> **1847** Instructions have been received from England for the abolition of all the **convict establishments**, Hyde Park Barracks, the Factory, Cockatoo Island, &c. A number of the convicts who are not near the expiration of their sentences, will, we believe, be sent to Van Diemen's Land; some of the clerks and superintendents are also to be sent to that colony, but we have not heard what will be done with those officers whose services are not required any longer. The buildings, we understand, will be handed over to the colonial authorities. *Maitland Mercury* 29 Sept. p. 3

convict gang a group of prisoners who worked together. [First recorded 1832.]

Convict gangs were often set to work on public works, such as clearing the bush, or building roads and bridges. Gangs that undertook particular types of work were given particular names, such as CLEARING GANG or bricklayers' gang.

> **1862** J.B. had an interview with the Governor on the subject of gaining access to the prisons and **convict** or chain-**gangs**. It was arranged that we should visit a chain-gang on First-day next, distant about eleven miles, and which has no

regular means of religious instruction. BACKHOUSE & TYLOR *Life and Labours of George Washington Walker* p. 40

convictism 1 the CONVICT SYSTEM; the use of an Australian colony as a place of penal servitude. New South Wales, for example, might be seen as being a place of convictism. [First recorded 1834.]

> **1838** Next to the delightful mildness of its climate and the simple state of its society, there is nothing which so strongly recommends the new Colony of South Australia, as its entire freedom from convicts and **convictism**. Perhaps it might be called the most distinguishing feature in the whole picture, and the very one which gives it so vast a superiority over the old penal Colonies of New South Wales and Van Diemen's Land. T.H. JAMES *Six Months in South Australia* p. 39

2 the convict population of an Australian colony. [First recorded 1847.]

> **1847** With the increasing scarcity and cost of labor, a very considerable immigration of exclusively male **convictism**, undiluted by any admixture of free and untainted persons, has been going on from Van Diemen's Land and from England, subscription societies having introduced 2500 probation and expiree convicts from the former country, besides 500 estimated to have immigrated at their own expense, whilst the British Government has sent from England nearly 500 exiles from the Pentonville and Parkhurst prisons. *Port Phillip Herald* 7 Jan. (Supplement)

convict labour work undertaken by prisoners. [First recorded 1827.]

Convict labour was essential in the early years of Australian colonial society. Before the advent of free immigration to Australia, labour was in short supply. Convicts made up the bulk of the workforce and were essential to the building of colonial infrastructure. Conditions of their labour varied greatly. Later, however, free settlers came to resent the fact that convict labour undercut the labour market, especially in times of economic depression, and this was one of the arguments used in the lobbying for the end of TRANSPORTATION.

> **1822** The hours of **convict labour** are from six till nine, and from ten till three in summer; and from eight till one o'clock without intermission in winter. On Saturdays the convicts leave their work at ten in summer and eleven in winter, to enable them to attend at the store to draw their rations, and on Wednesdays one hour is allowed them for the same purpose. From one o'clock, therefore, in winter, and from three o'clock in summer, the convicts at Hobart Town have the remainder of every working day in the week to themselves. The reason of this dispensation from work, is to enable them by their own labour to provide lodging and washing for themselves. J.T. BIGGE *Report of the Commissioner of Inquiry into the State of the Colony of New South Wales* p. 43

1835 The abundance of **convict-labour** in this colony has reduced the wages of all free persons in the capacity of servants, to a rate even lower than that of England; and when young women, whose expectations have been raised unreasonably by exaggerated reports of the state of the colony, are offered such wages on their arrival in Sydney, they become dispirited through disappointment. We have even been told that there are no fewer than fifteen unmarried female emigrants confined at present in the Lunatic Asylum, in consequence of mental aberration, induced by this and other causes. *Colonist* (Sydney) 15 Jan. p. 1

convict labourer a convict employed in unskilled manual work. [First recorded 1824.]

Most of the convicts in the Australian colonies worked as labourers performing unskilled manual work. Historians have found that convict labourers in New South Wales were generally well fed and well treated in comparison to other workers (for example, free workers in England) at the time. They worked on average five and a half days a week to perform about fifty-six hours of work. Convict labourers also had a relatively generous clothing allowance.

1822 Instances very frequently occur of the marriage of convicts with emancipated convict women, and with young women who are born in the colony, to which the latter are as much prompted by their early dispositions to marriage, as by the associations into which they are led, from the admission of the **convict labourers** to the houses and tables of the lower classes of emancipated convict settlers, to whom they are assigned. J.T. BIGGE *Report of the Commissioner of Inquiry into the State of the Colony of New South Wales* p. 195

1840 Farmers usually get **convict labourers** assigned to them by government, which is of much consequence, where free labour is yet scarce. Extensive establishments are provided with one or more mechanics, they being of greater value, are estimated as worth two or three labourers, and assigned accordingly. Female convicts are also assigned; the parties binding themselves to furnish all such servants with rations and clothing, agreeably to a government scale furnished them. A. RUSSELL *A Tour Through the Australian Colonies* p. 108

convict-made made or constructed by convict labour. [First recorded 1852.]

1852 The few brief chapters which compose our history thus inform you, how the shackled felon has become the instrument of human progress, in clearing the way for the corn-grower and sheep-feeder; how in their turn they had furnished food for the gold-digger, who now travels comfortably along the **convict-made** roads. S. MOSSMAN *A Voice from Australia* pp. 3–4

convict mechanic a convict with a trade or particular skill. [First recorded 1837.]

Those convicts who had a skill or a trade often practised them in the colonies. One term used to refer to those with such skills was 'convict mechanic'. Generally, such convicts had the opportunity to gain more privileges, and formed something of an elite within the convict work system.

1837 The lumber-yard, as it was called, was an establishment containing workshops for **convict mechanics** of various descriptions, in the employ of government, and was also a depot for materials and stores used in the carrying on of the government works. The mechanics (of course all convicts) employed by far the greater portion of their time in working, not for the government, but for the felon overseers and clerks of the establishment. The robbery thus practised upon the government was not confined to the misappropriation of labour, but extended to every description of materials. J. MUDIE *The Felonry of New South Wales* p. 28

1838 Convicts, who are mechanics, are as well, if not better treated, than those who are domestic servants; for as every kind of domestic labour is very scarce in New South Wales, a convict who has been a blacksmith, carpenter, mason, cooper, wheelwright, or gardener, is a most valuable servant, worth three or four ordinary convicts. … As a mechanic can scarcely be compelled by punishment to exert his skill, it is for the interest of the master to conciliate his **convict mechanic**, in order to induce him to work well. W. MOLESWORTH *Report from the Select Committee of the House of Commons on Transportation* p. 9

convict overseer a convict in government or assigned service appointed to supervise convict labourers. [First recorded 1829.]

OVERSEERS, or supervisors, for convicts were generally appointed from among the convict population itself to oversee the work of convicts. In return, convict overseers had extra privileges such as not having to do physical labour and the possibility of gaining an early PARDON.

1856 Their breakfast was of flour and water; no midday meal was prepared. At the close of their daily toil they were conveyed to their island gaol, and a more substantial repast afforded. But the double twisted and knotted cords applied to the excoriated back lashed forth the usual evening music. The brutality and injustice of **convict overseers** were the chief cause of such inflictions, and the exciting motive to escape from the cruelties of man to the heartlessness and horrors of surrounding natives. J. BONWICK *The Bushrangers: Illustrating the early days of Van Diemen's Land* p. 21

convict police a force of CONVICT CONSTABLES. [First recorded 1838.]

1849 Although a stern kind of mechanical discipline was carried out, yet there were moral evils of a most appalling nature in existence. The sleeping arrangements led to practices of the grossest description. Some of the worst prisoners were selected as constables and sub-overseers. Perfidy and treachery towards fellow prisoners were considered meritorious. Acts of brutal violence could be practised by the **convict police** on the men in gangs, not only with impunity but with approbation. T. ROGERS *Correspondence Relating to the Dismissal* p. 63

convict population that part of the colonial population made up of those serving sentences for which they had been transported to the colonies. [First recorded 1834.]

The nature and length of sentences varied, as did the experiences of convicts once they reached the colonies, however, what united the convict population was that they had not come to Australia by choice and were not free to do what they wished once they arrived; they were PRISONERS OF THE CROWN.

1834 For some time after the original establishment of the colony of New South Wales in the year 1788, the whole of the **convict-population**, with the exception of those individuals who were retained as house-servants by the Government officers of the settlement, were employed on account of the Government, either in agriculture or in the public works. J.D. LANG *An Historical and Statistical Account of New South Wales* vol. 2 p. 1

1838 For eight or nine months in the year, the climate of Sydney is delightful, but unlike Hobart Town and Launceston, where the same class of men are almost unknown, the **convict population** of Sydney is a great annoyance to the respectable emigrants from England. Owing to the excessive countenance afforded them by the late Governor Macquarrie, who seems to have given himself up, body and soul, to the convict party; they are now the principal landholders in the neighbourhood of the town, and more than one half of the Sydney houses belongs to them. T.H. JAMES *Six Months in South Australia* p. 164

convict servant = ASSIGNED CONVICT. [First recorded 1790.]

1822 As long as the great disproportion continues to exist between the male and female population in New South Wales, the temptations to illicit intercourse in both, and all the crimes that are committed for the purpose of supporting it, must be expected to prevail. Female **convict servants** will continue to be seduced from the houses of their masters, and will find asylums in the houses of single men, under the pretence of service; and the still greater evil will continue, of the seduction of the native-born young women by the male convicts, and their marriage with them. J.T. BIGGE *Report of the Commissioner of Inquiry into the State of the Colony of New South Wales* p. 106

1838 Domestic servants, transported for any offence, are assigned as domestic servants in Australia. ... They are well fed, well clothed, and receive wages from 10*l.* to 15*l.* a year, and are as well treated in respectable families as similar descriptions of servants are in this country. In many instances, masters have even carried to an illegal extent their indulgences to their **convict servants**. W. MOLESWORTH *Report from the Select Committee of the House of Commons on Transportation* p. 9

1843 TORTURE—The *Australasian Chronicle* of yesterday accuses a settler ... of having caused a **convict servant** to be tied up all night under the dripping of a cask of brine placed above him. *Sydney Morning Herald* 10 May p. 2

convict settlement any settlement established for the purpose of locating convicts. Also called CONVICT STATION. [First recorded 1831.]

The first convict settlement was Port Jackson, established in 1788. Some of the other principal convict settlements included Coal River (now Newcastle) in 1804, Port Macquarie in 1821, and Port Arthur in Van Diemen's Land, established in 1832.

1836 The connection of adult blacks with the **convict settlements** imparts to them all the vices of the convicts. Settlers employ them in harvesting for a small compensation, and they have proved willing, occasionally, to work, provided they be starved into it, and the liquor and food be withheld till nearly night, or delivered in such small quantities as barely to sustain the laborer and provoke his appetite. J.F. O'CONNELL *A Residence of Eleven Years in New Holland* pp. 87–8

1852 Neither South Australia nor Victoria have ever been used as **convict settlements**, and are consequently for the most part free from the moral taint which has infected the elder colony. W. HUGHES *The Australian Colonies* p. 110

convict settler a person transported as a convict who subequently took up land in Australia. [First recorded 1792.]

Convicts who were pardoned (EMANCIPISTS) or who had served their sentences (EXPIREES) were free to settle in the colonies. They were granted land, and from the 1830s could obtain land through the method of squatting on equal terms with the free settlers. From 1831 land was also available through sale, and those convicts with adequate finances could buy land. A large number of the early settlers of Australia, then, were convict settlers.

1817 [Governor Macquarie to Earl Bathurst] I respectfully recommend that all Persons, that have Come out as Convicts and may be deemed deserving of Grants of Land from the Crown ... should themselves and Families, with one Male Convict Servant to each such Settler, be Victualled at the Expence of Government for Six Months, at the Expiration of Which Period they will be able to Maintain themselves. ... By Victualling them for Six Months, they will have Sufficient time to reap and gather in part of their Crops, such as Maize, Potatoes, Peas &c. &c. I am however at the same time of opinion that it will be unnecessary even to Victual Emancipated **Convict-Settlers** for any Length of time. *Historical Records of Australia* 1st series IX p. 237

1826 [Surveyor-General Oxley to Governor Darling] From the first Settlement of the Colony, up to the Year 1810, the successive Governors had granted to Individuals 177,500 Acres of land, principally to **Convict Settlers**, the Grants seldom exceeding 100 Acres. *Historical Records of Australia* 1st series XII p. 379

convict shepherd a convict assigned to watch flocks of sheep for owners of rural properties. [First recorded 1834.]

Convict shepherds were an essential labour force underpinning the early pastoral industry. However, it was an occupation that was seen to be the lowest of the agricultural jobs—the harshest and most degrading. As settlement in the interior increased in the 1830s, the labour force was sometimes inadequate to the demand and masters might resort to flogging as well as profit sharing with his convict workers to keep them working effectively—often supervision on large rural properties was limited and valuable property had to be entrusted to the convict workers.

1834 On my first journey along with the Hunter's River settler,—who was better acquainted with the route,—we rode about nine miles down the valley after sunset, and bivouacked on the side of a hill near a pool of water. We happened to be near the sheep-station of a respectable free-emigrant settler; and the **convict-shepherd** or overseer in charge of it—a very obliging sort of person—brought us a bucket to hold water for our tea, and a piece of salt pork to relish it. J.D. LANG *An Historical and Statistical Account of New South Wales* vol. 2 pp. 110–11

convict ship a ship in which convicts were transported from Britain and Ireland to Australia. [First recorded 1812.]

Conditions on the ships varied, but were fair for most journeys. The second and third fleets were the worst of the transports, with a high death and illness rate. Ships were provided by private firms, which were later made to sign contracts with the government so as to prevent a recurrence of the early tragedies. A surgeon had to be provided and hygiene standards met. Over the years, the death and illness rate on board the convict ships improved significantly.

1812 *The appearance and regulations of a **convict ship** are as* singular as the novel punishment of transportation, or as a regulated colony of very lawless convicts. Order and discipline, necessary to such an abandoned society, prevails in every part of the ship. The men are ranged in one long line, the women in a second; but the sexes are separated. The former dine up on their bedsteads, the latter sleep on a species of table, three longitudinally, and two collaterally. To preserve subordination and regularity, a soldier in his regimentals is placed at the interval of ten convicts as their guard. E.H. BARKER *Geographical, Commercial, and Political Essays* p. 193

1822 I think the allowance of spirits to the soldiers composing the guard in a **convict-ship** is too much by half. I am confident there was not a night, while they had full allowance in the Neptune, but some were intoxicated; and on some occasions more than half of them were found quite unfit for duty, notwithstanding their commanding officer did all he could to keep them in good order. This scene of debauchery was heightened by the very abandoned conduct of their wives, who, in fits of intoxication, would offer themselves indiscriminately for prostitution; which kept up constant jealousy, and excited quarrels between the soldiers and sailors that often assumed a very serious aspect. T. REID *Two Voyages to New South Wales and Van Diemen's Land* p. 87

convict slave a convict servant. [First recorded 1829.]
The CONVICT SYSTEM was often compared to the system of slavery. Those who opposed the system of transportation often equated the two systems in order to make the convict system seem more abhorrent. In particular, the system was denounced as being like slavery in that private individuals controlled the system and benefited from it. This was seen to make masters corrupt and thus threatened to degrade the whole of colonial society. Arguments used to support the abolition of slavery were used in the campaigns that led to the abolition of transportation, and one of the key images of the rhetoric was to label convicts 'convict slaves'.

1838 Transportation, though chiefly dreaded as exile, undoubtedly is much more than exile; it is slavery as well; and the condition of the **convict slave** is frequently a very miserable one; but that condition is unknown, and cannot be made known; for the physical condition of a convict is generally better than that of an agricultural labourer; the former is in most cases better fed and better clothed than the latter; it is the restraint on the freedom of action, the degradation of slavery, and the other moral evils, which chiefly constitute the pains of transportation, and of which no description can convey an adequate idea to that class in whom Transportation ought to inspire terror. *Report from the Select Committee of the House of Commons on Transportation* p. 21

convict station = CONVICT SETTLEMENT. [First recorded 1834.]

1854 The settlement was formed on a small island twenty-five miles from the 'Gates,' or entrance, and continued in being, as the double or most severe **convict**

station, from the 2nd January, 1822, (the day the first party landed under Lieut. Cuthbertson, of the 48th Regiment,) until November, 1833, when it was partly abandoned, and finally ceased to be a settlement on the 11th January, 1834. H.B. STOREY *A Year in Tasmania* p. 4

convict stock-keeper a convict who worked tending livestock, especially cattle. [First recorded 1833.]

1833 One would imagine that a residence in such a lone place would be liable to cause a change of some consequence in the mind and habits of any person; and it would be an interesting point to ascertain the effect on the **convict stock-keepers**, who, for weeks together, can have no opportunity of conversing with a white man, except their sole companion; for there are always two in a hut. The time cannot hang very heavily on their hands, as they are almost constantly engaged in riding after cattle, in order to drive them within certain boundaries; or in hunting the kangaroo, of which there are great numbers on the hills, and the emu. W. BRETON *Excursions in New South Wales* p. 108

convict system the transportation of convicts and the treatment of them during confinement. [First recorded 1834.]

The entire system of transportation of prisoners from Britain and Ireland to the Australian colonies was referred to as the 'convict system'. This included its various facets, such as TRANSPORTATION, ASSIGNMENT, and PROBATION. The term was often used in a derogatory sense by its opponents, the ANTI-TRANSPORTATIONISTS.

1834 Until the banks of the Swan River were opened for settlement, the great natural advantages of Australia had been counteracted by the moral evils of the **convict system**. For fear of the degrading and corrupting influence of transportation, the emigrant who was possessed of a decent pride, and of some regard for the morals of his children, preferred the dense forests and long winters of Canada ... to the fine climate and grassy plains of Australia. E.G. WAKEFIELD *The New British Province of South Australia* p. 134

1847 The motion was seconded by Major St. John, and was as follows: That whilst this meeting acknowledges and sincerely regrets the scarcity of labour in this district, and the injury to property resulting therefrom, it cannot, under any circumstances, entertain any proposal for a system of importation of British criminals, coinciding, as this meeting does, in the declaration made by the Legislative Council of the colony, in 1844:—'That the moral and social influences of the **convict system**, and the contamination and vice which are inseparable from it, are evils for which no mere pecuniary benefits would serve as a compromise.' *Port Phillip Herald* 2 Mar. p. 2

convict woman a woman transported to Australia after having been convicted of a crime in Britain or Ireland. [First recorded 1827.]

A number of the convicts transported to the Australian colonies were female. Between 1787 and 1852, nearly 25,000 convict women arrived in Australia. The majority were sent to New South Wales, their average age was 27, and they were generally convicted of crimes such as theft and prostitution. Convict women were often first placed in the female FACTORY upon arrival, from which they might be ASSIGNED. Many women married in the colonies and were able to start new lives. Those who observed the CONVICT SYSTEM (usually its opponents) were often scathing of the women, labelling them as debased and morally corrupt, or, as in the title of Joy Damousi's 1997 study, 'depraved and disorderly'. Concerns over the moral status of women often led to them being more closely controlled and their lives, even after having been freed, more circumscribed.

> **1838** In a private family … **a convict woman**, frequently the only one in the service, perhaps in the neighbourhood, is surrounded by a number of depraved characters, to whom she becomes an object of constant pursuit and solicitation; she is generally obliged to select one man, as a paramour, to defend her from the importunities of the rest; she seldom remains long in the same place; she either commits some offence, for which she is returned to the Government; or she becomes pregnant, in which case she is sent to the factory, to be there confined at the expense of the Government; at the expiration of the period of confinement or punishment, she is re-assigned; and again goes through the same course; such is too generally the career of convict women, even in respectable families. W. MOLESWORTH *Report from the Select Committee of the House of Commons on Transportation* p. 12

cove a man, a bloke, a chap; a boss; the owner or manager of an establishment. [This term derives from thieves' cant, but its ultimate origin is unknown. While sense 1 exists in standard English, the OED points out that in the twentieth century it appears most frequently in Australasian sources.]

In the first 1812 citation below, Vaux demonstrates how **cove** was typically used in FLASH language, and this sense is recorded from the sixteenth century. In the second 1812 citation Vaux gives a second sense, one that is not recorded outside Australia (although Vaux must have known it from England), and it was this underworld sense that led to an especially Australian use of the term—from a generalised 'boss' to the specific sense of the owner or manager of a sheep station (recorded in Australian English from 1837 to the beginning of the twentieth century). It seems likely that the development of Vaux's 'master of a house or shop' into the general sense 'boss' occurred in convict contexts, as the 1837 and 1879 citations suggest.

> **1812** [W]hen joined to particular words, as a *cross-**cove***, a *flash-cove*, a *leary-cove*, &c., it simply implies a man of these several descriptions. J.H. VAUX *Memoirs* (1964) p. 233

1812 COVE: the master of a house or shop. J.H. VAUX *Memoirs* (1964) p. 233

1837 You must not go on as you have done with the **cove**; that is the master, the masters are called coves by the convicts. *Report from the Select Committee of the House of Commons on Transportation* p. 32

1879 The party consisted of eleven men, one boy, one overseer and the master, or '**cove**', as he was called. 'AN OLD HAND' (G. HAMILTON) *Experiences of a Colonist Forty Years Ago* p. 3

croppy a convict (originally an Irish convict). [From standard English *croppy* 'a person who has his hair cropped short'. The OED points out that the term was applied especially 'to the Irish rebels of 1798, who wore their hair short as a sign of sympathy with the French Revolution'. Some of these political prisoners were transported to Australia for their part in the rebellion, and arrived in Australia between 1800 and 1802. They were regarded as being particularly difficult and dangerous prisoners. The term was then extended to Irish convicts more generally, and was ultimately also applied to any convict who was at large and had turned to bushranging. First recorded 1800.]

1800 [Inquiry *re* the attempted Irish conspiracy] That a fortnight since the Witness ment'd the above conversation to Dogherty that he hath often been in company with Holt when drinking inflammatory and seditious Toasts—'Success to the **Croppies**' and other improper Expressions were made use of by Holt, that he asked the Witness if there was a rising of the Irish if he would not join them. *Historical Records of Australia* 1st series II p. 581

1833 While it [a meeting] lasts, all the blacks of the respective districts are on the most friendly terms; but as soon as it is concluded they become extremely shy of each other, and soon separate. The settlers are allowed to be present, but not the convicts, whom they call **croppies**, of course a word which they have learnt from the whites. W. BRETON *Excursions in New South Wales* p. 234

cross *noun* illegal practices. Especially in the phrase **on the cross** *adverb* illegally; *adjective* illegal. [These meanings all originate in British thieves' slang (see FLASH), and *on the cross* is first briefly recorded in a British text from 1802, but Vaux provides the next evidence.]

This term is well attested in texts from Britain, America, and Australia in the nineteenth century, and it is typical of underworld slang. In Australian sources it does not have a specifically convict sense, but it is included here as being representative of the kind of language that would have been well known to the more hardened criminals among the convict population.

1812 Illegal or dishonest practices in general are called *the **cross***, in opposition to *the square*. ... Any article which has been irregularly obtained, is said to have been *got upon the cross*, and is emphatically termed as a cross article. J.H. Vaux *Memoirs* (1964) p. 234

1847 I recall going up to their [the shepherds'] hut when I had been hurdle-making about three months, and they had come to know me well enough to have no fear of any foul play from me. It was night, and the dogs, who had been starved for several days, had just got hold of the entrails of a sheep the men had been killing '**on the cross**', so that they did not hear me till I came close up to the hut, and then all rushed barking at me in a mob. A. Harris *Settlers and Convicts* (1953) p. 186

crown labourer a convict worker. [First recorded 1824.]

A crown labourer could be working for the government (i.e. the crown) or be assigned to a free settler. It was typical of a number of euphemistic terms for convicts.

1824 The advantage of encouraging tillage agriculturalists will appear from this circumstance:—a settler possessing 200*l.* capital, living on and cultivating his farm, will employ and subsist four **crown labourers**, or convicts, making a saving to the government of 56*l.* per annum, the expense of subsisting those convicts. E. Eagar *Letters to the Rt. Hon. Robert Peel* p. 41

crown prisoner a convict. [First recorded 1819.]

'Crown prisoner' was another term for a CONVICT. All those transported to the colonies were subject to the law of the crown, that is, the British government. See also PRISONER OF THE CROWN.

1824 The public buildings in Hobart Town are not numerous, nor much dis-proportionate in their nature to the state of the colony. They are chiefly erected by the prisoners of the Crown in their hours of labour. No plan has as yet been adopted to compel this class of people to work as they ought to do. In fact, a **Crown prisoner** in Hobart Town does not perform one third of the daily task of a labourer in this country. E. Curr *An Account of the Colony of Van Diemen's Land, principally designed for the use of emigrants* pp. 9–10

crown servant a convict. [First recorded 1815.]

'Crown servant' was another term that referred to convicts, not just those who were employed as actual servants (domestic workers), but to all who were 'servants to the crown'. In terms of British law, all convicts were to be regarded as servants to the British crown. As the term 'convict' was not used very often, terms such as 'crown servant' were more widely applied to prisoners sent to the colonies.

1815 1st.—The whole of the **Crown Servants** are to be mustered every afternoon at sunset at the lumber-yard by the Superintendent of Public Works, after which they are to retire to their respective habitations and there remain until sunrise the following morning. M. Hookey *Bobby Knopwood and his Times* 25 Apr. p. 111

1827 If Government were to give an order, that all convicts (or as they are styled in New South Wales, **crown servants**,) should be worked in irons, and kept on bread and water, when in Government employ, they would be thankful to be employed as servants, and labourers by the colonists; at present they are supplied with a good ration, equal to that of His Majesty's troops, with tea, sugar, and tobacco; this of course attracts great numbers of them to be maintained by Government, and consequently it is necessary to have a large establishment of officers, superintendants, &c., which is a source of convenient patronage. It is extraordinary, however, that the Treasury has never interfered with it. One or two simple orders, relative to the rations and comforts issued to the convicts, would save the Treasury many thousands per annum. *Sydney Monitor* 6 Aug. p. 566

D

dark cell a prison cell (or small confined area) without light, used as a severe form of solitary confinement. [First recorded 1831.]

Solitary confinement in a darkened cell was a severe form of punishment for convicts kept in prisons, often with rations being restricted as well. Such punishment was increasingly common in the 1820s and 1830s—it aimed to deprive the prisoner of contact with all others and was only used as a short-term punishment. It should not be confused with the 'SEPARATE system' which was introduced in the 1830s and designed to keep prisoners individually in separate cells so as to prevent contamination and immorality.

> **1831** What do you mean by the term 'protracted confinement,' as referrable to a confinement in a light cell with bread and water?—For trivial offences, generally the light cells are had recourse to, and the confinement is of *short* duration; for the more heavy offences, the **dark cells** are of course adopted, with bread and water as diet, and it has generally been found that at the expiration of a fortnight, indeed in some instances after a few days, necessary for a resident surgeon to increase the quantity of bread, that quantity I mean which is allowed for a prisoner under the circumstance of punishment. *Report of the Select Committee on Secondary Punishments* p. 5

Derwenter An ex-convict (or runaway convict) from Tasmania. [From the *Derwent* River in Tasmania. A penal settlement was established on the banks of the Derwent where present-day Hobart stands, in 1804. First recorded 1827.]

The term is especially associated with the gold rushes in Victoria in the 1850s and 1860s, when ex-convicts and runaway convicts from Tasmania were blamed for increases in crime (see the 1863 citation). They were also called VANDEMONIANS.

> **1827** The ***Derwent-ers*** were as scantily provided with Spiritous Liquors as ourselves, previous to the late arrivals; a single puncheon of Rum remained in

the King's Stores before the last supply commenced landing. Shame on the Colony or the Government! That those Colonies should be forty years old and yet not able to manufacture all their own beverage! *Sydney Monitor* 16 Mar. p. 349

1863 The one prominent cause of crime there was the presence of runaway convicts and expirees, known commonly as Van Demonians, or **Derwenters**, as Hobart Town stands upon the river Derwent. The share which these Derwenters took in such proceedings may be ascertained from the police records. Although after all but a small fraction of the population of Victoria, they managed almost to monopolize the crime. *Meliora* (London) vol. 5 p. 68

detached (of a convict or party of convicts) separated for a particular purpose from the main body. [The term derives from the military and naval sense of *detach* 'to separate and send off (a part from a main body) for a special purpose; to draw off (a regiment, a ship, or the like) for some special mission'. The Australian sense is first recorded in 1821.]

Detached convicts might be sent to work on certain tasks, for example, repairing public works such as roads, or on detachments clearing tracts of land for settlement.

1825 [Sir Thomas Brisbane to Earl Bathurst] As Convicts in **Detached** Parties draw their rations for a week in advance, when removed from one Detached Station to another, they are not permitted to draw Rations with the latter, excepting from the Saturday of the week in which they join; if removed to Barracks, or to an Establishment in which Rations are issued daily, the Superintendent of such Establishment will account for the rations in their possession, which they must have drawn up to the Friday inclusively of the Week in which they join. *Historical Records of Australia* 1st series XI p. 505

1835 It would tend much to the public welfare, if H.M. Government would not permit overseers of road-gangs to send out **detached** gangs to repair *some* parts of the road, without a responsible person being in charge of the detached parties. The road-gang is properly stationed near the stockade, a few miles from Paddy's River, and the detached party near the Township of Bungonia, *a distance of at least* from fourteen to fifteen miles; and scarce a day passes but one may observe either one or more passing along the road from the chief gang to the detached party. *Colonist* (Sydney) 16 July p. 228

double cat-o'-nine-tails a whip used for physical punishment.

This was a more severe version of the CAT, and was intended to inflict a more brutal punishment. Cats often varied in nature, although in the 1830s a Sydney superintendent of convicts persuaded Governor Bourke to issue standard instruments of punishment throughout the colony of New South Wales, in an attempt to standardise the punishment of FLOGGING.

1838 Was the cat with which the floggings were inflicted at Macquarie Harbour of the same description as the ordinary cat-o'-nine-tails? No, it was a much heavier instrument, and larger; the cat which is generally used in the colony for the punishment of convicts is what is called a single cat, such as is generally employed for the punishment of soldiers and sailors, but that which was used at Macquarie Harbour is what is called a thief's cat, or a **double cat-o'-nine-tails**; it did not comprise more than the usual number of tails but each of them was a double twist of whipcord, and each tail contained nine knots; it was a very formidable instrument. *Report from the Select Committee of the House of Commons on Transportation* p. 38

double convict *noun* a transported convict found guilty of an offence commited in the colony, and sentenced to more severe punishment.

1836 The Phoenix was condemned at Port Jackson, as unseaworthy, purchased by Government, and made a receiving ship for **double convicts**, sentenced to penal settlements. J.F. O'CONNELL *A Residence of Eleven Years in New Holland* p. 35

1854 Port Arthur was next selected as a sawing establishment, to supply the Engineering Department with timber: however, the advantages the place afforded for the formation of a penal settlement becoming more apparent, the convicts were removed to it from Macquarie Harbour and Maria Island. It remained strictly a **double convict** station: no communication being allowed, except through the Government, until 1841, when the agricultural farm was established at Salt Water River. H.B. STONEY *A Year in Tasmania* p. 48

double convicted (also **doubly convicted**) to be sentenced for a criminal offence committed after arrival in Australia.

Punishment for a SECONDARY offence (see also COLONIAL OFFENCE) might range from being flogged to being sentenced to a term at a PENAL SETTLEMENT. To be convicted of a crime committed in the colonies was known as a DOUBLE CONVICTION. The rate of second conviction was quite high, although most were for minor crimes, such as drunkenness or gambling and other minor breaches of discipline. Statistics suggest that in New South Wales about half of all convicts were brought before a magistrate; in Van Diemen's Land this statistic was even higher, about three-quarters—but few (perhaps a fifth) had committed serious offences. Minor crimes might lead to a sentence of lashes; more severe crimes were often punished by death or by a sentence to a place of SECONDARY punishment such as Port Arthur. Prior to the 1823 New South Wales Act, sentences of transportation for colonial offences varied, but after this they could be no longer than three years. The rate of reoffence and double conviction varied, but was exacerbated by economic depressions and lack of employment for those pardoned or on TICKETS OF LEAVE.

1840 It appears that in 1837, a batch of those **doubly-convicted** from Norfolk Island, and from chain-gangs, were assigned to the trustees of the late Dr. Redfern, and sent to a remote district on the Lachlan river, where they were placed under the superintendence of Dr. Redfern's nephew ... on the arrival of these twice-convicted felons, five or six at a time, so well initiated in every species of wickedness, released from former restraint, and removed from the seat of Government, this establishment was thrown into a state of the utmost insubordination, inasmuch that, for a considerable time the place became like a garrison, the superintendent himself being obliged to go out armed with pistols, in passing from the house to the store. *Sydney Morning Herald* 31 Aug. p. 6

1843 Now, there is another class of **double convicted** felons—that is, those who, after being in this ironed gang, are again found guilty of robbery. They are then sentenced for seven or fourteen years or life, to a penal settlement, where they slave from morning till night, and no recompense for their labour. *Sydney Morning Herald* 7 Sept. p. 2

1847 Banishment from Australia, for the natives and free persons, is now to Norfolk Island, if for the first offence; but **doubly convicted** felons,—that is, prisoners transported from this country convicted of new crimes there, are now all sent to Van Diemen's Land. A. MARJORIBANKS *Travels in New South Wales* pp. 104–5

double conviction a conviction for a criminal offence committed after arrival in the Australian colonies. [First recorded 1827.]

1827 At the dinner, too, given ... to Sir Thomas Brisbane, a sort of Board of Green Cloth sat upon all applications for tickets, rejecting every one who had been punished or convicted by any colonial court—in order that His Excellency might not be exposed to the unpleasant dilemma of rubbing his immaculate shoulders against a man who had been sullied by a ***double*** conviction. P. CUNNINGHAM *Two Years in New South Wales* vol. 2 p. 140

double ironed see DOUBLY IRONED.

double irons fetters that were heavier than SINGLE IRONS. [First recorded 1811.]
Double irons consisted of iron fetters around the ankles, usually riveted in place so that they could not be easily removed. They were used as a more severe or additional form of punishment (e.g. for breaches of discipline or negligence) and to prevent absconding by those working on the GANGS.

1811 Whereas the following Persons have absconded from Government Labour, this is therefore to caution the Inhabitant in general, against harbouring, encouraging, secreting, or employing the said Absentees, under pain of the Penalties on that head:

Sayd, a Moorman, who effected his escape from the Governor Hunter, bound to Newcastle, while she was wind-bound in Broken Bay, by jumping overboard in the night (although in **double irons**) and swimming on shore; he has been many times advertised as a Runaway, for which offence he was sentenced to Newcastle, and is now supposed to be in or about Hawkesbury. *Sydney Gazette* 30 Mar.

doubly ironed (also **double ironed**) (of a convict) punished with DOUBLE IRONS.

1835 These prisoners consisted of workers, Pennel, M'Kan, Jones, Ferguson, and a carpenter (with the exception of the latter), who assisted the ship's Carpenter at his work, all these men were **double ironed**! H. MELVILLE *History of the Island of Van Diemen's Land* p. 91

E

educated (of a convict) fitted by some training or experience prior to transportation for employment in a clerical or professional capacity.

A convict might be described as educated if he had a skill, training, or profession prior to transportation that could then be put to use in the colonies. Such skills might include carpentry, boat-building, stonemasonry, tailoring, and shoe-making, to name but a few. Such convicts were often given pardons or tickets of leave fairly soon after arrival so as to make them more useful for colonial society. See also GENTLEMAN or SPECIAL convicts.

> **1830** [Governor Darling to Sir George Murray] '**Educated convicts**' as they are termed, which includes those transported for *Forgery* ... have until the present Moment been sent to Wellington Valley, a Government Establishment in the Interior 250 Miles from Sydney. These people have been kept there, in order to their undergoing a reasonable probation, and, when recommended by the Superintendent, have been from time to time assigned as Clerks or for such other situations as they appeared qualified to fill. *Historical Records of Australia* 1st series XV p. 832

> **1851** It is to this station [Norfolk Island] that **educated convicts** are sometimes transported from the mother country: the sufferings therefore such men are necessarily compelled to undergo, is indeed awful and unjust. The education they have received, it is true, should operate for the prevention of crime, but persons of this class have usually friends and connections from whom their punishments, generally speaking, separate them forever. This is punishment to the mind—and mental sufferings are far worse than those of the body. H. MELVILLE *The Present State of Australia* pp. 159–60

emancipate 1 *verb* to discharge as free a convict who has received a conditional or absolute pardon. [Specialised use of *emancipate* in the sense 'to set free from control; to release from legal, social, or political constraint'. The OED points out that in modern usage 'the word suggests primarily the liberation of slaves'. In Australia the term was not used in this loaded way (see ABOLITIONIST) but was simply another term for making a prisoner free. First recorded in the convict sense in 1787.]

Generally, a convict was emancipated through the granting of an absolute or conditional pardon—each of which provided varying degrees of freedom.

> **1787** [Phillip's Instructions] And whereas we have by our Commission, bearing date [2nd April] 1787, given and granted upon you full power and authority to **emancipate** and discharge from their servitude any of the convicts under your superintendance who shall, from their good conduct and a disposition to industry, be deserving of favour: It is our will and pleasure that in every such case you do issue your warrant to the Surveyor of Lands to make surveys of and mark out in lots such lands upon the said territory as may be necessary for their use; and when that shall be done, that you do pass grants thereof with all convenient speed to any of the said convicts so emancipated. *Historical Records of New South Wales* vol. 1 II p. 90

2 = EMANCIPATED. [First recorded 1829.]

> **1829** The population of Van Diemen's Land is about equal to one third of New South Wales, from which a pannel of 2000 persons, fit for Jurors could be obtained, and in about the like proportion of Emigrants, Colony born and **Emancipate** Settlers, as New South Wales. From these circumstances it is apprehended that the free population of these Colonies is capable of fully supplying the material in such a number of persons, fit and proper to serve on Juries, as will ensure the effective operation of the system there. *Sydney Monitor* 12 Jan. p. 1458

3 = EMANCIPIST. [First recorded 1838.]

> **1848** Some time since a diabolical effort was made to antagonise the free population and the **emancipates**. It failed, happily failed, as we trust all such unprincipled designs must. Now it is advised that the native youths should originate a class movement. It would be less mischievous only in degree. *Britannia* (Hobart) 20 July p. 4

emancipated (of a former convict) discharged as free, having been granted a conditional or an absolute pardon, or (loosely) having completed the sentence imposed.

Although this term referred to a convict who had been granted a conditional or an absolute pardon, it was occasionally used to refer to those who had completed their sentences (also known as EXPIREES) and therefore sometimes applied generally to the ex-convicts (as in the 1847 citation below), known as EMANCIPISTS. See also FREE, FREED.

> **1834** The widow having sworn, moreover, to one of the men as the person who fired at her husband, they were both found guilty and condemned to death. The men acknowledged that they had gone down the river in a boat on the night of the robbery, with an intention to rob the marine's house, but not to commit murder. On arriving at the spot, however, they found they had been anticipated; another party of desperadoes being actually engaged in robbing the house. ... But the whole story was apparently so improbable that nobody believed it, and the men were executed forthwith. Several years afterwards, however, an **emancipated** convict-settler of the name of Fitzpatrick ... was found guilty of some capital offence and condemned to death. Before his execution, Fitzpatrick ... confessed that it was he who had robbed and murdered the marine. J.D. LANG *An Historical and Statistical Account of New South Wales* vol. 2 pp. 68–9

> **1847** No invidious feeling of animosity exists between the **Emancipated** and those who have never been convicts. H.P. FRY *Letter to the Householders of Hobarton* p. 22

emancipation 1 The act of discharging as free a convict who had received a conditional or an absolute pardon. [First recorded 1787.]

> **1787** [Phillip's Instructions] And whereas it is likely to happen that the convicts who may after their **emancipation** ... be put in possession of lands will not have the means of proceeding to their cultivation without the public aid: It is our will and pleasure that you do cause every such person you may so emancipate to be supplied with such a quantity of provisions as may be sufficient for the subsistence of himself, and also of his family, for twelve months, together with an assortment of tools and utensils, and such a proportion of seed-grain, cattle, sheep, hogs &c., as may be proper, and can be spared from the general stock of the settlement. *Historical Records of New South Wales* vol. 1 II p. 91

2 A document certifying that a convict had received a conditional or an absolute pardon. This allowed ex-convicts to prove their status as free.

> **1822** Conditional pardons, or **emancipations**, were not to be granted to convicts for life until they had been 10 years in the colony; nor to convicts for limited terms, until they had resided at least two-thirds of their original sentences. The same regulation that was declared in the year 1811, respecting tickets of leave, was repeated. J.T. BIGGE *Report of the Commissioner of Inquiry into the State of the Colony of New South Wales* p. 119

emancipist a convict who had been pardoned or whose sentence had expired.

'Emancipist' was a term used to denote convicts who were free, usually through being pardoned, but sometimes through having served their sentence (this latter group were also known as EXPIREES). Ex-convicts came to make up a substantial proportion of the colonial population and many achieved considerable success, contributing much to the colonial community and economy. They sought to have the same rights and privileges as free settlers and lobbied for social acceptance and their political rights. There was some opposition from those not of convict origin who resented the emancipists' power in colonial society and sought to limit or withdraw the rights of emancipists. They also feared emancipists would continue to support transportation to the colonies. Early colonial politics was dominated by conflicts between these two groups.

1822 [Edward Eagar to Lord Bathurst, 6 November] The population of New South Wales consists of three descriptions of persons—first, Those who came free to the Colony as Settlers and retired Civil Officers military Officers and Men who are designated in the Colony 'Emigrants', secondly, those persons who came under sentences of Transportation, but have become free by Pardon or Service of the Term, and designated '**Emancipists**', and thirdly, of those who are now Convicts under the sentence of the Law. The two former Classes only, can be and are possessed of any property, real or personal. J. RITCHIE *The Evidence to the Bigge Reports* vol. 2 (1971) p. 212

1825 [Governor Darling to Under Secretary Hay] The Colony is deeply involved in the most serious dissension, and … Party feeling never was before carried to such height as at present. It is quite clear that the **Emancipists**, in the late struggle, have gained an ascendency, to which their opponents are not likely to offer any effectual Counterpoise. These people will not be *put down*, or rather *kept down* by the old Settlers, who are Comparatively few in number. They now feel their strength and importance in the Colony, and the union of superior talent, wealth and numbers in any one Body must preponderate, however the Community may be composed. … I can discover no just or reasonable ground for treating the Emancipists, as a Body, with indiscriminate contumely, which I apprehend has too generally been the practice of the old Settlers, or making them feel that reformation is unavailing. *Historical Records of Australia* 1st series XII pp. 81–2

1844 Of course a large proportion of the population are **emancipists** (convicts who have served their allotted years of transportation), and their families or descendants; and a strong line of demarcation is in most instances observed between them and the free emigrants and settlers. Wealth, all-powerful though it be,—and many of these emancipists are the richest men in the colony,— cannot wholly overcome the prejudice against them, though policy, in some instances, greatly modifies it. MRS CHARLES MEREDITH *Notes and Sketches of New South Wales During a Residence in that Colony from 1838 to 1844* pp. 50–1

emancipist class that group of the Australian population made up of ex-convicts. See EMANCIPIST. [First recorded 1823.]

1823 [Mr Edward Eagar to Earl Bathurst] This general union and harmony between the Emigrant and **Emancipist Classes** continued unabated and undisturbed until the end of the year 1819, down to which time they were cordially united in the formation, conduct, and management of every public measure and institution of the Colony. *Historical Records of Australia* 4th series I p. 462

1825 [Sir Thomas Brisbane to Earl Bathurst] There is another point, upon which I must reserve my opinion for the present, which is, how far it would be proper to admit the **Emancipist Class** of the Colonists to a participation of the privilege of sitting in Juries; I rather incline to think that it would be expedient under certain limitations, and that the principle limitation should be the unincumbered possession of real property to a given annual value. *Historical Records of Australia* 1st series XI p. 894

emancipist party a very loose term referring to those who championed the cause of the emancipists. See EMANCIPIST. [First recorded 1834.]

1838 The EMANCIPIST PARTY originated under the government of General Macquarie, in 1809. That gentleman had acted upon the principle, that the colony of New South Wales was founded for the sake of convicts, and not for emigrants; he endeavoured, therefore, to introduce the wealthier emancipists into the society of the officers, clergy, and other respectable inhabitants of the colony; and he even made magistrates of some individuals who had been convicts. This attempt gave rise to the two parties, of those who were for, and those who were against, the emancipists. The former party is a numerous one, as the number of emancipists in 1834 amounted to between 15,000 and 16,000, while the remainder of the free population did not much exceed 21,000; and of the latter number a considerable portion were probably connected, either by parentage or marriage, with persons who had been prisoners of the Crown. Many of the emancipists have … acquired considerable wealth, and they form, therefore, a powerful political party, whose chief object is to maintain the position, that all the free inhabitants of the colony, both those who have been convicts and those who have not, ought to possess equal rights. This party, however, is not merely composed of persons that have been convicts, but it includes in its ranks a considerable portion of the free settlers, some of whom are persons inclined, by their habits, to associate with the criminal population, and to participate in the feelings of that class; others, however, are amongst the most respectable inhabitants of the colony, and on the ground of political principle, join the emancipists' party. W. MOLESWORTH *Report from the Select Committee of the House of Commons on Transportation* p. 31

emigrant a person who chose to leave their country of origin in order to settle in Australia. [First recorded 1820.]

Most emigrants were of British origin. In the convict period, emigrants were usually contrasted with either CONVICTS or EMANCIPISTS (ex-convicts). Some emigrants were very defensive of their rights in the colonies, and resentful of the convict and emancipist populations. James Mudie's *The Felonry of New South Wales* (1837) was a denunciation of the non-emigrant population and a call to see the emigrants as the superior class of colonial Australians. The emigrants were also active in the formation of the ANTI-TRANSPORTATION movement that led to the termination of the transportation of prisoners to Australia.

1832 In Governor Macquarie's time, there *was* ill-feeling between the two classes, in consequence of that good-natured Ruler having paid very special attention to the Emancipists, and patronised them beyond all former Governors. ... But after Governor Macquarie left the Colony, the extraordinary attention paid the Emancipists was not continued; and since that period, the Emancipists and the **Emigrants** have lived in amity with each other. *Hill's Life in New South Wales* 23 Nov. p. 2

1849 Convicts often address an **emigrant** thus—'Oh, you great fool! *we* came out here because we could not help it; but you, you long-tailed donkey, were *lagged* with your own consent!' The phrase 'long-tailed' is in allusion to the emigrant's carefully-kept church-going coat, which is here considered the badge of a novice. Certain it is that many, both gentle and simple, come to the colony without any sufficient reason, impelled by restlessness, and, as they conceive, by the spirit of romance! J.P. TOWNSEND *Rambles and Observations in New South Wales* p. 168

exclusionist a person opposed to the integration of ex-convicts into Australian society. [Specialised use of *exclusionist* in the sense 'one who would exclude another from some privilege'. First recorded in the Australian sense in 1826.]

An exclusionist was a member of the EMIGRANT group in colonial society who objected to the ex-convict or EMANCIPIST being given the same rights and privileges as emigrants, and particularly wanted to prevent them being part of 'acceptable' society. Exclusionists sought to distinguish themselves and gain status through this exclusion of the ex-convicts. Governor Lachlan Macquarie angered many emigrants when he sought to treat some emancipists as equal—Macquarie believed that emancipists as much as, or even more so than the emigrants, could further improve the development of New South Wales.

> **1827** The grand division, however, of the free classes here, without reference to colonial technicalities, is into that of *emigrants*, who have come out free from England, and *emancipists*, who have arrived here as convicts, and have either been pardoned or completed their term of servitude. It is between portions of these classes, that there has been so much bickering. One subdivision of the emigrant class alluded to, is termed the ***exclusionist*** party, from their strict exclusion of the emancipists from their society. P. CUNNINGHAM *Two Years in New South Wales* vol. 2 p. 118

> **1852** The difference of opinion and feeling between the Governor and the military, led to the combination of emancipists, who did not veil their former condition, but ennobled it by raising it to a political interest; who adopted a designation, and formed a system of morality, to which it is useless to look for a parallel. ... The champion of this system, Mr W.C. Wentworth, turned the artillery of his wrath against the **exclusionists**: 'and shall not,' he exclaimed, in the ardour of his youth, 'shall not the sole efficacious remedy be administered (the restoration of civil rights, capacity to become magistrates and legislators), because a set of *interlopers*, in nowise connected with the purposes for which this colony was founded, wish to monopolise all the respectable offices of the government, all the functions of emolument, dignity, and power, themselves'. J. WEST *The History of Tasmania* vol. 2 p. 152

exclusive = EXCLUSIONIST. [This noun was formed from the adjective *exclusive* in the sense 'of a class of society disposed to resist the admission of outsiders'. First recorded 1836.]

'Exclusive', like EXCLUSIONIST, referred to those who sought to deny emancipists an equal place in Australian society. They generally consisted of wealthy settlers and all those of high status in New South Wales. The term was one applied to this group by their enemies, and generally was used in a derogatory sense. While the exclusives certainly had an influence on colonial politics, it should be noted that the lines between the groups in society were not so rigid, and often practicality led to a great deal of interaction between emigrants and emancipists, something the exclusives could not deny or prevent.

> **1836** On the impropriety of allowing the press in this colony to be in the hands of Emancipists, we took high ground some time since, we spoke out fearlessly, we perilled every thing; just because we felt convinced that so preposterous a system was ruinous to the best interests of the colony—ruinous to the respectable and virtuous Emancipists themselves as well as to the Free Emigrants. We got very little thanks indeed for our pains; but we established our

principle, we virtually annihilated the convict press; and the literary and general character of the colony rose fifty per cent in consequence in the estimation of all honest men. But what is it that our contemporaries of *The Herald*—our *Pure Merino*, our **Exclusive** contemporaries, who have been abusing the Governor and the Chief Justice in almost every number for the last eighteen months for their alleged Emancipist predilections—what is it that they have been doing all the while? *Colonist* (Sydney) 28 Jan. p. 27

1841 We did not of course suppose that Mr. Snodgrass, who is a gentleman, a member of the Melbourne Club, and moreover one of the '**Exclusives**,' who ruled the roast at the late St. Andrew's Dinner, would either tell a falsehood, or wilfully mislead the public, and therefore we inserted the information he communicated. It is for him to explain how he fell into such an unaccountable mistake. *Port Phillip Patriot* 10 May p. 2

exile 1 *noun* a person convicted and imprisoned in Britain and sent to the Australian colonies on either a conditional pardon or ticket of leave under a scheme beginning in 1847.

After transportation had ceased to New South Wales in 1840, plans by the British government to send 'exiles' to the Australian colonies were proposed. These exiles were prisoners who had served part of their sentence in Britain already and could be given a TICKET OF LEAVE (some were given conditional pardons at first, but it was decided that giving a ticket of leave would allow for greater control over the exiles) upon arrival. They were meant to be at least partially reformed. They were supposed to fill up labour shortages, but many colonists believed that this was merely the resumption of transportation by another name and there was much protest. Nearly all were sent to Van Diemen's Land at first due to protest in the other colonies. It is clear that the British government still wanted to get rid of the criminals crowding its prisons and needed some place to send them (and to be guaranteed that they would not return free to Britain), but was not willing to pay the costs of keeping the exiles. Some of these exiles served time in the British prison, Pentonville, and thus were dubbed PENTONS or PENTONVILLIANS. Many of these were sent from Van Diemen's Land to the Port Phillip district to work. Opposition in the eastern colonies led to the scheme's abandonment there, but from 1850 to 1868 Western Australia welcomed a convict labour force to help the young colony survive and grow.

1844 [Sir George Gipps to Lord Stanley] The result of our deliberations on the subject is first of all to convince us that there is no sufficient reason why the better class of Prisoners, who have served the prescribed period of secluded punishment at Parkhurst and Pentonville should be transported as Convicts at all. We apprehend that they may with equal advantage to Society at large and with greater benefit to themselves be sent to Australia as **Exciles**. That is, it appears to us that this class of persons should leave this Country with Free pardons qualified only by the condition of their not returning hither until the expiration of their Sentences. *Historical Records of Australia* 1st series XXIII p. 700

2 *verb* (also as participial adjective **exiled**) to send a person convicted and imprisoned in Britain to the Australian colonies on a conditional pardon or ticket of leave.

1862 In 1840, urged by the strenuous remonstrances of the Colony, the Government, by an Order in Council, put a stop to transportation to New South Wales. The whole body of newly exiled convicts was consequently thrown upon Tasmania. In 1841, or soon afterwards, an order was issued that the Settlers who employed convicts, should pay the full value of their services to the Government. This new law was productive of great inconvenience, so that in 1845, there were 12,000 convicts in the Islands on the hands of the Authorities, of whom more than 3000, having passed through their term of probation, were entitled to hire themselves out to labour, but were unable to obtain masters. Meanwhile a new scheme of Transportation was projected. The convicted offender who was sentenced to a long term of punishment, was, under this system, to serve, first, a year of probationary discipline in one of the 'Separate' prisons, Pentonville or Millbank, next, a three years' term of hard labour in an 'Associated' prison, as Portland or Dartmoor, and lastly to be '**exiled**' to Tasmania, there to commence anew his civil life, freed from the severe hardships and degrading conditions of the old transported convicts. But almost before any time had been allowed for the trial of this plan, Tasmania, like its sister colony of New South Wales, protested so energetically against being made any longer a sink for the refuse of the mother-country, that the Home Government also abandoned transportation to that colony under every form. BACK-HOUSE & TYLOR *Life and Labours of George Washington Walker* p. 517

exileism the practice of sending EXILES or conditionally pardoned British prisoners to the colonies as a labour force. See EXILE. [First recorded 1847.]

1847 The scheme for the punishment and reformation of criminals, about which the Whigs have made so much fuss, is, after all, but another form of the 'probation system' of Lord Stanley. The only material difference is, that the probationary course is to be gone through at home, instead of in Van Diemen's Land. It is astonishing what flimsy subterfuges will satisfy the consciences of statesmen generally, and of the Whigs in particular. They have abolished transportation in the open and straightforward form in which it has hitherto been carried on, only to renew it under the sentimental guise of **exileism**. They might as well whitewash a number of Ethiopians, and then try to persuade themselves and the community that they had accomplished a change of race and of colour. Exileism, as at present contemplated by the Whig Ministry, is, in fact, only deferred transportation; and under this system the Australian colonies will be, as much as they ever have been, the penal settlements of the empire. The colonists must not be deceived by the flimsy and dishonest pretensions of the Whigs: transportation is about to be renewed, is in fact already renewed to a limited extent, to this colony, and by the very men who abolished it seven years ago. *Maitland Mercury* 20 Oct. p. 2

1849 Notwithstanding 'Despatch' deference to the wishes of the colonists, and the re-echoed rumours that the last act in the moral masquerade of **Exileism** has been performed, we see quite enough to satisfy us of the insincerity of one, and to expect that the curtain will again shortly rise upon the other. ... The 'Anti-Transportation' agitation of the last six or seven years, throughout the entire of these dependencies, instead of leading to a better, has led to worse results. ... The colonists have now Transportation in its worst forms—felony without its fetters—convicts without coercion—and pollution without protection. *Britannia and Trades' Advocate* (Hobart) 22 Feb. p. 4

expiree a convict whose term of sentence had ended. [First recorded 1829.] Such convicts could return to Britain, and were restored to full civil rights. The term 'expiree' was not politically loaded or used as part of the EMANCIPIST–EXCLUSIONIST debates, and was usually a neutral term referring to an ex-convict. Those whose terms had expired were usually given a CERTIFICATE OF FREEDOM to prove that they were now of free status.

1835 The services of free labourers are usually the most valuable, from their being conversant with farm business; the master has, however, a more perfect control over the convict. But the point, more immediately now under consideration, is this; should the emancipist, or **expiree**, or the ticket-of-leave labourer, be placed on the same footing with the immigrant labourer? Should he, in fact, upon the expiration, or partial remission, of his sentence, in respect of having a property in his labour, be absolutely restored to freedom? A. RUSSELL *A Tour Through the Australian Colonies* p. 46

1855 During the last three years Victoria has been almost as remarkable for the number and atrocity of its crimes as for the yield of its Gold Fields. ... The real cause of the abundance of crime in Victoria is its proximity to that sink of England's felony, that dreadful den of depravity,—Van Diemen's Land. ... Victoria is the Land of Promise to the Van Diemen's Land convict, *Expirees*, or those whose sentence has run out ... flock over hither, and are soon lost in the crowd of Melbourne or of the Mines. G.H. WATHEN *The Golden Colony: or Victoria in 1854* p. 178

expiree convict = EXPIREE. [First recorded 1843.]

   1843 The Colonial Secretary laid upon the table a return to an address moved some time since by Dr. Nicholson, for returns of the number of **expiree convicts** who had landed in the district of Port Phillip from Van Diemen's Land. The Colonial Secretary regretted that there were no means of complying with the address, and the only return which he had it in his power to make was a letter which had been received from the Superintendent of Port Phillip on the subject. *Sydney Morning Herald* 19 Oct. p. 2

F

factory 1 (also **female factory**) a place for the confinement of female convicts. [First recorded 1806.]

The most well-known of the factories was the female factory at Parramatta, although there were factories established in Van Diemen's Land and around New South Wales, including at Moreton Bay. Women kept in these factories were put to work producing cloth, blankets, clothing and other items, and made an important contribution to the colonial economy. These factories were designed to keep women under close surveillance as they were seen to be morally dangerous (many CONVICT WOMEN were accused of being prostitutes) and thus a potential threat to the morality of the colonies. The Parramatta factory was formally established in 1821 (although women had been employed there from 1800). Here women were divided into CLASSES depending on their crimes and behaviour. The factory was also the place from which women were put into ASSIGNMENT (and returned to if they misbehaved, became pregnant, or needed to escape cruel employers). The women incarcerated in the factories often rioted and defied authority in attempts to show their contempt for the system. The factories were an essential part of the CONVICT SYSTEM and the control of female convicts.

1806 *John Bluneir,* for having in his possession a quantity of tea stolen from the *Criterion* American ship, which he could only account for by saying he had removed it from a place in which it had been concealed under circumstances that it was criminal to conceal, was sentenced 300 lashes and three years to labour for the Crown; and *Catherine Eyres,* otherwise *Macbeth,* as his accomplice in having sold a part of the tea in small quantities to different persons, was ordered to the **Factory** at Parramatta for the term of six months. *Sydney Gazette* 13 July p. 4

1822 The removal of the female convicts from Sydney to Paramatta has already been mentioned. On their arrival there, they are allowed to remain in a wooden building that is near the **factory**; and if they have succeeded in bringing their bedding from the ships, they are permitted to deposit it there, or in the room in which the female prisoners are confined for punishment. The first of these apartments is in the upper floor of a house that was built for the reception of pregnant females. It contains another apartment, on the ground floor, that is occupied by the men employed in the factory. It is not surrounded by any wall or paling; and the upper room or garret has only one window, and an easy communication with the room below. No accommodation is afforded for cooking provisions in this building; nor does there exist either inducement to the female convicts to remain in it, or the means of preventing their escape. The greater portion, therefore, betake themselves to the lodgings in the town of Paramatta, where they cohabit with the male convicts in the employ of government, or with any persons who will receive them. Their employment in the factory consists of picking, spinning and carding wool. They are tasked to perform a certain quantity in the day, and when their task is finished, which is generally at one o'clock, they are allowed to return to their lodgings. ... The factory itself consists of one long room that is immediately above the gaol, having two windows in front that look into the gaol yard, one in the end of the building, and two windows looking into a yard that is immediately behind. The dimensions of the room are 60 feet by 20; and at one end are store-rooms, where the wool, yarn and cloth are kept. There is one fire-place, at which all the provisions are cooked. The women have no other beds than those they can make from the wool in its dirty state; and they sleep upon it at night, and in the midst of their spinning wheels and work. J.T. BIGGE *Report of the Commissioner of Inquiry into the State of the Colony of New South Wales* p. 69

1847 In the **factory** too, there is a good chance of getting married, for the convict swains scattered amongst the settlers, when they obtain the consent of their masters, or choose, when they become free, to enter into the connubial state, usually apply for permission to go to the factory in quest of a fair helpmate. On the arrival of one of these at the abode of the *recluses*, the unmarried frail ones are drawn up in line for the inspection of the amorous and adventurous votary, who, fixing his eye on a vestal to his taste, with his finger, beckons her to step forth from the ranks, and if, after a short conference, they are mutually agreeable, the two are married in due time. A. MARJORIBANKS *Travels in New South Wales* p. 228

2 (used adjectivally in compounds) produced by, associated with, a factory. See sense 1.

1829 [Governor Darling to Sir George Murray] As it is desirable to provide employment for the Females in the penitentiary at Parramatta, the Board have recommended that a sufficient quantity of materials for the shirts and summer clothing of the Convicts should be sent from England to be made up here, instead of being ready made clothing as formerly. The winter clothing being entirely composed of **Factory** Cloth, the quantity of wool (the raw Material) used for its manufacture has been estimated for in the Abstract. *Historical Records of Australia* 1st series XV p. 4

1836 Such is the first lesson of the married convict, the burden of whose punishment government has shifted to her husband. She may run away to the bush within a week, she may stay a fortnight before she elopes, she may remain 'till death do them part,' as the liturgy hath it. The above is a faithful picture of too many '**factory** weddings.' J.F. O'CONNELL *A Residence of Eleven Years in New Holland* p. 55

felon a convict. [The term *felon* in the sense 'a person who has committed a felony (or crime)' has existed in standard English since the late thirteenth century. It was adopted in the Australian colonies as a synonym for a CONVICT or PRISONER OF THE CROWN. It had more pejorative connotations than terms such as PRISONER. It was first recorded in the Australian sense in 1826.]

1837 The second caste of the society of New South Wales consists of convicts who have been sent thither from England, by sentence of the law, for crimes committed—sent thither, not as *colonists*,—not as retaining the attributes of British subjects,—not for the purpose of bettering their social condition,—but as **felons**,—as men whom the violated law has divested of their natural and legal rights,—sent thither, in short, as to a place of punishment,—where they are not only to remain divested of the protection of the ordinary laws of the realm, but where they are to be subjected to *new laws*, having for their object both their punishment and their reformation, but regarding their *punishment* as a means of deterring other persons in England from the commission of similar crimes, and therefore justifying the prolongation of the *punishment*, even in cases in which the reformation may already have been accomplished. J. MUDIE *The Felonry of New South Wales* p. 18

felon colony a colony established for the placing of transported prisoners, such as New South Wales and Van Diemen's Land. [The term appears relatively late (first recorded 1851), and is used to compare convict-free colonies with convict colonies—it is an especially derogatory and stigmatising term.]

1853 [On one of the effects of the discovery of gold in Victoria] It is evident that the thieves have found an El Dorado in the very country to which they had originally been banished as a punishment; for although Victoria has never had the penal stigma upon it, yet it is so close in the neighbourhood of the **felon**

colonies, that it now affords shelter to a large share of their population. J. SHERER *The Gold Finder of Australia* p. 167

felon constable = CONVICT CONSTABLE. [First recorded 1835.]

1835 On the first trial there were three convict witnesses for the prosecution, who swore to the guilt of the prisoner, Mr. Bryan. The three witnesses were felon constables, John Boswood, a convict attaint, being a prisoner for life— Richard Gough, also a **felon constable** and a convict attaint, and George Scandlebury, a man of most infamous character, who in his cross-examination said, 'I am a prisoner; my sentence was seven years—my sentence has been extended three years; I was at Port Arthur (the penal settlement) until last May twelve months, since which I have been a constable; I was tried for absconding, and was either dismissed or suspended'. H. MELVILLE *The History of the Island of Van Diemen's Land* p. 217

felonise to taint with the human degradation associated with the convict system. [First recorded 1827.]

1827 Acts of Parliament to work men in chains on their arrival in this colony, will only scare our children, brutalize our youth, and blast the growth of moral sentiment. The sight of human woe and degradation continually before our eyes, will gradually impress upon our imaginations the feelings of gaolers, and *felonise* as it were every conception of our minds—will impede the march of philosophy, and drag down the soul aspiring to Heaven, to the abyss of Hell. *Sydney Monitor* 20 Apr. p. 388

felon overseer = CONVICT OVERSEER. [First recorded 1835.]

FELON OVERSEER and CONVICT OVERSEER are synonymous in terms of the position they refer to, and both terms appear in contexts where the overseers are criticised for performing their jobs poorly (either being extremely harsh in their treatment of prisoners, or, at the other extreme, very careless, lenient and open to bribery). CONVICT OVERSEER often appears in neutral contexts while FELON OVERSEER is always pejorative.

1835 The Government paper has thought proper to introduce again to the Public, the case of the lad *Berry*, in the shape of an article published at Sydney, which we verily believe was written at Hobart Town. ... All the bolstering of the *Courier*, will never make British free subjects believe, that under any circumstances they are liable to be scourged by **felon overseers**, at the caprice of a Subaltern of a marching regiment—let the man Berry's conduct have been, however mutinous, he did not, deserve to be degraded by convicts—and we are firm in our opinion, that the circumstances could never have happened under any British government, save ours—nothing however astonishes us, in this Colony. *Cornwall Chronicle* (Launceston) 14 Nov. p. 2

felon police = CONVICT POLICE. [First recorded 1834.]

FELON POLICE and CONVICT POLICE are synonymous in terms of the position they refer to, but while CONVICT POLICE often appears in neutral contexts FELON POLICE is always pejorative. (See also CONSTABLE, CONVICT CONSTABLE, CONVICT POLICE, FELON CONSTABLE.)

1836 Under *such* a Government, what community could be happy? We are bound to the observance of existing enactments, that cannot produce happiness—the main spring of the disorganization of our society is, the employment of England's outlaws in this police. In this country we have a **felon police** riding rough-shod over the liberties and rights of free British subjects. *Cornwall Chronicle* (Launceston) 2 Jan. p. 1

felonry the convict and ex-convict population, conceived of as a class.

The term was coined by James Mudie, an emigrant settler who attacked the transportation system and the giving of rights to convicts and ex-convicts in his book *The Felonry of New South Wales* (1837). It was subsequently used quite frequently to infer the low status of convicts, and sometimes ex-convicts, as a group or class.

1837 The author has ventured to coin the word *felonry*, as the appellative of an *order* or class of persons in New South Wales,—an order which happily exists in no other country in the world. The major part of the inhabitants of the colony are felons now undergoing or felons who have already undergone their sentences. … Hitherto there was no single term that could be employed to designate these various descriptions of persons, who now bear the denominations of 'convicts' and 'ticket-of-leave-men'; as also, 'emancipists', (as they are absurdly enough called), who again are subdivided into 'conditionally pardoned convicts', 'fully pardoned convicts', and 'expirees', or transported felons whose sentences have expired; together with 'runaway convicts', subdivided into 'absentees', (a name foolish for its mildness), and 'bushrangers'. The single term, the *felonry* (which comprehends all these descriptions of the criminal population), though new, is evidently a legitimate member of the tribe of appellatives distinguished by the same termination, as *peasantry, tenantry, yeomanry, gentry, cavalry, chivalry, &c.* J. MUDIE *The Felonry of New South Wales* p. vi

1847 Mr. Stawell, barrister, proposed the next resolution, and commenced by reading the despatch of Mr. Gladstone, the late Secretary of State for the Colonies, and contending that such a document did not at all contemplate the forcing of criminals upon the people of Port Phillip, but left it optionable with themselves whether they would have them or not. They had met there that day to consider this very important question, whether or not they wished to have a renewal of transportation? He would then ask them if they intended to nip their brightest prospects in the bud—to convert this province into a receptacle of British **felonry**, and themselves so many unpaid gaolers. *Port Phillip Herald* 2 Mar. p. 2

female convict = CONVICT WOMAN.

1822 Although, in the transportation of **female convicts** to New South Wales, the preservation of their health has been more easily and generally accomplished than that of the males, yet no scheme of superintendence has yet been devised by which their intercourse with the crew can be entirely prevented. From the evidence of Mr. Cordeaux, Mr. Gyles, and Mr. Walker, who were passengers on board the convict ship Friendship, prostitution appears to have prevailed in a great degree, and the captain and surgeon at last connived at excesses that they had not the means to resist, or any hope of suppressing. J.T. BIGGE *Report of the Commissioner of Inquiry into the State of the Colony of New South Wales* p. 3

1822 The marriage of the native born youths with **female convicts** are very rare; a circumstance that is attributable to the general disinclination to early marriage that is observable amongst them, and partly to the abandoned and dissolute habits of the female convicts, but chiefly to a sense of pride in the native-born youths, approaching to contempt for the vices and depravity of the convicts, even when manifested in the persons of their own parents. J.T. BIGGE *Report of the Commissioner of Inquiry into the State of the Colony of New South Wales* p. 105

female factory see FACTORY.

fifty the punishment of fifty lashes. [First recorded 1830.] See also FLOGGING.

1852 Some curious examples of magisterial equity are often told: one rose from the bench, when he heard his waggon in the street, and delivered his sentence in his progress towards the door—'I can't stop: give him **fifty**'. A cattle stealer owed his life to the same impatience of enquiry: before the charge was half investigated, the magistrate said, 'give him fifty'—an easy compromise with the hangman. J. WEST *The History of Tasmania* vol. 1 p. 105

first fleet the eleven British ships under the command of Arthur Phillip that arrived in Australia in January 1788. [First recorded 1791.]
Arthur Phillip commanded the first fleet of ships that arrived to establish the first British settlement at Port Jackson. Phillip was to be Governor of the new settlement. The fleet, which set out from England in 1787, was led by the flagship

HMS *Sirius*, and included the HMS *Supply*, the *Lady Penrhyn*, the *Prince of Wales*, and the *Charlotte*. Altogether 1023 settlers completed the voyage, of whom 751 were convicts and their children. See also FIRST FLEETER.

1817 Died, at Sydney … Mrs. Martha Jones, wife of Edward Jones, baker. They both arrived in the **first fleet**, and were the first couple married in that Colony; which ceremony was performed on the 23rd March, 1788, under a marquee. The deceased was always much esteemed as an honest and industrious woman. *Hobart Town Gazette* 11 Oct.

1834 The little fleet which was thus placed under the command of Captain Phillip, and which has ever since been designated by the colonists of New South Wales *the first fleet*, set sail from Portsmouth on the 13th of May, 1787. J.D. LANG *An Historical and Statistical Account of New South Wales* vol. 1 p. 26

first fleeter a person who came to Australia aboard one of the ships of the first fleet. [First recorded 1826.]
    The people who arrived on the first ships to settle New South Wales were gradually granted a special status in the colony.

1847 John Limeburner, the last of the *first fleeters*, as they are called in this Colony, died at Longbottom on Thursday week last, at the advanced age of 104 years. Poor old Jack retained his faculties to the last, and the day before his demise polished off two gills of *Niech's* pure *Jamaica*. He helped to pitch the first tent in Sydney, and pointed out the precise spot, the corner of Hunter and George streets, now occupied as a shop, and formerly known as the sign of the Crooked Billet public-house. Jack remembered the British Flag being first hoisted in Sydney on a swamp oak-tree, which was placed in the spot, at the rear of Cadman's house, now occupied as the Water Police Court. The tree stood until the government of General Darling, when it was ordered to be cut down. *Bell's Life in Sydney* 11 Sept. p. 2

flash of or pertaining to the language used by the criminal underworld, including convicts. Usually in combinations such as **flash language**. The adjective is sometimes used as a noun, such that 'flash' by itself can stand for 'flash language'. [The term itself is not Australian. It developed among the underworld of England, especially London, and appears in printed sources in the eighteenth century. Various theories have been proposed about the origin of the term. The OED notes: 'A statement made by Dr. Aitkin, *Country round Manchester* (1795), 437, that "flash" language was so called because spoken by pedlars from a place called Flash near Macclesfield, is often repeated, but is of no authority.' It is likely that the term derives from *flash* in the sense (OED) 'Gaudy, showy, smart. Of persons: Dashing, ostentatious, swaggering, "swell"'. The term first appears in the Australian records in 1793.]

The major characteristic of flash language is not its grammar and syntax, but its vocabulary. This is derived from many sources, including British dialects, Celtic (especially via Shelta, an ancient secret language used by Irish and Welsh tinkers and gypsies, and based largely on altered Irish or Gaelic words), Latin, Yiddish, and Romany (the Indo-European language, related to Hindi, of the gypsies). While the language is not specifically Australian, it is clear that it was much used by the underworld (especially the convicts) in the early colonial period (see the 1793 citation below). In 1812 the convict James Hardy Vaux, a thief who was transported three times to New South Wales, wrote his *Memoirs*, to which was appended *A New and Comprehensive Vocabulary of the Flash Language* (not published until 1819). Vaux dedicated the work to Thomas Skottowe, the commandant at the penal settlement of Newcastle, and he clearly believed that it would help the commandant to understand the language used by the convicts in his charge. Because flash language was obviously commonly used in the early colonies, some examples of its vocabulary are included as headwords in this book. The principles of selection are twofold: (i) a word is included if it is well attested in the Australian records; (ii) a word is included if it was significant in the development of Australian English. See also BELLOWSER, COVE, CROSS, FLASH MAN, FLASH MOB, GAMMON, PLANT, SCRAG, SWAG, SWELL MOB, TRAP.

1793 A leading distinction, which marked the convicts on their outset in the colony, was an use of what is called the *flash*, or *kiddy* **language**. In some of our early courts of justice, an interpreter was frequently necessary to translate the deposition of the witness, and the defence of the prisoner. This language has many dialects. The sly dexterity of the pickpocket; the brutal ferocity of the footpad; the more elevated career of the highwayman; and the deadly purpose of the midnight ruffian, is each strictly appropriate in the terms which distinguish and characterize it. W. TENCH *A Complete Account of the Settlement at Port Jackson* (1961) p. 297

1838 [Address by Patrick Grant, Maitland, NSW, 25 Oct. 1837] With respect to that spirit of association in guilt which is understood among you by the slang term of 'flash,' I would entreat all those who are not bent on getting hanged, to beware of giving into it. *Cornwall Chronicle* 4 Aug. p. 1

1838 What is the effect of congregating them [convicts] in large bodies? The mutual interchange of bad qualities; what is called the **flash** thief teaches the robber craft, and the robber instructs the other man again in acts of daring and boldness. *Report from the Select Committee of the House of Commons on Transportation* p. 60

1847 On the same evening, a little earlier, a bushman was drinking at the same house, and having treated some of the 'flash' fraternity was proceeding to his lodging through some infamous right of way when he was dogged by his former bar mates and one of them coming up, to use one of their own classical expressions, 'mugged' him by placing his hand upon the man's mouth. Another seized him by the legs and held him down gently, when a third party, pulled out a knife and cut off his pocket, which contained a cheque for £3 10 s., one ditto for £1, and 15 s. in silver, with which they decamped. *Port Phillip Herald* 14 Dec. p. 2

flash man an experienced criminal.

1837 He had frequent opportunities of observing the large sums of money that were spent in the tap-rooms of public-houses on the road-side, both by convicts, by ticket-of-leave men, and by emancipated convicts, who were engaged in cattle-stealing. ... The term he applied to them was **flash-men**. *Report from the Select Committee of the House of Commons on Transportation* p. 219

flash mob a group or gang of experienced criminals.

1840 There is a class of persons in this colony, the management of which produces more trouble to the Prison Disciplinarians than that of any other class. We refer to the Female Prisoners of the Crown, whose tricks, manouevres, and misconduct, have baffled the exertions of every person, appointed to control and correct them. We have ascertained that there is what is termed a 'mob,' always in the Factory, and that this mob has assumed the title of 'The **Flash Mob**.' *Colonial Times* 18 Feb.

1848 A few ... could not divest themselves of their true character, nor even disguise it for a time, as an expedient for the achievement of their liberty. These men were known amongst the rest as the '**flash mob**'. They spoke the secret language of thieves, were ever intent on robbing the stores, with false keys (called by them *screws*). T.L. MITCHELL *Journal of an Expedition into the Interior of Tropical Australia* pp. 419–20

flog to beat or whip (a person). See FLOGGING. [This standard English term is possibly related to Latin *flagellare* 'to whip, scourge, beat', although it does not appear in print until 1676 as a cant word. It is possibly onomatopoeic.]

1834 The same evening, Wednesday, that I had the conversation with Mr Mudie, before stated, but some time before it, I heard Mr Larnach say, 'that he had the name of Tyrant, and a tyrant he would be as long as he lived—and he'd **flog** a Government-man when he had one.' J. MUDIE *Vindication of James Mudie and John Larnach* p. 5

1847 There was one man being **flogged** for theft, whose crime it was acknowledged was the consequence of the hunger of a three days' fast. His miserable pittance having been stolen, and, after enduring his hunger as long as he could, he has swum the river in the night, and broken into an adjacent settler's granary. A. HARRIS *Settlers and Convicts* (1953) p. 69

flogger the person who administered a whipping, usually with a CAT, to a convict as punishment.

In colonial Australia, masters could not physically punish their convict servants but had to refer them to magistrates who could then order a punishment of FLOGGING. Punishments were carried out in barracks and gaols by the flogger, who was often a convict (or occasionally an ex-convict) paid a ration and small wage for performing this duty. There were opportunities for corruption as magistrates were often lax in their supervision, and floggers were sometimes bribed to lighten punishments.

> **1847** I heard the **flogger** say, 'Well, who's the first?' After an instant or two I heard the answer; it seemed to be the voice of a Scotch lad: 'Here, I'm the first, you —; but — my eyes if I don't have satisfaction one way or another, if I get hanged for it'. I heard, awhile after, the dull, heavy fall of the cat on the flesh, and the constable's count—ONE, TWO, THREE, FOUR, &c., mingling with the flogger's *hiss* each time, as he sent the blows home, dallying between each to spin out the punishment to the utmost. But there was no cry, no groan, no prayer for mercy. … I often heard people in Sydney afterwards expressing their astonishment and horror when some of these iron-gang overseers were killed by the men; but from this time I never found any difficulty in comprehending the how and why. A. HARRIS *Settlers and Convicts* (1953) p. 69

flogging the practice or system of punishing convicts by a beating or whipping with a CAT.

Flogging was a common form of punishment for minor crimes in the convict colonies. It was an important means of controlling convicts in the early days of settlement, along with incentives, in a system that was open rather than closed (that is, most convicts were not held in prisons under close supervision). From the 1820s in New South Wales, floggings usually took place inside GAOLS or CONVICT BARRACKS and were out of sight of the colonial population. Nevertheless, it remained an essential part of the system of convict discipline. The records show that in 1835 in New South Wales, there were 7103 floggings and 27,340 male convicts under sentence, an average of 25 per cent of convicts. Van Diemen's Land in the same year had a male convict population of 13,800 with an average of 11 per cent being flogged. According to A.G.L. Shaw, between 1830 and 1835 almost one male convict in six was flogged with an average of thirty-five lashes. The most common crimes or breaches of discipline that resulted in corporal punishment were 'neglect, idleness' and 'absenting'; drunkenness, disorderly conduct, and insolence also resulted in a whipping. Flogging in colonial Australia was, however, always controlled in that masters could not punish convicts indiscriminately and such punishments had to be ordered by a magistrate. This prevented great excesses.

> **1846** They closed the door after me and talked together for a few minutes outside, when the constable inquired if I would work, provided they would overlook my offense and not report it to Mr. Gunn, who would certainly flog me. 'Fifty lashes,' said he, 'is the least punishment he ever inflicts for such a crime.' 'I shall remain here and take the flogging,' I replied. The door, however, was re-opened, and I ordered out. 'Now,' said they, 'go to church and be d— to you; but depend on a **flogging** in the morning;' and I went to church. L.W. MILLER *Notes of an Exile to Van Dieman's Land* p. 281

> **1849** [Norfolk Island] On the 17th of February there must have been some eighty men 'packed' into these ten cells! In the new gaol, on the same dates, there would be at least some seventy or eighty men, including the gaol gang. In addition to these sentences there would be the '**flogging**' and sentences to the chain-gangs and reef-gangs. Besides these, there were also the 'extensions' of the period of probation on the island. These facts are incontrovertible, and show with what a lavish hand punishment was meted out for slight offences. T. Rogers *Correspondence Relating to the Dismissal* p. 99

fourteen-years' man a male convict sentenced to a fourteen-year term of penal servitude.

The evidence suggests that the most popular sentence was a sentence of seven years, which applied to more than half of those transported. A quarter were sentenced for life (although this proportion declined as time went on) and the remainder were likely to have a fourteen-years' sentence. However, after 1840 a ten-year sentence became more common.

> **1849** Men who behaved well, and had not been brought before a bench of magistrates, were, after a certain period of probation, entitled to an indulgence called a ticket of leave for a certain district, and were entitled to hire for wages within their district. Seven-years men received their tickets at the expiry of four years; **fourteen-years men** after six years' servitude; and life-men after eight, which gave the latter an additional indulgence. After the long-sentenced man held his ticket for six years, he received a conditional pardon, which entitled him to all the privileges of a free subject within the colony. J. PATTISON *New South Wales* p. 16

free 1 (of a person formerly a convict) released from penal servitude. See also FREED. [As with many of the terms associated with the convict system, this is a term closely associated with debates about slavery. As its first sense for *free* the

OED gives: 'Of persons: Not bound or subject as a slave is to his master; enjoying personal rights and liberty of action as a member of a society or state'. First recorded in the Australian sense in 1792.]

Such a convict would have completed their sentence or been given an ABSOLUTE PARDON. They were restored to all the legal rights of British subjects, for example, being able to own property.

1822 Yielding to the recommendations made to him by the captains and surgeons of the female convict ships, Governor Macquarie has given tickets of leave to some of the females on their arrival; and influenced also by a wish to economize the public expenditure, he has given the same indulgence to those who were represented to him as having money, by which they have established them in the town of Sydney, and at once been placed on a level with the emancipated and **free** convicts of their own sex. In this state, which cannot be considered as a state of punishment, and which tends to produce a belief that opulence can redeem the consequences of crime, these women form connections with convicts whom they have formerly known in England, or support themselves by any casual demand for their labour. Those also who have children, and have any means of supporting themselves, are furnished with tickets of leave. The government is thus relieved from the expense of their maintenance, and they are themselves benefitted by being saved from the consequences of consignment to the factory at Parramatta. J.T. BIGGE *Report of the Commissioner of Inquiry into the State of the Colony of New South Wales* p. 68

1847 [Thomas Ryan, Chief Clerk] I never have received a fee of any kind or amount from any one, upon any occasion for searches or for giving extracts or other information whatever from this Office, beyond the following, namely, where I am subpoenaed to produce any document before the Supreme Court in its Civil Jurisdiction, I receive a fee of one Guinea, and the like sum is given to me in every case when required to attend before a Notary Public or the Mayor to make Oath or declaration (for transmission to England or elsewhere) to the indentity [sic] of any person, who, having been transported to this Colony, had become **free**; and even these sums are given without any demand from me, and are I believe usual in such cases. I may observe that I do not consider proving the identity of a free man or the making of an oath or declaration as above mentioned as any part of my official duties. *Historical Records of Australia* 1st series XXVI p. 8

2 (of a settler in an Australian colony) not transported as a convict. [This sense of *free* is a version of OED sense 19: 'Of a person, his will, etc.: Acting of one's own will or choice, and not under compulsion or restraint; determining one's own act or choice, not motivated from without'. First recorded in Australia in the combination *free settler* in 1795.]

'Free' was also used to refer to those settlers who came to the Australian colonies as free emigrants, as opposed to those convicted and sentenced to transportation. Such persons hoped to find a new life, and hopefully success, in the colonies.

1824 Though the morality of the colony is generally speaking at the lowest ebb, instances of improvement are not wholly wanting, particularly among that class of persons who have received the benefit of education. Many of these rise to independence, and some to opulence; but that they often redeem their lost reputation, is more than I am prepared to state. In Van Diemen's Land, a line of demarcation has ever existed between convicts and **free** persons, which the future acquisition of their freedom has never enabled them to overstep. It has been otherwise in New South Wales. E. CURR *An Account of the Colony of Van Diemen's Land* p. 11

1844 First, the community is composed of three classes, the **free**, the *freed*, and the *bond*. The majority of the former class are men of intelligence and experience in their native country, and well acquainted with the rights and privileges of that free and mighty nation [Britain], and justly expect and require to be governed and treated as its subjects. *Colonial Times* (Hobart) 10 July p. 2

3 The word 'free' was used in a number of combinations to describe people as being of a free, rather than convict, status. However, these combinations used 'free' both in the sense of a FREED person (that is, someone who had been a convict and had been made free) and in the sense of one who had always been free (that is, someone who had come to the colonies as a free person; see sense 2). As time wore on, the freed population mingled with the free settlers, thus blurring the distinctions between the two groups and allowing both to be defined against those who still remained of convict status. See FREE COLONIST, FREE FEMALE, FREE LABOUR, FREE MAN, FREE PEOPLE, FREE POPULATION, FREE SERVANT, FREE WOMAN.

freebooter a runaway convict; a bushranger. [In standard English a *freebooter* is a person who goes about in search of plunder, especially a pirate. The transferred Australian sense is first recorded in 1817.]

In the Australian colonies, the term 'freebooter' was used to refer to runaway convicts who took to criminal activities. In order to survive in the bush, escaped convicts turned to crime. See also BUSHRANGER.

1817 The Crown Prisoners may well take warning from the present condition of these Men; the future Fate of some may perhaps be more Awful; and the whole may be assured that all who attempt to establish themselves in the

Woods as **Free-Booters** will meet the same Fate as those Men who have lately tried it. *Hobart Town Gazette* 16 Aug.

1855 A large reward was offered for the capture of the two bushrangers, and they were hunted through the island more hotly than ever. Driven to desperation, they seized upon a whaleboat; by threats pressed four boatmen into their service, and actually compelled them to work the boat across Bass's Straits to the opposite shores of Victoria. ... News of the escape of these formidable and blood-stained **freebooters** had been immediately transmitted to the authorities of Victoria. G.H. WATHEN *The Golden Colony; or Victoria in 1854* p. 147

free by servitude (of a former convict) released, having served the full sentence imposed. [First recorded 1813.]

1813 The Principal Surgeon, at Head Quarters; the Assistant Surgeons, at Out-settlements and Dependencies, and Magistrates and Clergymen in the Several Districts, to make quarterly reports to the Governor of all Deaths and Casualties occurring within their Districts: These reports to state the age, description, and country of the deceased; whether free settler, free or conditionally pardoned convict; **free by servitude**, or then a convict; the places, if possible, where tried, their sentences, and by what ships they arrived. *New South Wales Pocket Almanack* p. 63

1848 All free persons are supposed to carry credentials about them certifying their freedom. The emigrant must be able to produce a certificate of his ship's clearance; the emancipist, one who has served his conditional term, of his 'emancipation;' the '**free by servitude**,' he who has served his full sentence, is required to show his 'certificate of freedom;' and the ticket of leave-holder, his printed ticket. Should any one be so unlucky as not to possess any of these documents, he is supposed to be a convict illegally at large, and is liable to be taken into custody, and forwarded a close prisoner in irons to Sidney for identification; and should he eventually prove a free man, he is discharged, without the least possible chance of redress. C. COZENS *Adventures of a Guardsman* pp. 163–4

free colonist a member of a colony who came to Australia as a free person, or who was a convict who became free. See FREE sense 3. [First recorded 1832.]

1837 Commissioner Therry furnished the *Sydney Gazette* with '*retorts-courteous*' to the epithets applied to his convict associates and fellow labourers in the cause of misrule and insubordination, and by his '*Letter of an Unpaid Magistrate*,' and other writings, at once assisted to vilify and bespatter the respectable **free colonists**, and to vindicate and eulogize, even to nausea, every thing that was unprincipled, unwise, and unjust, in the conduct and proceedings of the colonial government. J. MUDIE *The Felonry of New South Wales* p. 127

1848 The exact population of Van Diemen's Land in this year [1835] was: —

Free colonists,	23,315
Under bond,	16,968
Total	40,283

The 'free colonists' included those who were originally convicts but had become free by servitude. W. Westgarth *Australia Felix* pp. 150–1

free colony a colony such as South Australia that was not established as a colony for the location of convicts, or was no longer used as a place of penal servitude. [First recorded 1828.]

1843 The rapidly improving state of New South Wales and Van Diemen's Land about ten years ago, and the important position which they began to assume among the Colonies of Britain, proved the means of drawing the attention of many gentlemen of capital and influence in that direction. The accounts of the climate and soil of these places, were very favourable; but their social condition, produced by their being penal settlements, was held by many as an insuperable objection to them as favourable fields for free emigration. A proposition was therefore made to form a new and **free Colony** in some other part of Australia which should be beyond the pale of convict contamination; and the southern coast, from its geographical position, added to such vague report as had been received regarding it, was looked on as a favourable locality wherein to found the proposed Colony. J.F. BENNETT *Historical and Descriptive Account of South Australia* p. 11

freed (of a convict who had served the sentence imposed, or obtained a remission of the sentence) restored to the possession of civil liberties. [First recorded 1829.]
The term 'freed' was used to refer to prisoners who were either free through having completed their sentences or through having obtained a pardon. Convicts were freed for numerous reasons before they had served their complete sentence; these reasons included good behaviour, having particular skills that were needed in the colony, or being of a high status before coming to Australia. See also EMAN-CIPIST, EMANCIPATE 2.

1844 It came out in evidence before the Court of Quarter Sessions yesterday, during the trial of nine prisoners of the Crown, attached to a probation gang, employed under the superintendence of Mr. Dark, the assistant Surgeon, and stationed at a place called Warranora, that their overseer, a **freed** man named

O'Hara, permitted them to range about the country at pleasure, committing depredations in every direction. *Parramatta Chronicle* 6 Jan. p. 3

freed convict a convict who had served the sentence imposed, or obtained a remission of the sentence, and was therefore restored to the possession of civil liberties. [First recorded 1832.]

1832 Such men would be employed in situations that require a degree of trust which cannot be committed to a convict, or *freed* **convict**, without, in most cases, the certainty of a loss, which a man, having his employer's interest at heart, would prevent. The stockholder is at present liable to very heavy losses from the fraud and carelessness of his servant. The employment of honester men would not only obviate these losses, as far as the individual's own conduct was concerned, but would also afford to his master a check upon the conduct of others. J. BUSBY *Authentic Information Relative to New South Wales, and New Zealand* p. 13

1837 After what has been stated ... as to the peculiar construction of society in New South Wales, and as to the legal and unalterable infamy of the convict population, regarded as a caste, it must excite no slight degree of astonishment that the admission of **freed convicts**, whether by pardon or expiry of their sentences, to the same social and legal rights and immunities as the emigrants, is not only a subject of discussion, but of bitter and well-grounded complaint. J. MUDIE *The Felonry of New South Wales* p. 220

freed man = FREED CONVICT. [First recorded 1830.]

1830 [Sir George Murray to Governor Darling] Much has been said of the equal Right to protection and legal privileges of the Freemen and **Freedmen**; I would be the last to promote any measure tending to render the Security afforded by the Law to all Classes of Men at all doubtful; and surely, whilst all Parties are subjected to the same Tribunal with equal Rights and Privileges in seeking Justice and protection from the Courts, there can be no failure as regards the one more than the other! But, on the contrary, should the unconvicted Freeman be subjected to a Tribunal of convicted Freedmen, I contend he would be deprived of one of the most valuable Birthrights of Englishmen, secured to them by the Constitution. The branded Felon can never be the Peer of the unconvicted Man, and, in my humble opinion, Honor, Integrity and Fidelity would be driven from the Community, in which a contrary principal could prevail. *Historical Records of Australia* 1st series XV p. 791

1849 'Working hands are working hands, up the country or down,' replied the black. 'The only difference I can see, is that everywhere there are some who are emigrants, and some who are **freed-men**: the emigrants are flats, and the others are sharps. Of the two, I think the sharps are a great deal best worth their wages; they want good looking after, but there's something to be got out of them. The emigrants they send over here always seem more dead than alive, till they've been five or six years in the country; then they begin to be like the rest of the people.' A. Harris *The Emigrant Family* (1967) p. 32

freedom = CERTIFICATE OF FREEDOM. [First recorded 1847.]

1848 Every ticket-of-leave man, expiree, or emancipated convict, on obtaining his partial or total freedom, receives from the convict department an official document bearing testimony to the fact. On demand, the production of this frees them from further molestation on the part of the police; but the free immigrant has nothing of the kind to produce, if required by the prying constable to 'show his **freedom**'; the consequence is generally, that unless the functionary of the law thinks fit to be satisfied with the exhibition of letters, or similar matters, the unfortunate free man, whose only fault seems his not having been 'lagged', is dragged to the nearest police station, and forwarded from lock-up to lock-up, till he reaches Sydney for 'identification'. J.C. BYRNE *Twelve Years' Wanderings in the British Colonies, from 1835 to 1847* vol. 1 p. 167

free emigrant = FREE SETTLER. [First recorded 1827.]

1827 Governor Macquarie ... forthwith began to look upon all who opposed his projects as *personal* enemies, and often indeed treated them as such. This line of conduct *at once* severed from him many individuals; while the more marked attention he paid to members of the emancipist body in comparison with the free inhabitants, made it be believed by others that it was his intention to exalt the emancipist *above* the emigrant, and thus disgusted those who might probably have countenanced the plan. Now, what has been the result in Van Dieman's Land, where a different course was pursued by the able and judicious Sorrell? An individual of the emancipist body has been lately elected there to the bank-directorship, in opposition to several most respectable emigrants, and by a body of proprietors too, the greater portion of whom are *free emigrants*. P. CUNNINGHAM *Two Years in New South Wales* vol. 2 pp. 132–3

free female a woman who came to Australia as a free person. See FREE sense 2. [First recorded 1837.]

1837 The numerical disparity between the sexes, which is still, amongst the prison population, as three to one, is the cause of indescribable evils. The government, with a view to remedy, has been sending out ship-loads of **free females**; but what must those females generally be, who, abandoning their country, go out such a voyage, unprotected, in the expectation of marrying convicts. The extravagant hopes held out to these poor creatures—the richness with which the colonial prospect is painted and gilded to their fancies—is of course followed by disappointment, and disappointment by self-abandonment. W. ULLATHORNE *The Catholic Mission in Australasia* p. 28

free immigrant = FREE SETTLER. [First recorded 1841.]

1841 The population of New South Wales consists of four classes; the **free immigrants** and their progeny; the convicts; the convicts who have become free through pardon or expiry of their term of service; and the progeny of the convict immigrants—persons who have always been free, but have a 'taint' in their blood. The third class is free, it occupies in numbers, intelligence, and wealth, a most important station in the society of the colony. But the free emigrants and their progeny, partly out of (perhaps an exaggerated) fear of the criminal sympathies of the emancipists, partly out of a more unworthy pride of class, hesitate to bestow on the others the privileges which they seek for themselves. *Port Phillip Patriot* 10 June p. 4

free labour labour provided by a person who came to Australia as a free person. See FREE sense 2. [First recorded 1832.]

1838 The circumstances of the labor-market in Van Diemen's Land are also singularly adverse to the moral character of free laboring immigrants into it. The demand for **free labor** is not as yet great in it, the proportion of prisoners to the means of employing them being considerably greater here than in New South Wales. The tendency of speculation among the settlers has also of late years been rather to Port Philip, than to develop the resources of their own Island. A. MACONOCHIE *Thoughts on Convict Management* p. 156

free labourer a free person who worked as a labourer. See FREE sense 2. [First recorded 1805]

1842 In regard to transportation and assignment he objected entirely to both. It might be very advantageous to those gentlemen who had their millions of acres and their thousands of sheep, to perpetuate slavery in the land, but to the **free labourer** the recurrence to transportation would be the death blow of his hopes, and to those like himself who had only a few pounds in their pockets it would be no benefit at all, but the reverse. *Colonial Observer* (Sydney) 2 Feb. p. 142

free man a man who came to Australia as a free person, or who was a convict who became free. See FREE sense 3. [First recorded 1789.]

1789 Notwithstanding little more than two years had elapsed since our departure from England, several convicts about this time signified that the respective terms for which they had been transported had expired, and claimed to be restored to the privileges of **free men**. Unfortunately, by some unaccountable oversight, the papers necessary to ascertain these particulars had been left by the masters of the transports with their owners in England, instead of being brought out and deposited in the colony; and as, thus situated, it was equally impossible to admit or to deny the truth of their assertions, they were told to wait until accounts could be received from England; and in the mean time, by continuing to labour for the public, they would be entitled to share the public provisions in the store. D. COLLINS *An Account of the English Colony in New South Wales* (1798) vol. 1 p. 74

1811 On Monday the 25th, and Tuesday the 26th, the whole of the **Free Men** on and off the Stores, such as have become free from their Sentence of Transportation being expired, and such as are free by Absolute Pardon or Conditional Emancipation, residing at Sydney, or any of the Districts adjacent thereto, at which time if any of the above Descriptions of Persons are Settlers or Landholders, they are to give in an Account of their Land in Cultivation, &c. together with the Stock and Grain in their Possession. *Sydney Gazette* 19 Jan. p. 1

free pardon = ABSOLUTE PARDON. [First recorded 1794.]

1812 The muster occupied two whole days, and, being ended, Mr. Marsden told me that his clerk having received a **free pardon** from Governor King, was about to quit the colony in a few days, and that it was his intention to appoint me his successor, promising, if I behaved well, to shew me every indulgence in his power. J.H. VAUX *Memoirs* vol. 1 p. 190

1838 We went to the Penitentiary to see the convicts from on board the Elizabeth, examined by the Lieut. Governor, who spoke to several of them individually … he gave them counsel regarding their future conduct, warning them particularly against the influence of bad company, and of drunkenness; and told them they might regard the door of a public house, through which many of them had come into their present situation, as the entrance to a jail; that their conduct would be narrowly watched, and if it should be bad, they would be severely punished, put to work in a chain-gang, or sent to a penal settlement, where they would be under very severe discipline; or their career might be terminated on the scaffold. That, on the contrary, if they behaved well, they would in the course of a proper time, be indulged with a ticket-of-leave, which would permit them to reap the profit of their own labour: that if they should still persevere in doing well, they would then become eligible for a conditional pardon, which would give them the liberty of the colony: and that a further continuance in good conduct, would open the way for a **free pardon**, which would liberate those who received it, to return to their native land. J. BACK-HOUSE *Narrative of a Visit to the Australian Colonies* (1843) pp. 19–20

free people those who came to Australia as free persons, or who were convicts who became free. See FREE sense 3. [First recorded 1789.]

> **1795** The report of the general muster which was ordered in the last month having been laid before the governor, he thought proper to make some regulations in the assistance afforded by government to settlers and others holding grants of land. ... To the settlers who arrived in the Surprise he allowed five male convicts; to the superintendants, constables, and store-keepers, four; to settlers from **free people**, two; to settlers from prisoners, one; and to serjeants of the New South Wales corps, one. D. COLLINS *An Account of the English Colony in New South Wales* (1798) vol. 1 p. 432

> **1802** [Governor King to the Duke of Portland] Before the Governor quits this subject, he feels it necessary to remind those convicts who are allowed to go off the store that any insolence to an officer, soldier, or constable, imposition in their demands for labour, neglect of doing the work they have been engaged to perform, or idleness, will subject them to be recalled to Government labour and otherwise punished: and although there are many who have obtained their free pardons and emancipations, or who have expiated their sentence of the law, or are otherwise ranked as **free people**, yet they will recollect that the Governor possesses ample power to restrain and punish every act tending to disturb the peace, good order, and tranquility of this colony, which he is at all times ready to enforce, as it is his study to seek for occasions to reward and protect the industrious and well-behaved. *Historical Records of Australia* 1st series III p. 473

free population that part of the population made up of people who came to Australia as free persons, or who were convicts who became free. See FREE sense 3. [First recorded 1791.]

> **1852** The additions ... made to the **free population**, were generally of persons connected with the merchant service or the military profession; and who, by a residence intended only to be temporary and official, contracted a preference for the climate; where they found great respect and deference, by the paucity of their numbers. It was their example which finally overcame the reluctance to settle, which no mere offers of the crown were sufficient to conquer. J. WEST *The History of Tasmania* vol. 2 p. 186

> **1851** What would be thought were a gang of some two hundred men wearing heavy chains on their legs to pass up and down the pavement of New Bond street some four or five times a day? The bare idea would be actually horrifying to the minds of some, and yet the inhabitants of the city of Hobart are obliged

to submit to the degradation, for gangs are almost continually passing along their most fashionable thoroughfares, and the promenades of their city. The Governor soon after his arrival in the colony becomes habituated to the sound of the rattling of chains, for gangs pass frequently before the front entrance of Government House, and other gangs are now constantly working at the rear— besides, how many thousands of convicts are there mingled among the **free population**? H. MELVILLE *The Present State of Australia* p. 182

free servant a servant who came to Australia as a free person, or who was a convict who became free. See FREE sense 3. [First recorded 1808.]

1831 We are perfectly satisfied with prison labour, and humbly conceive, that the introduction of paupers among them would tend to work the most serious evil. We all of us, have brought out more or less of these ***Free Servants***, and we have found them invariably, not only a great expense, but a source of injury. By such illiterate ignorant beings, the very term *free* is construed (particularly among a prisoner population,) as a power given them exclusively of being lazy, impertinent, and licentious. We would also observe, that the greatest possible incentive to good conduct is the hope of indulgence after a certain probation. If labour is poured in upon us at such a rate as to become of little value, what inducement has a prisoner to conduct himself well? *Sydney Monitor* 13 Aug. p. 3

1847 No humane person can have seen the working of the assignment system in New South Wales without seeing that it is of good effect, to one party at least; and it is some presumption that masters have been also benefited or pleased, or so many ticket-of-leave men would not be seen about the Colony, who have been placed in good and improving situations by their former masters, and who are assisted by those they formerly served. That system must have some merit whose reformatory effects are shown by a convict becoming a **free servant**, and then a small settler, and many afterwards landowners, and in all these gradations, assisted, too, by those they formerly served. R. WELCH *Observations on Convict and Free Labour* p. 16

free settlement 1 = FREE COLONY.

1840 The sister provinces of South Australia and Australia Felix, have both presented a state of advancement and prosperity, unknown to the older colonies. Three years have enabled these flourishing districts to acquire a degree of importance, arising from their population and commerce, which a period of twenty had scarcely established either in Van Diemen's Land or Sydney. Two distinct causes may be assigned for these examples of successful colonization.—The first, originates in the difference between the results of a *penal* and a *free* **settlement**; the second, in the experience obtained by the mercantile communities, in establishing and carrying out a communication with British Ports. *Port Phillip Gazette* 12 Feb. p. 2

2 part of a penal colony that was not used, or was no longer used, as a place of penal servitude.

1843 As a Native of the Colony, and Voter for the new Legislative Council, I beg leave to mention my reasons for not voting for Mr. W.C. Wentworth. ... He is not a native candidate, and consequently has no claim on the score of nationality, he being a native of Norfolk Island when it was a **free settlement** ... which island will soon be transferred to the government of Van Diemen's Land, if it is not so already, according to advices received from England recently. *Sydney Morning Herald* 12 June p. 3

free settler an emigrant to Australia who came of his or her free will (i.e. was' not transported as a convict). [First recorded 1795.]

1837 Governor Bligh exerted himself, but in vain, to bridle the rapacious New South Wales corps, and especially to destroy their monopoly in the sale of ardent spirits. There being now a few **free settlers** in the colony, he also did every thing in his power to promote their interests. He received their agricultural produce into the public stores at a fixed and liberal price, furnishing them, beforehand, and while their crops were still growing, with whatsoever articles they required for the consumption of their families, at charges very greatly below those at which they could obtain them from the dealers in those commodities in the colony, whose prices, in consideration of the credit they gave the distressed settlers, were most exorbitantly high. J. MUDIE *The Felonry of New South Wales* p. 33

free woman a woman who came to Australia as a free person, or who was a convict who became free. See FREE sense 3. [First recorded 1798.]

1829 Ann Baker, a **free woman**, was sentenced by the Police Magistrate on Saturday for being found at her old tricks in the street, to one months' hard labour in the 3rd class factory. *Sydney Monitor* 23 Feb. p. 1512

1836 The government of the convicts at this institution [Factory] is intrusted principally to a female, whose title is 'The Matron.' The matron must be a **free woman**; not a freed transport, but a person whose character has never been endorsed by a judicial tribunal. She selects, from each class, convicts as monitresses. No males are employed about the institution, except two or three superannuated old men as sentinels or porters. The sway of the matron is not despotic; she cannot even degrade a convict to a lower class without preferring a formal complaint to the magistrate at Parramatta. J.F. O'CONNELL *A Residence of Eleven Years in New Holland* pp. 46–7

G

gammon *noun* guile, deceit; nonsense, pretence, humbug; *verb* to deceive, fool, or cheat (a person); to pretend. [From British thieves' slang, first recorded in the eighteenth century.]

These senses are not specifically Australian, but the term is closely associated with FLASH language, and is typical of the kind of language that would have been used by some of the convicts. The term is also of significance in the development of Australian English. 'Gammon' in the sense 'nonsense, pretence, humbug' is chiefly attested in Australian pidgin English in the nineteenth century. While 'gammon' in all of its senses is archaic in contemporary English, it is still widely used in Australian Aboriginal English as a noun meaning 'nonsense, bullshit' and as a verb meaning 'to pretend, to lie, to bullshit'. These senses have re-entered the wider Australian community in the Northern Territory.

1812 GAMMON: flattery; deceit; pretence; plausible language; any assertion which is not strictly true, or professions believed to be insincere, as, I believe you're *gammoning*, or, that's all *gammon*, meaning, you are no doubt jesting with me, or, that's all a farce. To *gammon* a person, is to amuse him with false assurances, to praise, or flatter him, in order to obtain some particular end; to *gammon* a man *to* any act, is to persuade him to it by artful language, or pretence; to *gammon* a shop-keeper, &c., is to engage his attention to your discourse, while your accomplice is executing some preconcerted plan of depredation upon his property. J.H. VAUX *Memoirs* (1964) p. 243

1827 The perfect command of countenance and profound tact which the higher graduates display when accused of offences, baffle description. They have almost succeeded in persuading me that I was mistaken as to things I have actually seen them doing! ... Yet all these *innocent* rogues are in truth the perpetrators of the offences, and laugh and vaunt most immoderately, when sitting among their comrades, how they have **gammoned** you over. … As the person they palm the robbery upon is always some simple country fellow, with but little *bounce* or *gammon* in his composition, he gets confused, blushes, stammers, and contradicts himself; and you are often convinced from these signs alone, that he is really the purloiner. P. CUNNINGHAM *Two Years in New South Wales* vol. 2 pp. 231–3

gang a detachment of convicts detailed to public labour, under the supervision of an overseer. [First recorded 1789.]

Gangs of CONVICT LABOUR were essential in constructing public buildings and working on the public works such as roads that were necessary for the colonies' infrastructure. The term 'gang' is often found with an epithet describing the type of work the gangs did, for example, bricklayers' gang, or for gangs worked in IRONS, the terms IRON (and IRONED) GANG and CHAIN GANG were common. See also BATTERY GANG, CAMP GANG, CARRYING GANG, CLEARING GANG, CONVICT GANG, GAOL GANG, GOVERNMENT GANG, INVALID GANG, LOAN GANG, PENAL GANG, PROBATION GANG, PUBLIC GANG, PUNISHMENT GANG, ROAD GANG, TOWN GANG, and WORKING GANG.

1789 If the overseers, or the greatest part of any **gang**, should have reason to complain of the idleness of any one man belonging to that gang, and the complaint should be found just, the offender will be severely punished. J. HUNTER *Transactions at Port Jackson* p. 379

1822 Since the improvement of the roads and bridges was undertaken by Major Druitt, the chief engineer, in the year 1819, several **gangs** of convicts, amounting in the month of November 1819 to 362, under the superintendence of overseers, have been employed in this service. The gangs vary from 30 to 60 each; and as their work proceeds, they remove their huts, which are always constructed of the branches and bark of the eucalyptus, from one station to another. This operation is attended with very little difficulty and no expense. J.T. BIGGE *Report of the Commissioner of Inquiry into the State of the Colony of New South Wales* p. 26

gaol gang A punishment gang to which a convict is sentenced. [First recorded 1796.]

A gaol gang was a working party that consisted of prisoners who worked on the GANG by day and were kept in the gaol or PENITENTIARY at other times. Being sentenced to a gaol gang was a form of punishment, usually for offences committed in the colonies. These were usually the gangs that undertook the most severe work and were often heavily IRONED. For example, the gangs in Port Arthur worked on felling, cutting, and transporting timber, and worked in quarries and on road construction.

1796 In a settlement which was still in a great measure dependant on the mother country for food, it might have been supposed that these people would have endeavoured by their own industry to have increased, rather than by robbery and fraud to have lessened, the means of their support: but far too many of them were most incorrigibly flagitious. The most notorious of these were formed into a **gaol gang**, which was composed of such a set of hardened and worthless characters, that, although Saturday was always given up to the convicts for their own private avocations, as well as to enable them to appear clean and decent on Sunday at church, this gang was ordered, as an additional punishment, to work on the Saturday morning in repairing the roads and bridges near the town. D. Collins *An Account of the English Colony in New South Wales* vol. 2 pp. 2–3

1821 [Governor Macquarie to Earl Bathurst] From the worst description and most refractory Convicts, you are to form a **Gaol Gang**, who are to be worked in Irons, be employed on all the most heavy and disagreeable Labour, and always sleep in the Gaol. Men sentenced to work in this Gang must feel it a severe Punishment, and it ought not therefore to be frequently resorted to for petty offences. *Historical Records of Australia* 1st series X p. 484

gentleman convict a convict with either a liberal education or some training requiring literacy (acquired prior to transportation) and so fitted for employment in a clerical or professional capacity. [First recorded 1830.]

The records indicate that 'gentleman' in the compound **gentleman convict** often served to designate those convicts who possessed skills superior to the general run of convicts, although some were members of the British upper classes. These were convicts who had some education and were literate, and therefore could be employed as clerks or professionals. Such people were also known as EDUCATED convicts or SPECIALS. Like those of high status, they were often pardoned soon after arrival so as to be more useful to the colony. There were fears, however, that educated convicts were potentially disruptive and might be likely to be a threat to law and order. They were thus sometimes exiled to penal settlements such as Port Macquarie, which after 1831 became a place of exile for invalid convicts and specials.

1830 I propose to divide culprits generally into two classes; 1st, those who commit crime with free inclination, and from actual depravity; and 2dly, those who are driven to evil courses by sheer want and destitution. Amongst the former I would class all cases where culprits had acted in gangs (except poachers), all repeated offences, all pickpockets from London and populous towns; and, above all, that most useless class, generally designated as *gentlemen convicts*, persons guilty of minor cases of forgery, of breaches of trust, as merchant's clerks, &c.; for these, an entirely new species of punishment should be devised; but for the agricultural labourer, driven to the commission of crime by circumstances I have already detailed, transportation for life, under the name of colonization, is the best and most humane remedy; and this on the ground that his errors chiefly resulting from want of employment, reformation, the great object of punishment, will be best obtained by placing him in a new course of life, where profitable employment is certain. T.P. MacQueen *Thoughts and Suggestions on the Present Condition of the Country* p. 33

1835 It is hither the class of convicts, called '**gentlemen convicts**,' educated men, who have fallen from their high estate, are transported: their employment consists of gardening and work of that kind; they are dressed in the prisoners' garb, and treated as regards food, &c. in every way like the other convicts. It is almost unnecessary to say, that such punishment is more severe to them than it is to the uneducated prisoner, and so I think it should be, for it must be remembered that their education makes their crimes of a double die. Ignorance, though not an excuse for any crime, in a measure may palliate some offences; but erudition not only does not extenuate or mitigate, but makes the delinquency more heinous and atrocious. H.W. Parker *The Rise, Progress and Present State of Van Diemen's Land* pp. 132–3

good man a convict whose behaviour in custody is exemplary. [First recorded 1788.]

A convict who behaved well was deemed to be a 'good man'. Such good behaviour could lead to an ABSOLUTE or CONDITIONAL PARDON or the granting of a TICKET OF LEAVE. See also BAD, where there is evidence that the convicts themselves used the terms 'good man' and 'bad man' ironically.

1788 The detachment also finding it convenient to collect vegetables, and being obliged to go for them as far as Botany Bay, the convicts were ordered to avail themselves of the protection they might find by going in company with an armed party; and never, upon any account, to straggle from the soldiers, or go to Botany Bay without them, on pain of severe punishment. Notwithstanding this order and precaution, however, a convict, who had been looked upon as a **good man**, (no complaint having been made of him since his landing, either for dishonesty or idleness,) having gone out with an armed party to procure vegetables at Botany Bay, straggled from them, though repeatedly cautioned against it, and was killed by the natives. D. Collins *An Account of the English Colony in New South Wales* vol. 1 p. 43

1850 All the consolation that we got, was the assurance that if we continued to be **good men** till our probation of two years was expired, we should have tickets-of-leave—not to leave the island—but to go any where on it we chose, so long as we should make weekly returns to some peace officer, of our doings and whereabouts. This privilege, he assured us, was a great privilege, and the next thing to freedom. W. GATES *Recollections of Life in Van Diemen's Land* p. 124

government the governing power in a penal colony; the body of instrumentalities responsible for the administration of a penal colony.

While part of standard English, this term is of special significance in the early history of Australia. Due to the nature of early Australian society, that is, its nature as settlements established as places to which convicts were transported, government played an important role. The term was used in numerous phrases and combinations, reflecting the pervasive presence of the government in colonial society. One of the important phrases was **returned to government** (see 1 below). In many combinations 'government' is a euphemism for 'convict' (see 2 below).

1 The phrase **returned to government** was frequently used and referred to a convict, usually out on ASSIGNMENT and under the supervision of a MASTER or MISTRESS, who was sent back into the custody of the colonial government. The return may have been for any of various reasons—for example, the servant was no longer required, or the servant had misbehaved and the master or mistress requested punishment.

> **1847** Twenty-sixth day, Bong-Bong.—As we neared this settlement we passed a female prisoner on foot going down, in charge of a constable, to the Female Factory (Penitentiary) of Paramatta. She had been giving her mistress what they here technically term 'cheek', and was sentenced to some months' confinement and be **returned to Government**. She was a rough brutal creature, but the cutting off of her hair, which would be one of the consequences of her return to Government in this way, she seemed to feel very acutely. A. HARRIS *Settlers and Convicts* (1953) p. 138

2 Government was used as a euphemism for 'convict'. Typical uses include **government workman** (1803), **government stockman** (1813), **government mechanic** (1816), **government sawyer** (1833), and **government dress** (1846), where in each case 'government' is synonymous with 'convict'. Some of the more common combinations are given separate entries—see GOVERNMENT GANG, GOVERNMENT LABOUR, GOVERNMENT LABOURER, GOVERNMENT MAN, GOVERNMENT SERVANT, GOVERNMENT WOMAN.

> **1840** Being on board a colonial vessel, I may give a few specimens of what is to be met with in the like situations, where *slang terms* and a little *bouncing* is the order of the day with the convicts, while passing up and down the river. By the bye, these worthies are very indignant at the name of convict being applied to them. *Government people* is the appellation most suited to their fancy. A. RUSSELL *A Tour Through the Australian Colonies* p. 126

1851 There may be, among the **Government** hands, or rather among those men that have just received their indulgences, a difficulty in obtaining work; but if so, it is merely because such men have, during their probation, been instructed in no other knowledge than that of breaking stones, and who are, consequently, unfit for anything else. H. MELVILLE *The Present State of Australia* p. 295

government gang a detachment of convicts assigned to public labour. [First recorded 1808.]

1808 On Monday morning last this vessel was missed from her anchorage in Farm Cove, which was directly in view of captain Campbell's house there. Between 8 and 9 the captain reported the extraordinary circumstance to his Honor the Lieutenant Governor, who issued immediate orders for a search to be made to discover whether any of the **Government gangs** were absent; the result of which was, that one Robert Stewart, and several others had not joined their work that morning. Upon further enquiry it next appeared, that a vessel had been seen at day-light from South Head, standing off, from which joint circumstances, no further doubt was to be entertained of her having been taken away by a body of desperadoes. *Sydney Gazette* 22 May p. 2

1827 It is melancholy indeed to witness the number of fine young men that are ruined by the inefficient discipline now in vogue in the **government gangs,** it being a common trick to station a sentinel on a commanding eminence to give the alarm, while all the others divert themselves, or go to sleep. P. CUNNINGHAM *Two Years in New South Wales* vol. 2 p. 329

government labour = PUBLIC LABOUR. [First recorded 1802.]

1803 [Government and General Orders] It is known that many Settlers have been in the habit of employing those who have left **Government Labour**. Settlers and other Persons employing any Prisoner without seeing his Certificate, will incur the Penalty pointed out by former Orders, and the prisoners who leave their work will not escape their part of the punishment. *Historical Records of Australia* 1st series IV p. 325

government labourer a convict assigned to PUBLIC LABOUR. [First recorded 1807.]

1807 *George Wilson* settler at Prospect was also examined, on a charge of employing *John Campbell*, a **Government labourer**, without demanding his certificate or pass: whereupon he was fined in the penalty of 5l. and 2s. 6d. per diem for nine days he was in his employ. *Sydney Gazette* 5 Apr. p. 2

1822 Since the establishment of the convict barrack at Sydney, in the month of June 1819, a considerable number of convicts, varying, and gradually increasing from 600 to 1,000, have been lodged there. Previous to this period, there existed no place either of lodging or temporary confinement for any of them; and after the inspection of those that had newly arrived was concluded, they were told by the principal superintendent 'to go and provide lodging where they could for the remainder of the day, and to come to their work in the morning.' All the **government labourers** and convicts, at this period, were allowed to leave their work at three o'clock every day, and were enabled by their own labour to pay for their weekly lodgings and washing. Those who are now permitted to remain out of barrack, are compelled to work the whole of the day, but are allowed to employ themselves after the hours of government work, and on the whole of Saturdays, for their own benefit. J.T. Bigge *Report of the Commissioner of Inquiry into the State of the Colony of New South Wales* p. 21

government man a convict. [First recorded 1797.]

1850 At ten a.m., they began to call over the names, and in half an hour, I was startled by hearing the name Charles King, come forth, I obeyed the mandate, and a gentleman receiving me, I took my bed upon my back, and followed him to the bottom of George Street, where I beheld my future master, sitting in his office, he was a true English looking gentleman; I cannot forget his first salutation. Where do you come from? I answered Manchester; well said he, I will tell you what I do with my **government men**, I feed and clothe them well, and if they deserve it I flog them well. C.A. KING *Life of Charles Adolphus King* pp. 15–16

government servant a convict. [First recorded 1802.]

1819 Yesterday Thomas Whitear was brought before the Superintendant of Police, charged by his master, Mr. E.S. Hall, of Surry Hills, with having embezzled upwards of £40 of the complainant's money.—The prisoner was Mr. Hall's **government servant**, and had been his milk carrier, as which he had obtained the sums alleged.—He confessed his offence, and was sentenced to three months solitary imprisonment on bread and water, and to Newcastle for the remainder of his term of transportation. *Sydney Gazette* 17 Apr.

1834 Some of the lower orders contrive to get **government servants** assigned to them, ostensibly for the purpose of cultivating the soil, but in reality to assist in plundering. … As a veil to such practices, and to lull any suspicion that might be created, they dig, and plant a few potatoes and other vegetables, in a small spot of ground, laid out near their bark residence, as a garden; and the crown prisoners are procured ostensibly to assist in cultivating this 'bit of earth'; and thus the vegetable garden affords a cloak to many crimes. G. BENNETT *Wanderings in New South Wales* p. 91

government stroke a deliberately slow pace of working. [From *stroke* in the sense 'an amount of work', in negative contexts meaning 'a minimum amount of work', as in 'I have not done a stroke of work today'. First recorded 1842.]

1842 Although of the immigrants who have thus arrived, are not of the most useful description, a very small portion of them being available as farm labourers, still they are likely to meet with speedy engagements. In the mean time the men are employed on the public works; but we are sorry to say that they do not appear to be of much use, apparently from the want of an active overseer. The '**government stroke**' is soon learned; and the proficiency of the new hands appears to exceed that of the oldest gang in the colony. *Geelong Advertiser* 7 Mar. p. 2

1847 Gangs of men … were seen … some resting on their shovels, some riding in hand carts, some lying on the ground smoking their pipes … having acquired what was emphatically termed 'the **Government stroke**', as descriptive of the slovenly and tediously measured way in which they learned to work. Z.P. POCOCK *Transportation and Convict Discipline* p. 8

government woman a convict woman. [First recorded 1834.]

1834 I was brought once to Court since I came to Mr. Mudie, but not punished; the complaint was about ploughing, and made to the Bench, but I was acquitted; in fact I was not punished since I came to the employment of Mr. Mudie; I heard, about three weeks ago, from a woman, that Mr. Larnach was determined to send me to an iron-gang for twelve months; she was Mr. Larnach's **Government woman**. J. MUDIE *Vindication of James Mudie and John Larnach* p. 8

1844 Two **government women**, one assigned to Dr. Forster, and the other to Dr. Cartwright, were, on Saturday last, each sentenced to two months' imprisonment in the third class of the Female Factory for drunkenness and disorderly conduct—both cases being the consequence of the Christmas revels. *Sydney Morning Herald* 31 Dec. p. 2

guard house a place where prisoners or convicts were detained and kept under guard. Generally people were kept in the guard house temporarily until further action was taken.

1800 It having been for some time observed, indeed more particularly since the late arrivals from Ireland, that a number of idle and suspicious persons were frequently strolling about the town of Sydney at improper hours of the night, and several boats having been taken away, and much property stolen out of houses; in order to put a stop to such practices, the centinels on duty were directed not to suffer any person, the civil and military officers of the settlement excepted, to pass their posts after ten o'clock at night, without they could give the counter-sign; in which case the sentinel was to detain them until the relief came round; when, if the corporal should not be satisfied with the account which they might give, they were to be taken to the **guard-house**, and there detained, until released by proper authority. D. COLLINS *An Account of the English Colony in New South Wales* vol. 2 p. 286

H

hand 1 In the phrase **on** (or **upon**) **one's own hands** (of a convict) permitted to work for one's interest or benefit rather than working in public or private service. [First recorded 1801.]

In the early period of settlement, prior to Macquarie's governorship (1810–22), convicts were given time to work for themselves and earn wages. Although control of convicts and their time tightened in later years, those assigned to private service might still be given time to work for themselves for wages.

1801 [Government and General Orders] It having been represented to the Governor that several settlers and others who have been allowed to take prisoners off the stores have abused that indulgence by receiving payments from the prisoners to allow them to be **on their own hands**, or have let such prisoners out for hire, if any person cannot support or employ the prisoners they have taken off the stores they are to be returned to Government labour before next Monday, the 8th instant; and if any person is detected in letting out a prisoner to hire, or allowing him to be on his own hands, they will, on conviction before a magistrate, be fined the sum of two shillings and sixpence for each day such prisoner has been assigned to them. *Historical Records of Australia* 1st series III p. 254

1818 All Female Prisoners not assigned to Service, and who are allowed to be at large **on their own Hands**, must have regular Tickets of Leave; they are required to apply at the Secretary's Office on Wednesday next, the 7th Instant, between the Hours of Ten and One o'Clock, and to bring with them in writing the Names of the Ships in which they left England, the Years in which they arrived from Europe, and the Names of the Vessels by which they arrived at this Colony; also, the Periods and Places of Trial, and the periods of Sentence. Such Women as neglect or disobey this Notice will be ordered in to Government Employ. *Hobart Town Gazette* 3 Jan.

2 In the phrase **on the hands of government** (of a convict) in official custody. [First recorded 1829.]

> **1829** [Governor Darling to Sir George Murray] I have the honor to acknowledge the receipt of your Despatch of the 17th of July last, No. 125, in reply to mine of the 18th February, representing the inconvenience which was experienced at that time from the Number of female Convicts who remained **on the hands of the Government**. *Historical Records of Australia* 1st series XV p. 309

hard labour physically hard labour imposed on a convict. [*Hard labour* in the sense 'labour imposed upon certain classes of criminals during their term of imprisonment' (OED) is standard English, although the OED's first recorded usage is 1853. It is first recorded in Australia in 1803.]

Hard labour was a sentence given to some convicts, and consisted of physically difficult work, often undertaken in IRONS or CHAINS. Hard labour was usually a punishment for SECONDARY offences, that is, crimes committed in the colonies, or for bad behaviour. PENAL SETTLEMENTS such as Norfolk Island and Port Arthur were notorious for the extreme nature of the hard labour to which prisoners were subjected.

> **1803** [Proclamation by Governor King] Whereas there is great reason to suppose some Persons not duly Authorised, do make a Practice of going to those Parts beyond the Nepean, where the Strayed Cattle Resort, for the purpose of Killing them, whereby several are Wounded—To prevent which, it is hereby Ordered That if any Person whatever frequent the Cow Pastures, or pass the Nepean, without a Permit Signed by the Governor, stating for what purpose that Permission is given, He or They will on Conviction, be put to **Hard Labour** for Six Months as a Vagrant, And if any Person whatever, not authorised, shall presume to Kill any of the above Black Cattle, Male or Female, they will be Punished to the utmost extent of the Law. *Sydney Gazette* 10 July p. 1

> **1851** Mr. P. O'Donohoe arrived here on Wednesday evening last, and was 'classed' on Thursday morning, for a hard labour party, but after some little 'cavilling' on the part of the Assistant Superintendent placed over him it was found that he (Mr. O'D.) was not in a fit state of health to undergo *hard labour*, in fact the poor fellow was scarcely able to stand, and was ordered into the hospital, where he now is, but it is hoped a week or two of retirement and kind treatment, which I have no doubt he will receive, as every officer (with three exceptions) on this station, pities the State Prisoners, and despises the man who ordered them, contrary to law, to undergo three months hard labour at this vile spot. *Irish Exile* (Hobart) 18 Jan. p. 3

home sentence a term of transportation from the United Kingdom to an Australian colony. [First recorded 1848.]

A home sentence was a term of punishment given to convicts while still in Britain, as opposed to sentences or punishments that were incurred in the colonies (known as COLONIAL SENTENCES). The typical sentence given in Britain was transportation and the serving of a three-, seven-, or fourteen-year period as a convict (after which a convict could be FREED), or transportation for life.

> **1848** Whenever any convict incurs a sentence to an ironed gang, the treadmill, or cell, the term of punishment, whether it be three years or seven days, is added to the original or **home sentence**. C. COZENS *Adventures of a Guardsman* pp. 164–5

> **1848** Send even to England for fifty superior constables, if necessary—as it is now intended to do in New South Wales; do anything rather than longer permit the gross inconsistency of having constables—the sworn conservators of the peace—in townships, the lockers-up of free and bond men and women, in many instances, doubly-convicted felons. Many a good man would join the police if the pay was better; at any rate, the practice of having men under **home-sentence** acting as headboroughs in the interior townships, walking into free men's houses with all the freedom and insolence possible, is an outrage upon public liberty and decency, although, here, it does not appear to be considered a matter deserving official consideration. *Britannia* (Hobart) 11 May p. 4

hulk the body of a dismantled ship (worn out and unfit for sea service) used as a prison. [Standard English term, first recorded in an Australian convict context in 1820.]

The use of hulks on the Thames River to relieve overcrowding in the prisons began in 1776 when transportation of prisoners to the New World was interrupted by the American War of Independence. When there were similar problems of overcrowding in the Australian colonies, a few hulks were established for housing prisoners. When transportation to New South Wales was stopped in 1840, the many women who then were sent to Van Diemen's Land had no place to stay, and were kept in the hulk of the ship *Anson* moored in the Derwent River from 1843. Over the period 1844 to 1849 the *Anson* held as many women as the Cascades female factory. The *Anson* was shut down on 31 January 1849. See also HULK DRESS and HULK LIST.

> **1835** [Sir Richard Bourke to Secretary of State] I have the honour to solicit your sanction to the expenditure, which I have found it necessary to commence of £100 per annum as the Salary of a schoolmaster, engaged for the instruction of the Convicts arriving under sentence to work in Irons for long

periods, and placed on Goat Island in Port Jackson for this purpose, and of those who, being sentenced here to a Penal Settlement, are detained in the **Hulk** (which is anchored abreast of Goat-Island) whilst awaiting a conveyance to Norfolk Island or Moreton Bay. *Historical Records of Australia* 1st series XVII p. 718

1838 We had a religious interview with the Hulk Chain-gang, in a long shed, in which they regularly assemble for worship, on First and Fourth days. The discipline of this gang is very strict; and from its local situation, the men are effectually kept from strong drink. The **hulks** on board of which they sleep, are kept clean, and are well ventilated: they are moored close alongside of the yard in which the men muster. These prisoners are employed in public works of improvement on the side of Sulivans Cove, and are kept constantly under an overseer and a military guard. J. BACKHOUSE *A Narrative of a Visit to the Australian Colonies* p. 158

hulk dress the clothing worn by convicts imprisoned on a HULK.

1843 The next move was to the washing ward, where we were stripped, under-went an ablution, and a complete transformation, by the assumption of the '**hulk dress**,' consisting of a coarse, spotted guernsey frock, hemp shirt, and a pair of short knee breeches, jacket, and waistcoat, of coarse thin gray cloth. A thin pair of gray long stockings, a coarse check cotton neckerchief, a pair of low cowskin shoes, to *cap* all a coarse stiff wool hat; every article of which was marked, re-marked and marked again, with the 'crow's foot' (broad arrow). When last, though not least, a large iron band of near four pounds weight, extremely rusty, was put on each right leg the following day. Thus carrying out to the fullest extent their *iron* policy. B. WAIT *Letters from Van Dieman's Land* p. 204

hulk list a list of the prisoners kept on a HULK.

1822 As no information is transmitted in the **hulk lists**, of the single or married state of the convicts, and when there are so many motives in New South Wales for concealing it, it is very difficult, almost impossible, to ascertain it. Two affect-ing consequences of a second marriage, contracted in New South Wales during the life-time of a first and absent husband, are mentioned by Mr. Marsden in his evidence; and he states such marriages to have been of frequent occurrence. These consequences may be greatly obviated, by requiring the gaolers of the dif-ferent prisons in England to communicate the information that they may receive respecting the single or married condition of the convicts sent to the hulks; and by adding these particulars, corrected by subsequent inquiry there, to the com-munications transmitted in the hulk lists. J.T. BIGGE *Report of the Commissioner of Inquiry into the State of the Colony of New South Wales* p. 105

hut a building for the accommodation of a convict (or convicts). [First recorded 1793.]

A hut was a building, often small and sometimes temporary, in which convicts were housed. They were usually built near where convicts worked when assigned to public works—this allowed more supervision of them. In some cases, however, especially where convicts were assigned to large properties, they built huts for themselves, which allowed them some measure of independent living.

> **1825** The Government House stands nearly in the centre of the town, on a handsome esplanade, open to the sea. To the northward, on a rising ground, which commands the whole town, are the military barracks, calculated to hold 150 men, each of the married men having a small cottage and garden. On the right of the hill are two handsome cottages, which are used as officers' quarters. The remainder of the town, which is extremely clean, is entirely occupied by the prisoners, who are kept as distinct as possible from the military, and who have each a small but neat **hut**, constructed of split-wood, lathed, plastered and white-washed, with a garden attached. B. FIELD *Geographical Memoirs on New South Wales* p. 31

> **1833** The **huts** of the convicts are seldom notorious for cleanliness or comfort, and the inmates are not infrequently more numerous than those of an Irish cabin: the last that I inspected contained a multitude of noisy parrots, intended for sale; pet kangaroos and opossums, and a variety of kangaroo dogs, greyhounds, and sheep-dogs: on the fire was a huge boiler filled with the flesh of a kangaroo, and close by were suspended the hind-quarters of another of these animals; in one corner was a large pan of milk, in another, a number of skins partially dried; while, a few feet from the ground, were the filthy bed-places or cribs of the people themselves. W. BRETON *Excursions in New South Wales* p. 315

I

imperial convict (in Western Australia) a convict the cost of whose penal servitude was met by the British as distinct from the Colonial government. [First recorded 1873.]

An imperial convict was a transported prisoner or convict sent to Western Australia and whose care was paid for by the British government. Unlike New South Wales and Van Diemen's Land, established primarily as penal settlements, Western Australia (the Swan River Colony) was initially established in 1831 as a free colony. For many years it struggled to be viable. While New South Wales and Van Diemen's Land saw increased opposition to transportation, it was decided that convict labour would be necessary to make Western Australia a successful settlement. In June 1850, therefore, convicts began to arrive in Western Australia. Convicts sent to Western Australia from Britain had served part of their sentence in Britain; upon arrival they were kept in confinement in Fremantle or Perth and employed on public works, after which they might receive their TICKETS OF LEAVE. The scheme helped to improve the fragile Western Australian economy through Britain's financial support for convict food and clothing, jails and the wages of guards and administrators. Transportation continued until 1868, and some 9718 convicts were brought to the colony.

> **1873** The prison, which, as I have said, can hold 850 inmates, now contains 359 men. Of these 240 are **imperial convicts,**—convicts who have been sent out from England, and who are now serving under British sentences, or sentences inflicted in the colony within twelve months of the date of their freedom. For all these the expense is paid from home. And there are 119 colonial convicts,—convicts with whom the colony is charged, as being representative of colonial crime. But even of these about four-fifths came to Western Australia

114

originally as convicts from home. A. TROLLOPE *Australia and New Zealand* vol. 2 p. 112

incorrigible a recalcitrant convict. [*Incorrigible* in the sense 'bad or depraved beyond correction or reform' is used in standard English from the fourteenth century, and as a noun it is recorded from the mid eighteenth century. In the Australian convict context it is first recorded in 1827.]

An incorrigible was a convict who was difficult and uncooperative, and who often continued to participate in criminal and rebellious behaviour. Such convicts were usually seen as beyond redemption. They were often those located in places of SECONDARY and severe punishment, such as Norfolk Island and Port Arthur, where they were sentenced to HARD LABOUR and often worked in IRONS.

> **1827** [Newcastle] possesses a great advantage over most of the other colonial ports in the quantity of excellent coal wherewith the surrounding country abounds; inasmuch as vessels are always sure of a return cargo. The coal shaft is sunk upon the summit of the hill, and the coals carted down by bullocks; but from the defective nature of the working, and the lazy habits of the ***incorrigibles*** who are sentenced to this labour, the produce does not at all correspond with what may be expected when a more efficient system is introduced. P. CUNNINGHAM *Two Years in New South Wales* vol. 1 pp. 148–9

indent a document recording the names of a party of convicts transported to Australia and transferring a property in these convicts to the relevant governor, usually detailing name, date of trial, etc. [In the sense 'official or formal list, inventory' *indent* is a shortened form of *indenture*. In its specific Australian convict sense it is first recorded in 1802.]

Convicts had their names and details listed on indents when they were transported as property of the government. Such indents were used to check the claims of convicts when they declared that they had completed their sentences. However, the quality of information varied, and it was not until the convict system was well established that accurate and full lists of convict particulars were made. From 1830 to 1842 volumes of indents were printed and distributed to magistrates and officials, so they would have access to relevant information about convicts and be able to identify them.

> **1812** [Governor Macquarie to Earl of Liverpool] The Musters do not stand as Authentic Documents for the other Circumstances of 'Time and place of Trial' or 'Time of Transportation', which, being taken merely on the personal Reports of the Convicts themselves, Cannot be fully relied on; whilst on the other Hand, Misrepresentations, if Made, Could not always be Corrected, as Reference Could not be had to the regular **Indents**, which frequently do not

arrive until long after the Landing of the Convicts. *Historical Records of Australia* 1st series VII p. 615

1828 [Governor Darling to Right Hon. W. Huskisson] The **Indents** or Assignments of Convicts by the Lord Lieutenant of Ireland to the Governor of New South Wales, specify the Term of Years for which each Convict is Sentenced to be Transported, but do not mention the Time of Trial, or the Day from which the Term of Transportation is to be reckoned. Consequently when Convicts from Ireland apply for Certificates of Freedom, their own Statements of the times of Trial are necessarily adopted in the Colonial Secretary's Office as the periods from which their sentences are to be calculated. *Historical Records of Australia* 1st series XIV p. 117

indented (of a convict) assigned into private service. [The standard English sense is 'bound by an indenture', *indenture* here originally referring to the contract by which an apprentice was bound to his master, and later to the contract by which a person bound himself to service in the colonies. Its use in the Australian convict context is first recorded in 1804.]

Convicts were bound as indented servants to private masters. This obliged them to remain with the master to whom they were assigned. 'Indented' was often used in a similar sense to ASSIGNED.

1804 [Governor King to Lord Hobart] I propose ... cultivating as much of the 700 acres clear at Castle Hill, as I shall be able to reserve convicts to labour it, as there is now a great demand for **indented** convicts in consequence of my late Order. *Historical Records of Australia* 1st series IV p. 480

indented servant a convict bound over by a contract of service to a private person. [First recorded 1809.]

1809 [Hawkesbury Settlers' Address to Governor Bligh] We had no sooner began to feel the benefit of your Measures, and see the reform they were led to produce, than we were alarmed at your being arrested; and we solemnly protest against that Act and declare we had no foreknowledge, act, or part in the said Rebellion; and some of us who did sign an Address to Major Johnston after the Act was committed on the 26th January, 1808, was under the impression of Fear and Terror, the Colony being then under Martial Law, with Bands of men going round ... using various threats (among which to take our **Indented Servants** from us), and that our property should not be worth sixpence in the Colony. *Historical Records of Australia* 1st series VII pp. 147–8

indented service (of a convict) the state of being bound over by a contract of service to a private person.

1843 Yesterday, an urchin named Richard Duggan *alias* Tizzy, was brought before the Police Court, charged with having absconded from his **indented service**. It appears that the defendant will be sixteen years old next July, that he has already undergone a sentence of six years in the New Penitentiary in Britain, and that he, with about one hundred boys from the same establishment, was sent to Auckland, where they were apprenticed off to such of the new colonists as chose to apply for them. The prisoner's master having occasion to come to Sydney, transferred him for the time being to Captain Rough, but as soon as the real master left, Duggan contrived to get stowed away on board a vessel coming to Sydney, where he remained concealed until hunger forced him to appear on deck. The captain, on arriving here, immediately surrendered him to the Water Police as a prisoner at large. In the interim Mr. Jamison, his master, arrived in Sydney, and having recognised him, had him brought before the bench. Mr. Windeyer told the prisoner that his sentence of seven years, although mitigated to six years' service in the Penitentiary, was still acting against him, and that he must fulfil his indentures, as it was in mercy to him that the law allowed him to get off on an indenture. The prisoner was then ordered to be kept in custody until a ship could be found by which he might be forwarded to Auckland. According to the prisoner's own account of himself, he was sent to the new Penitentiary for taking a few pence from a shop till, but it was the first thing of the sort he had been engaged in. *Sydney Morning Herald* 16 May p. 2

indulge to grant a convict some mitigation of the conditions under which a sentence was being served. See INDULGENCE. [*Indulge* in its standard English sense (separate from the earlier senses of *indulgence* and *indulgent*) first appears in the seventeenth century, and means 'to treat (a person) with such favour, kindness, or complaisance as he has no claim to, but desires or likes'. In the Australian convict context the assumption is always that the convict has done something to deserve the indulgence. First recorded 1805.]

1805 Several of the Prisoners under Sentence of the Law who have been **indulged** with Permission to be off the Stores on Tickets of Leave, having neglected to attend the Muster of Yesterday, are ordered to Public Labour, and to be sent to some other Settlements. *Sydney Gazette* 14 July p. 1

1849 A man transported for seven years obtained a ticket-of-leave at the expiration of four years' servitude; and one transported for life at the lapse of eight years, provided no punishment had been incurred during that time. Each punishment deferred this indulgence for a year, during which period he remained in his master's service; and this was a severe, and certainly a very impolitic

regulation. When a 'lifer' had held a ticket-of-leave for six years, and could produce good testimonials to character, he was further **indulged** with a conditional pardon. J.P. TOWNSEND *Rambles and Observations in New South Wales*
pp. 220–1

indulgence A mitigation of the conditions under which a convict's sentence was
served. [First recorded 1794.]

An indulgence was a reward granted to a convict who had behaved well. It often
took the form of a PARDON, such as a TICKET OF LEAVE. It might also consist of being
given material rewards, such as better rations or better jobs. Indulgences were an
incentive for convicts to behave well and to reform themselves. By obtaining such
indulgences, convicts were able to contribute more to the colony than they would in
government service. It was also a relatively successful way of reducing the financial
burden on the government for the care of convicts. See also INDULGE.

> **1794** At the latter end of the month some warrants of emancipation passed
> the seal of the territory, and received the lieutenant-governor's signature. The
> objects of this **indulgence** were, Robert Sidaway, who received an uncondi-
> tional pardon in consideration of his diligence, unremitting good conduct, and
> strict integrity in his employment for several years as the public baker of the
> settlement; and William Leach, who was permitted to quit this country, but
> not to return to England during the unexpired term of his sentence of trans-
> portation, which was for seven years. D. COLLINS *An Account of the English
> Colony in New South Wales* vol. 1 p. 391

> **1828** The Lieut. Governor having reason to fear, that the Instructions which
> have from time to time been given respecting the employment of the Convicts
> on Saturday, are not duly attended to, all Persons in charge of Prisoners,
> whether employed in the Towns or in the Country, are distinctly to under-
> stand, that, with the exception of married men, or men of particular good con-
> duct, who are not permitted the **indulgence** of sleeping out of Barracks, and
> allowed the benefit of One Day in the Week for the purpose of providing their
> own Lodgings, all Convicts are to be employed until the dinner hour on Sat-
> urdays:—the afternoons to be set apart for the washing and mending of their
> clothes. *Tasmanian* (Hobart) 12 Dec. p. 4

> **1849** It had been the custom at Norfolk Island to grant an *indulgence* to such
> prisoners as performed the office of hangman. The indulgence consisted in
> remitting their sentence of penal probation, and sending them up to Van
> Diemen's Land, by the next ship after the executions where, I am told, they
> were generally made constables or turnkeys. T. ROGERS *Correspondence Relat-
> ing to the Dismissal* pp. 153–4

invalid gang a detachment of convicts unfit for hard work. [First recorded 1832.]

The invalid gang was a working party of convicts who due to age or infirmity were unfit for doing hard work or physical labour.

> **1848** There was what was called the **invalid gang**, picking up brush, &c. I was put with them but did not stay long. Pringall the superintendant had marked me for severe treatment. R. MARSH *Seven Years of my Life: Or Narrative of a Patriot Exile* p. 118

> **1862** About two miles before we arrived at Deep Gully, where the huts of an **Invalid Gang** are situated, we overtook a large party at work on the road. The overseer caused them to be drawn up by the road side, where we had a full opportunity of extending religious counsel to them. ... These poor men greatly excited our commiseration. Many of them are labouring under debility or indisposition, the result of intemperance, others are crippled or superannuated. BACKHOUSE & TYLOR *Life and Labours of George Washington Walker* p. 47

iron collar a band of iron worn around the neck of a convict as punishment. [First recorded 1791.]

An iron collar was ordered as a form of punishment for convicts who misbehaved, rebelled, tried to ABSCOND, or participated in criminal behaviour.

> **1791** On his majesty's birth-day an extra allowance of provisions was issued to the garrison and settlements; each man receiving one pound of salt meat, and the like quantity of rice; each woman half a pound of meat and one pound of rice; and each child a quarter of a pound of meat and half a pound of rice. And to make it a chearful day to every one, all offenders who had for stealing Indian corn been ordered to wear **iron collars** were pardoned. D. COLLINS *An Account of the English Colony in New South Wales* vol. 1 pp. 164–5

ironed gang = IRON GANG. See also CHAIN GANG. [First recorded 1832.]

> **1847** He is perfectly correct, however, in describing the horror which the prisoners have of an **ironed gang**; and so desperate do they become, that it is necessary to have a soldier for every twenty or thirty men, who attends them at their work with loaded muskets, ready to fire upon them if they attempt to escape, and many have been shot in making the attempt. Most of the stone quarries around Sydney are worked with ironed-gangs; a guard of soldiers being stationed all round the quarry. ... The quantity of work done by an ironed gang is just about the one-half of what would be done by free labourers, which shows the unprofitableness of compulsory labour. A. MARJORIBANKS *Travels in New South Wales* pp. 71–2

iron gang a detachment of convicts assigned to hard labour in fetters. See also CHAIN GANG. [First recorded 1829.]

An iron gang was a working party of convicts who had to perform their work while in IRONS or CHAINS. They wore ankle fetters and were chained together when moved about. This added to the severity of the convicts' punishment and also prevented their escape. Ironed gangs were largely responsible for road and bridge building.

> **1835** What is the Punishment adopted in **Iron Gangs**? It is this. The delinquents are employed in forming new roads, by cutting through mountains, blasting rocks, cutting the trees up by the roots, felling and burning off. They are attended by a Military Guard, night and day, to prevent escape; wear Irons upon both legs, and at night are locked up in small wooden houses, containing about a dozen sleeping places; escape is impossible; otherwise they live in huts surrounded by high paling, called stockades; they are never allowed after labour to come without the stockade under penalty of being shot; so complete is the confinement, that not half-a-dozen have escaped within the last two or three years; they labour from one hour after sunrise until eleven o'clock, then two hours to dinner and work until night; no supper. The triangles are constantly at hand to tie up any man neglecting work, or insolent. G.C. INGLETON *True Patriots All: or news from Early Australia—as told in a collection of broadsides* (1952) p. 160

> **1836** For the offences which come before the quarter sessions, the convicts are sentenced to **iron gangs**, to penal settlements, and to death. ... Iron gangs labor under heavy guards of soldiers in clearing tracts of land in the interior, all wearing gyves, proportioned in weight to their crimes. J.F. O'CONNELL *A Residence of Eleven Years in New Holland* p. 72

irons chains in which convicts were placed as a specific form of punishment and to prevent their escape. [This is the standard English sense, although clearly of great significance in the Australian convict context.]

Irons usually consisted of iron fetters around the ankles, of various weights depending on the severity of the punishment, and usually riveted in place so that they could not be easily removed.

> **1834** [Indulgences to the Port Macquarie men removed to Norfolk Island in July, 1830] Escapes being most commonly effected by Convicts first getting off their **Irons**, the Superintendent is personally to inspect and carefully Examine the Irons on each Prisoner before quitting the Stockade in the Morning, and on their return in the afternoon. *Historical Records of Australia* 1st series XVII p. 337

1838 The man was formerly a soldier: he had been sentenced to wear **irons** for life. Good conduct would have entitled him to have had the irons only on one leg, at the expiration of twelve months; but he had been concerned in a mutiny and had conducted himself improperly in other respects; his irons were therefore heavy, and attached to both legs. J. BACKHOUSE *A Narrative of a Visit to the Australian Colonies* pp. 262–3

K

King's stores the supplies of food and clothing that were rationed out to the convicts. [First recorded 1801.]

The government STORES coordinated the supply of food to the early settlers and convicts in the colonies, and in times of hardship even those who were self-sufficient otherwise might need to turn to the government stores. The King's stores also supplied tools and equipment, and purchased much of the produce of private farms, and were thus central to the early colonial economy. Items from the King's stores were often marked with the BROAD ARROW to identify something as government property.

1819 A prisoner for his labor receives 7lbs of beef, and 7lbs. of flour from the **King's stores**, and an overseer, half as much more as a common man. J. SLATER *Description of Sydney* p. 8

1852 The first expiree, James Rouse, who was established (1790) as a settler, was industrious and successful. Phillip, anxious to test the competence of the land to sustain a cultivator, cleared two acres for this man, erected his hut, and supplied him with food. Fifteen months after, he relinquished his claim on the **King's stores**, and received thirty acres of land, in reward for his diligence. It thus became common to offer similar facilities to expiree convicts, but generally in vain. J. WEST *The History of Tasmania* vol. 2 pp. 143–4

L

lag 1 *verb* to transport (a convict) from Britain to a penal settlement in Australia; to sentence (a criminal) to a term of imprisonment. [The term is recorded in James Hardy Vaux's vocabulary of the flash language written in Australia in 1812 and published in London in 1819 (see FLASH). In 1811 it is also recorded in *Lexicon Balatronicum* (London). It probably derives from *lag* in the sense 'to carry off; steal' (first recorded in the late sixteenth century, although the origin of the term is unknown).]

1812 LAG, to transport for seven years or upwards. J.H. VAUX *Memoirs* (1964) vol. 2 p. 185

1873 In New South Wales, with its enormous area, and in the absence of any sea barriers by which convicts could be hemmed in, the traveller does not at present hear much about convicts. They have wandered away whither they would. Now and then good-natured reference is made in regard to some lady or gentleman to the fact that her or his father was '**lagged**,' and occasionally up in the bush a shepherd may be found who will own to the soft impeachment of having lagged himself,—though always for some offence which is supposed to have in it more of nobility than depravity. But in Tasmania the records are recent, fresh, and ever present. There is still felt the necessity of adhering to the social rule that no convict, whatever may have been his success, shall be received into society. A. TROLLOPE *Australia and New Zealand* vol. 2 p. 21

2 *noun* a convict who has been transported to a penal settlement in Australia; any convict. [From LAG *verb*. The noun is first recorded in Francis Grose *A Classical Dictionary of the Vulgar Tongue* (1785). It also appears in James Hardy Vaux's vocabulary of the flash language written in Australia in 1812 and published in London in 1819 (see FLASH).]

1812 LAG, a convict under sentence of transportation. J.H. VAUX *Memoirs* (1964) vol. 2 p. 185

1845 The labouring population may be divided into two classes, the old hands and emigrants. The old hands are men who, having been formerly convicts, (or *lags* as they are generally termed,) have become free by the expiration of their sentences. C. GRIFFITHS *Present State and Prospects of the Port Phillip District* pp. 76–7

1852 We had about twenty-five cabin passengers, and a very motley assemblage we formed. There were civil and military and clerical, medical and legal and mechanical gentlemen, Jews and Gentiles, merchants and squatters. As for the 'civil condition' (as the Census papers call it) of the guests at the cuddy-table, there was really every gradation of the bond and the free, short of prisoners under actual restraint. One or two of them had '**lag**' so indelibly written on their hardened lineaments, that opulent as they might now be, it seemed monstrous that they should be permitted to jostle gentlemen of character on equal terms. G.C. MUNDY *Our Antipodes* vol. 3 p. 259

lagging a term of penal servitude; a sentence or term of imprisonment.

1857 We were then within the boundary of Hexham township, and in sight of the half-way house, at which we shortly after arrived. Mr. Smith, the owner of the place, and two brawny shoemakers with the leather aprons on, came out to receive us. These men had committed crimes, and were doing their **lagging** with Mr. Smith, who appeared to be a very humane man, and they seemed to have easy time of it. J. ASKEW *A Voyage to Australia and New Zealand* p. 297

lags' land Australia.

'Lags' land' was a term used to refer to the penal colonies or to Australia generally (literally, the land of LAGS). It appeared late in the convict period (the earliest citation is 1858), and indicates how the colonies' image was intimately tied to their being places established as settlements for convicts, a reputation difficult to overcome.

1858 What right have such as you to come here, to this island—to our country—to the **lags'-land**? What right have you, puppified, sneaking crawlers, to come to this 'ere place, as we've made a country of by sweat and labour, to rob us of our gold? 'A. PENDRAGON' (G. Isaacs) *The Queen of the South* p. 76

lash a stroke with a whip as a form of punishment; (as **the lash**) the punishment of flogging. See FLOGGING.

1822 The extent of punishments inflicted by the magistrates at Hobart Town appears to have varied greatly. In the years 1810 and 1811 as many as 500 **lashes** have been inflicted; but since the commencement of the year 1816, they have very rarely exceeded 100, and have generally been limited to 50. J.T. BIGGE *Report of the Commissioner of Inquiry into the State of the Colony of New South Wales*, p. 112

1827 The *veteran convict* will point out to the *rogue of yesterday* the tree, still green and flourishing near the house of the naval officer, dedicated in older times to the office of a triangle, under whose boughs many thousand **lashes** have been inflicted upon well-deserving backs. P. CUNNINGHAM *Two Years in New South Wales* vol. 1 p. 71

1845 The governor would order **the lash** at the rate of five hundred, six hundred or eight hundred; and if the men could have stood it they would have had more. I knew a man hung there and then for stealing a few biscuits, and another for stealing a duck frock. A man was condemned—no time—take him to the tree, and hang him. The overseers were allowed to flog the men in the fields. Often have men been taken from the gang, had fifty, and sent back to work. G.C. INGLETON *True Patriots All: or news from Early Australia—as told in a collection of broadsides* (1952) p. 240

leave In the phrase **on leave** in possession of a ticket of leave. See TICKET OF LEAVE. [First recorded 1811.]

1811 Persons whose Sentences of Transportation are expired, will be required to produce their Certificates; those who have received Emancipations or Pardons will be required to produce them, as will also those who are off the Store **on leave**, be required to produce their Tickets of Leave. *Sydney Gazette* 19 Jan.

1840 At times considerable fidelity and courage has been shown by individuals among them. A government servant having run away from his employer, was met by a native who stood high in favour with this employer. He stopped the man, and asked where he was going? The runaway telling him he was travelling on a message, the native, in a business-like manner, demanded a sight of the dingo (dog), meaning the unicorn in the royal arms of the passport, which every convict **on leave** carries. This was a complete set down; the man shewed a piece of paper, but no dingo was there, when the native gained the day, by carrying the man back to his master. A. RUSSELL *A Tour Through the Australian Colonies* pp. 184–5

leg-iron a shackle or fetter for the leg. [Used elsewhere (recorded 1861) but recorded earliest in Australia (1849).]

The term IRONS was the most common term to refer to the iron bands placed on convicts as a form of punishment and to prevent escape, but the word 'leg-iron' referred specifically to the part of the CHAINS that consisted of the band of iron placed around a convict's ankle. Leg-irons varied in weight, according to the severity of the punishment.

1849 Mile after mile in terror, day after day in hunger, night after night in damp, cold, and solitude—such was Beck's journey there; such was his journey back. ... The gaol, the dock, and the penal settlement, danced before his eyes; the clank of the **leg-iron**, the hiss of the scourger and the yell of the scourged sounded in his ears. A. HARRIS *The Emigrant Family* (1967) p. 310

legitimacy the fact of being sanctioned or authorised by law. [First recorded in an Australian convict context in 1827.]

The term 'legitimacy' gained a specific meaning within the Australian convict system. It referred to the notion of coming to Australia due to 'legal' reasons, that is coming under sentence as a convict. It thus took on ironic or negative connotations.

> **1827** *Legitimacy*, a colonial term for designating the *cause* of the emigration of a certain portion of our population; i.e. having *legal* reasons for making the voyage. P. CUNNINGHAM *Two Years in New South Wales* vol. 1 p. 16

> **1836 Legitimacy**, in all other parts of the world a coveted qualification, is in New Holland a term of reproach. J.F. O'CONNELL *A Residence of Eleven Years in New Holland* p. 34

legitimate a person who came to Australia as a convict. [First recorded 1827.]

A convict had legal reasons for coming to Australia (he or she had been sentenced by the law to transportation), and was therefore legitimate in the sense of conforming to, or acting under, the law. This slang term is ironic in its usage— implying that the state of being a convict was 'legal' rather than 'criminal'.

> **1827** We have, as I said before, first the *Sterling* and *Currency*, or English and Colonial born, the latter bearing also the name of *corn stalks* (Indian corn), from the way in which they shoot up. This is the first grand division. Next, we have the *legitimates*, or *cross-breds*, namely, such as have *legal* reasons for visiting this colony; and the *illegitimates*, or such as are free from that stigma. P. CUNNINGHAM *Two Years in New South Wales* vol. 2 p. 116

> **1829** But between the free emigrants and those who are born in the colony, that unity which is so essential to the prosperity of a community, especially of one that has its land to reclaim from a state of nature, and all the machinery of its domestic economy to put in motion, there are animosities arising from other causes. One of these is the application of generic names. Those who are born in the colony are called *Currency*, and those of English or European birth, and who have not found their way there in such a manner as to entitle them to the cant name of *Legitimates*, are called *Sterling*. It happened, too, that when some ideal officer, who had more pretensions to humour than title to understanding, imposed those names, the currency of the country was depreciated below the value of sterling money. The names, *Currency* and *Sterling* thus became at once badges of inferiority and superiority, and tended to set the two classes of the people against each other. R. MUDIE *The Picture of Australia* p. 355

lend to give to another the temporary use of the labour of a convict in one's charge. [First recorded in the Australian convict context in 1827.]

Masters were given much authority over the convicts assigned to their care, and might lend them to work on someone else's property. The government could also choose to lend a convict to an employer for short periods for particular work (for example, during harvest time), which was more temporary an arrangement than ASSIGNMENT, and also meant that the government retained power over the convict.

> **1827** The Government stands in a similar relation (to say the least) towards a prisoner, as a guardian towards a minor. In the latter case, the guardian may send the minor to a master, in any way or place he shall think proper for his improvement and advantage, and bind him to such master, in the most secure manner, till he comes of age; but, should the master treat the minor improperly, the same guardian has the power of cancelling the agreement, and withdrawing his ward. In the same *ratio*, the Government can either **lend** or assign the prisoner to a master; and, if that prisoner be not well treated, and can prove his complaint to be just and reasonable, the Crown has, and must have, the power of withdrawing him as a master. We argue, further, that, as the law now stands, the Government never ceases to have a control over the prisoners of the Crown. *Tasmanian* (Hobart) 18 Oct. p. 2

> **1837** General Darling had reclaimed a convict servant who had been ***lent***, not assigned, to a free emigrant in Sydney. The emigrant refused to give up the convict, on the ground that his having been lent was equivalent to his having been assigned, and that the governor had no power to withdraw or recall from any emigrant or settler a convict servant who had once been assigned to him. J. MUDIE *The Felonry of New South Wales* p. 54

> **1838** CONVICT MECHANICS MAY BE LENT, AND LABOURERS DURING HARVEST. —Convicts, being assigned as mechanics, may be lent by one master to another in the same district, for any period not exceeding three months. *Tegg's New South Wales Pocket Almanack* pp. 86–7

life a sentence of transportation to Australia and penal servitude for life; imprisonment for life. [Used elsewhere (recorded 1903) but used much earlier in Australia (first recorded 1833).]

Obviously, this was the most severe sentence one could receive short of execution. Those sentenced to life (see LIFERS) often had their sentences reduced, or were given a pardon such as a TICKET OF LEAVE, if they behaved well in the colonies. About a quarter of prisoners sentenced to transportation received a life sentence.

1833 That, the number of years, for a seven, fourteen, or **life** convict, to serve in the Gangs, before he can get his ticket-of-leave, to be mentioned, and the ticket-of-leave always to be granted, except the man should have conducted himself incorrectly, but his additional period to serve, to be defined. T. BANNISTER *A Letter on Colonial Labour* p. 12

1843 [quoting Mr Wixon in court] I learned in court, that my sentence is *fourteen years* after arrival in V.D.L.—Mr. Watson's is '**life**,' and the others are yet as ignorant as ever of what time they are *ordered, (not sentenced)* for. B. WAIT *Letters from Van Dieman's Land* p. 230.

lifer a person sentenced to transportation to Australia and penal servitude for life; a person sentenced to life imprisonment. [Used elsewhere (recorded 1832) but used earlier in Australia (first recorded 1827).]

In spite of the sentence, a lifer in the colonies had opportunities to gain freedom. Good behaviour and the need to lessen the burden on the public purse led to numerous mechanisms that gave lifers at least partial freedom, including PROBATION, PARDONS, and TICKETS OF LEAVE. A well-behaved lifer might therefore eventually achieve some form of freedom.

1827 As the law, affecting male Prisoners of the Crown, now stands, '**lifers**,' have either a very remote, or as it regards 999 out of every thousand of them, no chance whatever of being permitted to marry. We would therefore press upon Government the necessity of an early emendation of the laws on this behalf. *Sydney Monitor* 29 Oct. p. 728

1843 Perhaps you do not know that I have been in the colony for ten years. I was a **lifer**. It's bad that; better hang a man at once than punish him for life; there ought to be a prospect of an end to suffering; then the man can look forward to something; he would have hope left. C. ROWCROFT *Tales of the Colonies* (1858) p. 216

1847 [Statement no. 13 by J. S—, Cork 19 Feb 1846] As a token, I give you a letter received from my wife. As another token, my wife, her sister, and husband came to see me when I received sentence of death, for taking fire-arms from a constable in a tithe row. ... I was sent here as a *lifer*. I am now on my Ticket—not yet received my emancipation. MRS C. CHISHOLM *Emigration and Transportation* p. 38

loan gang a party of skilled convicts, artisans, or CONVICT MECHANICS, who were employed on public or GOVERNMENT WORKS, but might be lent to settlers for work on private property. [First recorded 1833.]

The evidence suggests that they were principally put to work for and by government officers, a practice that settlers objected to, as the labour of these skilled convicts cost nothing for government officers.

1835 Another great evil complained of loudly by the Colonists is, the manner in which the mechanics are employed. There is what is termed 'the **loan gang**,' consisting of a parcel of men, the best workmen in the Colony; these men it is understood, are lent on loan to the settlers generally, but this is not the case, these men are for the greater part employed by Government Officers, or men friendly with the chief authorities—such individuals, by the aid of this loan gang, are enabled to build fine palaces, and make fine improvements, with scarcely any cost to themselves. H. MELVILLE *The History of the Island of Van Diemen's Land* pp. 258–9

1852 The artizan, when not adapted for public works, was placed in the **loan gang**, and lent from time to time, chiefly to the officers of government, or to such settlers as were deemed worthy of official patronage. … Master trades-men complained, that their callings were followed by captains and lieutenants, whose journeymen were the prisoners of the crown, and who, beside the emol-uments of office, engrossed the profits of smiths and carpenters—of tailors and shoemakers. Those settlers, excluded from participation in the *loan* labor, denounced the venal partiality of its distribution. Long lists were published of workmen allotted to the relatives and confidants of the Governor, to display his unwearied nepotism. J. WEST *The History of Tasmania* vol. 2 p. 240

lock-up a place where a convict was detained if criminal behaviour had been alleged or had occurred. Also **lock-up house**. [In standard English this is a short-ened form of *lock-up house* 'a house or room for the detention (usually temporary) of offenders'. First recorded 1822.]

Lock-ups were important in colonial society where settlers were concerned about criminal behaviour among the convict population and wanted to ensure that there was adequate control of convicts. Should they misbehave or commit criminal offences, a convict would be taken to the lock-up until further action was taken.

1822 The prices of a weekly lodging in Hobart Town to a convict was esti-mated, in March 1820, at five shillings, and for this sum he is admitted to live and sleep in the house; but there are many who take up their abode in the back part of it, called the skilling, for which the labour of providing wood and water is taken as a payment. As soon as they are assigned to the working gangs after debarkation from the ships, they are allowed to look for lodgings where they please, and if they are not able to find them, the chief constable is directed to billet them for a short period on the houses of other prisoners, or they are lodged in a room in the gaol, or in the **lock-up house**. J.T. BIGGE *Report of the Commissioner of Inquiry into the State of the Colony of New South Wales* p. 42

1847 There is a lieutenant (a mere boy), who is now magistrate over a gang that are making a road not three miles from the farm where I stop. Whenever this lad means to send a man to the **lock-up** for the night, he makes the lock-up keeper start three or four buckets of water over the floor, under pretence of keeping it free from vermin, but really for the purpose of tormenting the culprit by compelling him to walk about all night and then he will have the poor wretch tied up to the triangles first thing in the morning, before breakfast. This I know to be true because I have it from the lock-up keeper himself. A. HARRIS *Settlers and Convicts* (1953) p. 12

long-sentence(d) man a convict who was serving a fourteen-year sentence or a life sentence. See FOURTEEN YEARS' MAN, LIFE, LIFER. [First recorded 1840.]

Half of all convicts had a seven-year sentence, the other half a long sentence. But sentences were likely to be reduced through the system of pardons and tickets of leave, unless a convict reoffended or did not behave well—such convicts might have their sentences lengthened as a form of punishment.

1875 [From Governor Weld's Report to Earl of Canarvon 1874] It has been for me to preside over the latter stages of the existence of the Imperial convict establishment in Western Australia. ... Although the residue of convicts are, many of them, men of the doubly reconvicted class and **long-sentence men**, discipline is well kept, serious prison offences are rare, the health of the men is excellent, whilst severe punishments are seldom needful. J. Forrest *Explorations in Australia* p. 334

M

magpie (of convict clothing) black and yellow. Often used as a noun. [First recorded 1841.]

The clothing in which convicts were dressed, generally yellow and black cloth, led to the use of the tag 'magpie' (a black and white bird) to describe convict clothing. Those dressed in straight yellow were dubbed CANARIES. As the citation evidence suggests, magpie uniforms were ascribed to prisoners as a marker of their disgrace. Better behaved convicts might graduate to uniforms of grey. However, it should be noted that convict uniforms were never standard issue in the colonies—convicts on first arrival brought their own clothes or were issued SLOPS. Various governors did attempt to introduce uniforms, especially in an attempt to distinguish the convicts from the rest of the population, and those in government work gangs and in penal settlements were among those who wore uniforms. Some uniforms were emblazoned with the BROAD ARROW indicating that the wearer was government property. Convicts on ASSIGNMENT had their clothing issued to them by their employer. The Australian colonies generally had no ordered system of appearance for convicts, and thus they were not always distinguishable from the rest of the population—a source of some anxiety for the free settlers.

1843 Hobarttown lies spread over a square mile of rising ground, and is well located for business, and romantic views. It is beautifully laid out, with streets intersecting at right angles, and from its center, may be had a full view of the river, harbor, shipping and docks, with the bustle of men and drays continually engaged upon them, enlivening the scene, and giving it an important appearance. But, alas! here to darken the picture, near the dock, you cannot but observe a mass of beings, dressed in **magpie** (black and yellow) carting the earth away to the water's edge, to form new docks and move extended warehouses. In one of the streets near by, you also observe another of those magpie companies, sitting upon piles of small stone with a small hammer in the hand, breaking them for macadamizing the streets. B. WAIT *Letters from Van Dieman's Land* p. 350

1846 After calling me ill names, and venting his spleen and rage, as he afterwards did to me personally, he told them that if they followed my vicious example, and absconded, they would be shot down without quarter; as he had given such orders to *his* soldiers. ... He then ordered them to be dressed in ***magpie*** (as a punishment for OUR absconding,) and removed to Green Ponds, a distance of only six miles. L.W. MILLER *Notes of an Exile to Van Dieman's Land* p. 349

1850 The day after the capture of our friends, we were ordered to be dressed in '**magpie**' and changed to another station, where were a number of soldiers stationed. This 'magpie' suit is intended for chain gangs and doubly convicted prisoners, and is ordered by government as a badge of the deepest disgrace. It is composed of black and yellow cloth, of the same quality as the grey. The left side of the front part of the body, with the front of the left arm and leg, together with the right side of the back part of the body were yellow, whilst the remainder was black. The suits were all of a size, or with but a slight variation, and were distributed to us as we stood in rank, without regard to their fitting our persons. The consequence was, we got all sorts of fits. W. GATES *Recollections of Life in Van Dieman's Land* p. 112

mark a point or unit of credit (or penalty) counting towards a total which may work towards the remission of a convict's sentence (or, in the case of a penalty, to its increase). [First recorded 1839.]

Convicts had marks ascribed to them, usually recorded in books, that could count as credit or discredit in their sentence. Good marks might help gain freedom for a convict; bad marks might lead to further punishment. Such a system of marks was used in several places, including Norfolk Island, in determining how convicts were to be treated and when they should receive rewards and punishments. Captain Alexander Maconochie instituted a mark system on Norfolk Island in 1840 (until 1844, when he was removed from the island) that used marks as a form of wages that could be used towards food and clothing, or could be lost through fines for bad behaviour.

1843 [Sir George Gipps to Lord Stanley, concerning Norfolk Island] The 'New Hands' appeared nearly as anxious as the 'Old' to get off the Island; and when I explained to them that, owing to the scarcity of employment in Van Diemen's Land, their condition probably would not be improved by being removed to it; they replied, 'perhaps not'; but that, having acquired the number of **Marks**, which they had looked upon as the price of their removal, they wished to get away from the place where they had seen so many of their comrades die; that they would rather go to New South Wales than to Van Diemen's Land; but that they would go anywhere rather than remain at Norfolk Island. *Historical Records of Australia* 1st series XXII p. 619

1845 But how remove the taint of Slavery from Transportation, and yet retain the element of punishment in it? For this purpose I propose that a form of *Wages* (**marks**) be introduced into all our Penal Establishments, whether settlements apart from free communities, or working parties in them—that an accumulation of these, proportioned to each man's crime or sentence, and over and above all lost by expense or misconduct, be the only terms on which he can procure his discharge—that he earn a fair proportion of them from day to day, according to his exertions, but be charged in them, at the same time, for every supply furnished him, whether of food or clothing—that if he is idle the cost of his maintenance shall thus go against his liberty—that if he is ill-conducted he shall in like manner be fined in proportionate amounts of progress already made towards it; and that thus, by no means possible, except by sustained exertion and good conduct combined, will he ever obtain his liberation. A. MACONOCHIE *On the Management of Transported Criminals* p. 2

mark system a system of using units of credit (or penalty) in calculating the length of a convict's sentence. See MARK. [First recorded 1862.]

1862 The experiments which were made on Norfolk Island and elsewhere, of the **Mark System**, which was a part of Captain Maconochie's scheme, were considered by some who expected more than was reasonable, to be unsuccessful, and seem to have thrown upon his humane principles a shade of discredit which they did not deserve. He continued his exertions for the amelioration of Penal Discipline until his death, which took place in 1861. BACKHOUSE & TYLOR *Life and Labours of George Washington Walker* pp. 272–3

master the person (usually a free settler) to whom a convict was ASSIGNED as a servant. [First recorded 1796.]

In contrast to the slave system, which many opponents of the convict system compared it to, masters did not own their convicts. While a master had considerable latitude in the treatment of his convicts, there were restrictions on what he could and could not do. For example, a master could not flog his convict servant—he had to send him to a magistrate who would order the punishment and it would be carried out by a person in the employ of the government. Masters wanted the best work out of their convicts, and abuse of the system (such as physical punishment, unreasonable demands for work, etc.), while it did occur, was limited by the need to extract the most use out of convicts. A system that consisted of both rewards and punishments was thus necessary. In general, the evidence suggests that most masters treated their convict servants fairly.

1838 As the lot of a slave depends upon the character of his **master**, as the condition of a convict depends upon the temper and disposition of the settler to whom he is assigned. On this account Sir George Arthur, late Governor of Van Diemen's Land, likened the convict to a slave, and described him 'as deprived of liberty, exposed to all the caprice of the family to whose service he may happen to be assigned, and subject to the most summary laws;' 'his condition (said Sir George) in no respect differs from that of a slave, except that his master cannot apply corporal punishment by his own hands, or those of his overseer, and has a property in him for a limited period.' W. MOLESWORTH *Report from the Select Committee of the House of Commons on Transportation* p. 10

1838 The relation between **masters** and servants in these Colonies is at present productive of almost unmixed evil to all concerned,—and the system of discipline by which it is supported is in no way morally more deleterious than by its complete indifference to *personal* reform as an ultimate object, and its consequent sacrifice at all times of moral and improving principle to temporary expediency. This not only lowers the standard of moral worth generally, but gives masters an indifference for the moral improvement of their servants, provided they can make them answer their immediate purposes. Under an opposite system, however, an opposite effect might be implicitly relied on. Did masters see the Government make personal reform its *chief* object, even the most indifferent of them would soon seek to share in so good a work. A. MACONOCHIE *Thoughts on Convict Management* pp. 123–4

mess a division of a party or group of convicts, primarily for the provision of meals. [A *mess* is a company of people eating together, originally groups of usually four people at a banquet. This was taken over into army and navy usage, meaning each of the several parties into which a regiment or ship's company is systematically divided, the members of each party taking their meals together. The convict use, first recorded in 1822, is a transfer from the army and navy usage.]

The convicts were divided into messes on the transport ships and groups of convicts were referred to as 'messes' once in the colonies, with relation to the organisation of accommodation and the taking of meals. The term was not used in reference to the organisation of the convicts' work.

1822 As a further check, however, upon any fraudulent change in the issue of provisions that may escape the attention of the surgeon superintendent, it will be found useful to establish a regulation, that one person from each of the **messes**, into which the convicts are distributed, should be required to attend in rotation at the delivery and weighing of the provisions. J.T. BIGGE *Report of the Commissioner of Inquiry into the State of the Colony of New South Wales* p. 2

1822   The ground floor of the principal building [of the carters' barracks] contains, on one side of the entrance, a large mess-room, at which 162 persons can be seated, in **messes** of six. J.T. BIGGE *Report of the Commissioner of Inquiry into the State of the Colony of New South Wales* p. 23

mistress the female counterpart to a MASTER. [First recorded 1813.]
In the Australian colonies, a convict could be assigned to a woman, although this was rarer than being assigned to a master. 'Mistress' could also refer to the wife of a master.

1843   Unfortunately, the suspension or deprivation of a ticket of leave is seldom caused but by some fortuitous circumstance which brings the prisoner holding this indulgence under the eye of the authorities; and, though instances of tickets being cancelled may be rare, I look on this as no test of the conduct of the class. They are less under control than any other class in the colony, and their misdemeanours in many cases not coming under the eye of domestic masters or **mistresses**, they escape the supervision of the Police. J. FRANKLIN *Confidential Despatch* pp. 15–16

1856   No female convict was allowed to be in the streets after dusk without her master or **mistress**. No such lady could, by the law of 1829, be permitted to marry until she had been in service one year, and given proofs of good behaviour. J. BONWICK *The Bushrangers: Illustrating the early days of Van Diemen's Land* p. 9

model denoting a prisoner who came from a model prison, especially Pentonville in London.

1845   Forgery is become of common occurrence in Melbourne—the last offender was one of the recently arrived '**model**' pets. On taking him in custody for a forgery, he was endeavouring to pass; no less than 3 forged orders were found on him, and 10 or 12 blank cheques, 'raw material for future manufacture.' *Parramatta Chronicle and Cumberland General Advertiser* 27 Dec. p. 4

muster 1 *noun* a routine assembling of convicts in order to ascertain that all are present.
[In standard English from the fifteenth century *muster* meant 'an assembly of soldiers, sailors, etc., for inspection, ascertainment or verification of numbers, exercise, display, etc.' In the early colony this sense was transferred to similar assemblies of convicts, and then to an assembly of all of the population of an area.

Such musters were usually a way of locating, identifying, and monitoring the whereabouts and activities of convicts. By the mid-nineteeenth century there was a further transfer of meaning, and *muster* was used to describe 'the gathering together of (frequently widely dispersed) livestock in one place for the purpose of branding, counting, etc.' In the convict sense it is first recorded in 1788.]

1804 [Governor King to Lord Hobart] Being anxious to take the last half-yearly **muster** before the Albion's departure, I have the honour to transmit the result of the free people and convicts' muster, and of every person who is not a settler or landholder; also the general muster of the settlers and landholders, with the quantity of ground they hold and stock, &c., throughout these settlements. *Historical Records of Australia* 1st series V p. 9

1843 The muskets were wrenched from the soldiers, and these, with their cartouch boxes, in each of which we found twenty rounds of ball-cartridge, furnished us with arms. We bound and gagged the soldiers as we had done the overseers, so that you see we accomplished our purpose without taking life; not that we should have hesitated to sacrifice them all, had it been necessary. … The next thing to be done was to get rid of our chains, for there was no time to be lost, as we knew that if we were not present at **muster**, the officer would send to look after us. C. ROWCROFT *Tales of the Colonies* pp. 219–20

2 *verb* to assemble (convicts) for counting, inspecting, etc.

1803 Every Prisoner Victualled from the Public Stores at Sydney will be **Mustered** at Government House, on Friday Morning next, the 8th Inst. at Nine o'clock. Officers, Settlers, and Others having Prisoners victualled by the Crown, who are employed in their domestic business, or on their Farms, will send Lists to the Secretary's Office before Thursday next. *Sydney Gazette* 3 July p. 1

1835 If a prisoner's good behaviour has entitled him to a ticket-of-leave, and his continued good behaviour justifies the Government in permitting him to enjoy the privileges of it, in God's name let him not be disturbed. The unhappy circumstances of many a ticket-of-leave man is unknown to the public—his dealings and connection with others in business is correct and upright—and while it is so, and while he traffics, and pursues his calling with honesty, let his next door neighbour, if so it be, remain in ignorance of it. **Muster** the men who justly enjoy tickets-of-leave, every Sunday morning, and march them to the church as the chain gangs are marched, and the indulgence will lose its virtue. It will, in fact, cease to be an indulgence. The holders may as well be wholly disgraced, as in part—and may as honestly be made members of the chain gangs at once, as to be shewn up every Sunday morning in military array. *Cornwall Chronicle* (Launceston) 20 June p. 1

muster bell a bell rung to summon convicts to an assembly. [First recorded 1846.]

1846 At half past four o'clock in the morning the bell rang for '*turn out*,' and there was a terrible rattling of nuisance-tubs, kids, pannakins, &c., until the breakfast hour was over. ... At six o'clock the **muster bell** rang, and about twelve hundred men answered to their names, took their places in their respective gangs, and under the charge of overseers marched out of the barracks to their daily labor. L.W. MILLER *Notes of an Exile to Van Dieman's Land* p. 263

muster book a register of the population of a colony; a register of the names etc. of convicts. [First recorded 1826.]

1822 I was not able to make a comparison of the number of convicts and their offences in any years preceding 1819, as I found on referring to the **muster-books**, that the number of convicts not victualled in each district, or rather those assigned to settlers, were not distinguished, but that they were included under the general head of 'persons not victualled,' and I was not able to learn their precise numbers from any other source. J.T. BIGGE *Report of the Commissioner of Inquiry into the State of the Colony of New South Wales* p. 99

muster ground a place where convicts were assembled to be counted, inspected, etc.

1848 The whole gang, except those at the out-huts, hear prayers read on the **muster-ground** morning and evening, before going to and after returning from work. The Protestants and Roman Catholics are attended by the religious instructor and catechist respectively. J. SYME *Nine Years in Van Diemen's Land* p. 277

muster master an official responsible for keeping a MUSTER-ROLL. [First recorded 1827.]

1830 [Mr F.A. Hely to Colonial Secretary Macleay] His Excellency is doubtless aware that, at Hobart Town, Van Diemen's Land, where the Police and Convict Departments cannot have more than one fourth of the business, which the corresponding Departments in this Colony have to perform, there is, besides a Superintendent of Police and a Superintendent of Convicts, an Officer called the '**Muster Master**', who is especially charged with all details connected with temporary remissions of the Sentences of Convicts, Records of Delinquincies, Musters of Ticket of Leave holders, etc., etc. *Historical Records of Australia* 1st series XV p. 766

muster roll a register of convicts. [First recorded 1802.]

1822 The muster and inspection of the convicts landed in Van Dieman's Land, is conducted nearly on the same principles as that which has just been described; but since the year 1817, a detailed description of the persons of the convicts has been made by the magistrate of police of Hobart Town, and kept in his office as a future guide to the identity of their persons, either on application for passes, tickets of leave or pardon. The lieutenant-governor's secretary proceeds on board the convict ships, attended by the lieutenant-governor's clerk, and makes a list or **muster roll** of the convicts, describing the number, name, time and place of trial, their sentences, age, native place, trade, description of person and character. This muster roll is derived from an actual muster of the convicts, checked and compared with their state and appearance after the voyage, but the inquiries respecting complaints are not so particular as those at Sydney, nor is any note made of them at the end of the muster roll. J.T. BIGGE *Report of the Commissioner of Inquiry into the State of the Colony of New South Wales* p. 15

1848 Another attempt to escape was made by three men who excavated a deep hole in the ground adjoining a sewer which emptied itself into the river. This they did by slow degrees during the hours of relaxation from their work, and when unobserved. Having hollowed out a hiding-place sufficient in extent to admit of containing the three, they one evening, prior to muster, concealed themselves in it, and awaited anxiously the success of their ingenuity. When the **muster-roll** was called at five o'clock, the three absentees were of course not forthcoming, and a general search ensued, but without success. C. COZENS *Adventures of a Guardsman* p. 255

muster station the office in which a MUSTER ROLL is kept. [First recorded 1820.]

1820 His Excellency's instructions, as to the holding of these Musters, being very strict in Regard to their being rendered as full and complete as possible, it is ordered and directed, for the Purpose of effecting the desired Object, that all Persons, of whatever Description herein enumerated, shall give their personal Attendance accordingly, at the Times and Places herein assigned for their Musters. ... It is further ordered and directed, that the Clerk of the General Muster do furnish to the Principal or Senior Magistrate at each **Muster Station**, a suitable Book and Form for the taking [of] the said Musters. *Sydney Gazette* 16 Sept. p. 2

N

new chum a prisoner who was newly arrived or admitted to a transport ship, gaol, or hulk. See also NEW HAND. [The term *new chum* appears only in Australian sources, though its earliest appearance in Vaux (see 1812 citation and FLASH) suggests that it may have been current in contemporary London underworld contexts. By the late 1820s the term was being used to describe any recently arrived immigrant, and by the 1850s it was used to mean 'novice; one inexperienced in a particular activity, occupation, etc.']

As made clear in the citation evidence, a new chum was particularly vulnerable to being taken advantage of by the older and more experienced prisoners, also known as OLD HANDS.

1812 CHUM: A fellow prisoner in a jail, hulk, &c.; so there are ***new chums*** and *old chums*, as they happen to have been a short or a long time in confinement. J.H. VAUX *Memoirs* (1964) vol. 2 p. 232

1845 In about a fortnight from their arrival the prisoners on board were again mustered preparatory to their going on shore and received each a new suit of clothing, after which they were placed in boats, by divisions, and rowed to a spot of land near Fort Macquarie, where, being landed, they waited until all had arrived and then proceeded through a part of the public promenade known as the Domain, up to the Prisoners' Barracks, where they were placed in a back yard by themselves, and shortly afterwards again paraded. On their dismissal a host of the older prisoners insinuated themselves among them for the purpose of bargaining for clothes, trinkets or other property, and many a poor ***new chum***—the distinctive name bestowed upon them by the old hands—was deprived of all his little stock of comforts by the artifices of the others, who appeared to pique themselves in no small degree upon the dexterity with which they could thus *pick up* (rob) the unwary new-comers. J. TUCKER *Ralph Rashleigh* (1962) pp. 69–70

1846 When he had done, we found a convict overseer, of the name of Sawyer, waiting for us. His first salutation was, 'Now you bloody **new chum**—! I have you! I will run your legs off, and have a dozen flogged before night, into the bargain'. L.W. MILLER *Notes of an Exile to Van Dieman's Land* p. 328

new hand = NEW CHUM. [First recorded in a convict context in 1817.]

1835 Nothing is more dreaded by the men than Iron Gangs; as when their sentence is expired they have *all that time spent in irons to serve again*, as every sentence is now in addition to the original sentence. If a man is nearly due for his ticket of leave, and is flogged, he is put back for a certain time, unless for theft, and then he forfeits every indulgence. If an iron-gang man has served any number of years in the country, he must begin again; he is the same as a **new hand**; he has to wait the whole term of years before he receives any indulgence. G.C. INGLETON *True Patriots All: or news from Early Australia—as told in a collection of broadsides* (1952) p. 160

1843 [Sir George Gipps to Lord Stanley, concerning Norfolk Island] The only definite reason, which can be assigned for the existence during the last three years of a greater degree of sickness and mortality among the '**New Hands**' than among the 'Old' or Penal Prisoners is that, at the time of their arrival, Dysentery, though in a mild form, prevailed among the 'Old Hands'; that from the 'Old' it passed to the 'New' before the latter had become accustomed either to the Climate or the Diet of the Island; and that it subsequently became chronic among them. *Historical Records of Australia* 1st series XXII p. 618

night watch a party of police, usually convicts, who went on patrol during the night hours as a means of preventing crime. See also CONSTABLES, CONVICT CONSTABLES, and FELON POLICE. [This is the standard English sense, except that in colonial Australia such night watches were often made up of convict police. First recorded in an Australian context in 1793.]

1798 The convicts who were employed in making bricks, living in huts by themselves on the spot where their work was performed, were suspected of being the perpetrators of most of the offences committed at Sydney; and orders had been given, forbidding under pain of punishment, their being seen in town after sunset. These depradations continuing, however, a convict of the name of Harris presented to the judge-advocate a proposal for establishing a **night-watch**, to be selected from among the convicts, with authority to secure all persons of that description who should be found straggling from the huts at improper hours. D. COLLINS *An Account of the English Colony in New South Wales* vol. 1 p. 77

1827 Sydney is divided into six police districts, with a lock-up house and a **night-watch**, under the orders of a conductor, attached to each. P. CUNNING-HAM *Two Years in New South Wales* vol. 1 pp. 60–1

Norfolk Islander a person who is, or who has been, a convict sentenced to penal servitude on Norfolk Island.

Norfolk Island was discovered by James Cook in 1774, and settled as a penal colony by Lieutenant Philip Gidley King in February 1788. The settlement was closed in 1814 and all prisoners there were moved to Van Diemen's Land. The decision to reopen it as a place of secondary punishment where the worst criminals and reoffenders were sent was made in 1824, with the first people arriving in 1825. The name of Norfolk Island thus came to be associated with the worst aspects of the convict system—the most incorrigible and brutal convicts, and the most sadistic punishments. 'Norfolk Islanders' were seen to be the worst and most irredeemable of all convicts. Settlers in Van Diemen's Land strongly resented the sending of Norfolk Islanders to Van Diemen's Land after the closing of the Norfolk Island penal colony, and this added to the momentum of the ANTI-TRANSPORTATION movement. Norfolk Island was closed as a penal colony in 1853.

1842 NORFOLK ISLANDERS—The Superintendent of Police some time since issued an order that expirees from Norfolk Island shall be visited at their residences once a week at least, by the inspectors of the parishes in which they reside. In pursuance of this order, Inspector Ryan went on Sunday last to the house of one John Cave, a notorious fence, resident in Pitt-street. On his entrance, a man rushed from the house by the back door, and knowing his customers, Ryan endeavoured to follow, but was seized by Cave, who struggled with him until the man had fairly got off. The obstruction was fairly repeated on Ryan's attempting to go into a room in which he heard some other parties conversing. Cave was brought up before Mr. Windeyer, and, on referring to the books, it was found that he had removed from Market-street to Pitt-street without having registered his residence, which, according to the law respecting expirees, constitutes another offence. *Sydney Herald* 21 Apr. p. 3

Norfolk-Islandised (of a convict) degraded and brutalised by the conditions at the penal settlement on Norfolk Island. [First recorded 1840.]

1840 No longer are British convicts to be landed in New South Wales and Van Diemen's Land immediately on their arrival in the Southern Pacific, and placed in circumstances—those of assignment to a master—under which many criminals have been reformed; but they are to be carried to a mere 'penal settlement,' kept there until ***Norfolk-islandised***—that is, utterly degraded and hardened in depravity, so as to have 'the heart of the beast,' … and then they are to be taken to New South Wales and Van Diemen's Land, and there turned loose on the virtuous settlers who may have emigrated thither in the meanwhile. And this is called 'reform!' D. BURN *Vindication of Van Diemen's Land* p. 34

nut-brown a name applied to a convict. [The term probably derived from the deep tan that convicts who worked at public labour in the sun acquired, thus making them the colour nut-brown. First recorded 1834.]

1834 The 'NUT-BROWNS'—It is a common saying 'spare the rod and you spoil the child;' this nursery proverb is fully verified in the spoiled *innocents* of the Government gangs, y'clept by Humanitas the 'Nut-brown faces.' The 'worse than death' system of the Home Government, as pathetically expiated upon by some of our sympathetic contemporaries, strikes the traveller with *horror* when he beholds the chubby but unfortunately 'Nut-brown' countenances ever and anon looking out for something to prig, or other equally profitable amusement. *Sydney Herald* 20 Oct. p. 2

O

off the stores see STORE.

old hand a convict with long experience of life in a penal colony (as opposed to one newly arrived); an ex-convict. [*Old hand* appears in F. Grose's *Classical Dictionary of the Vulgar Tongue* (1785) in the sense of one who is 'knowing or expert in any business', and while this is now standard English, it is interesting that most of the early evidence for the term in the OED is from Australia and New Zealand. The convict sense is first recorded in 1826.]

In contrast to a NEW CHUM or NEW HAND, an old hand was a convict who had spent a length of time in the convict system and had much experience of convict life. 'An old hand' might also refer to a former convict. Old hands had considerable knowledge of the system and how to operate within it to their best advantage.

> **1837** Attempts at escape ... are now seldom made, and in the technical phrase the '**old hands** declare it is no use to chance it.' Nevertheless such is the irksomeness of restraint, an endeavour is yet occasionally made to escape from it. In the verandah of the Commandant's residence we observed about a dozen most wretched attempts at boats and canoes which had been seized at different times, and the makers apprehended. To risk oneself upon the water of even the smoothest pond, unless a man could swim, in one of these frail structures would be next to madness, but to venture out to sea in them, as they sometimes do must be the feat of madness or desperation itself. *Elliston's Hobart Town Almanack* pp. 97–8

> **1848** We are annoyed by some fierce jealousies and feuds between the Vandiemonians and Pentonvillains, and the two *castes* can never agree. The '**old hands**' denounce the others as 'Johnny Newcomes,' and believe that the road-gangs of Port Arthur are a far more honourable martyrdom than the cloisters of Pentonville. *Maitland Mercury* 30 Sept. p. 4

old lag a former convict or LAG. [See LAG. The combination *old lag* is first recorded in Vaux (see 1812 citation and FLASH).]

The term was a colloquial one, and more pejorative than other terms for ex-convicts, such as EMANCIPIST.

> **1812** OLD LAG, a man or woman who has been transported, is so called on returning home, by those who are acquainted with the secret. J.H. VAUX *Memoirs* (1964) vol. 2 p. 193

> **1853** We reached the station of a Mr. Ross at an early hour. Here some shearers, who were rather the worse of their early potations, were inclined to be troublesome. Captain Cadell turned one of them out of the fore cabin without ceremony; and, shortly after, three of these men, endeavoring to aggravate some of the crew whilst taking in fuel, and to prevent the natives from giving their assistance, received from them a well-merited chastisement, which, though to a looker-on it might appear unnecessarily severe, was yet a well-timed and useful result. Nothing but a rough and summary mode of proceeding would be effectual with such people, whose conduct might destroy the comfort of all decent classes of passengers. They were probably *ci devant* convicts, or, as they are here termed, '**old lags**.' A. KINLOCH *The Murray River* p. 19

on the stores see STORE.

overseer a person appointed, frequently from the convict body, to superintend the work of a party of convicts. [*Overseer* in the sense 'one who oversees or superintends a piece of work or a body of workers' is standard English since the sixteenth century. The Australian convict sense is first recorded in 1788.]

In colonial Australia an overseer supervised the working parties of convicts, or GANGS, that laboured on public works. There were also overseers who supervised large groups of convicts who worked on large private properties. Overseers were often convicts or ex-convicts themselves (see CONVICT OVERSEER), and were frequently open to bribery. In government works, supervision of overseers' behaviour was often lax and they were thus given a great deal of latitude that resulted in extremes of both harsh and lenient treatment.

> **1788** One of this description made his week's allowance of flour (eight pounds) into eighteen cakes, which he devoured at one meal; he was soon after taken speechless and senseless, and died the following day at the hospital, a loathsome putrid object. The obvious consequence of this want of economy was, that he who had three days to live, and nothing to live on, before the store would be open to supply his wants, must steal from those who had been more provident. Had a few persons been sent out who were not of the description of convicts, to have acted as **overseers**, or superintendants, regulations for their

internal economy, as well in the articles of clothing as provisions, might have been formed which would have prevented these evils … But overseers drawn from among themselves were found not to have that influence which was so absolutely necessary to carry any regulation into effect. D. COLLINS *An Account of the English Colony in New South Wales* vol. 1 p. 33

1838 Overseers, selected from among the first-class men, have the time of their sentence reduced, by every two years counting for three; but if they misconduct themselves, and be removed from office in consequence, they lose the benefit of the previously reduced time. Two of the overseers at Norfolk Island are free men. A number who are called Volunteer-overseers, are prisoners, of New South Wales, holding tickets-of-leave, who have volunteered to become overseers on Norfolk Island, for salaries from 1s. to 2s. 3d. a day, with the hope of obtaining free or conditional pardons, as a reward for the faithful discharge of their duty. J. BACKHOUSE *A Narrative of a Visit to the Australian Colonies* p. 263

P

paper man a convict who held a ticket of leave. [First recorded 1848.]

'Paper' referred to the document providing evidence of the convict's status. It appears to be a term that was mainly used in Tasmania. Convicts were given a TICKET OF LEAVE, which was a form of conditional PARDON, and as is clear from the citation evidence, this privilege could be revoked for bad behaviour.

> **1848** Peter Allen, free, charged with having been drunk, was fined 5s. James Pearson, t.l., ditto, but not ditto as to punishment, (being a '**paper man**,') he was ordered 3 months road-making. *Guardian* (Hobart) 25 Mar. p. 6

> **1851** Instances could be adduced, showing the contempt with which anything like a claim to exercise his right on the part of an unfortunate ticket holder is treated by magistrates and others. Among other illustrations one may be mentioned, as a specimen: the holder of a ticket-of-leave was fined £10 by the Longford Bench; he had the audacity to appeal; and, furthermore, to give the sapient justice notice of an action at law for false imprisonment; conceiving in conjunction with an eminent Solicitor, whose advice was taken on the occasion, that the Statute before mentioned gave him power to do so. But how did that right operate? The moment the magistrate ascertained what was intended, he had proceedings taken, and recommended the unlucky wight of a '**paper**' **man**, to have his indulgence revoked; and revoked it was—meanwhile the appeal was heard and quashed; costs being given the appellant by the Quarter Sessions. Of course his ticket of leave has been restored! No such thing! In vain has he applied for it, and in vain has he claimed it. *Guardian* (Hobart) 26 Apr. p. 2

parchment a certificate issued to a pardoned convict. [Specific use of *parchment* in the sense 'a document on parchment'. First recorded in a convict context in 1848.]

In the Australian colonies, the word 'parchment' was used to refer to the document that was issued to convicts when they received their pardon or freedom. Such documents allowed convicts to provide evidence of their free status should they need to.

> **1848** We are now in Hobart Town and at the office receiving our **parchments** or pardon. As I receive mine, I ask the clerk if it is customary to give a prisoner a pardon before or after receiving a sentence; says he—'how is it done in America?' Well, says I, I never was a prisoner there, so I could not say for certain, but I always supposed that a man must be sentenced before he can receive a pardon; if not, how is he to know what the pardon is for? O! says he—'I think you know what your pardon is for; if you don't, the government does, and that is enough'. R. MARSH *Seven Years of my Life: Or Narrative of a Patriot Exile* pp. 175–6

pardon a remission of a convict's sentence; a document certifying this. [Specific use of *pardon* in the sense 'remission of the legal consequences of a crime'. First recorded in a convict context in 1793.]

From 1790, governors were granted the power to remit prisoners' sentences, that is, to pardon them. The pardons varied in nature, generally being either CONDITIONAL or ABSOLUTE. Such pardons gave convicts partial or complete freedom, and made the convicts of far more use in the development of the Australian settlements and in saving the government money. Convicts with skills and enterprise were more useful free than not. Pardons were freely granted until 1812, when a Select Committee on Transportation indicated concern about the ease with which convicts were being pardoned and subsequently tried to set limits on this. In general, during Macquarie's governorship, pardons along with TICKETS OF LEAVE were freely granted, partly to get people off the government STORES and to let them work more usefully in colonial society. Technically, however, after the 1823 New South Wales Act the governor could only recommend, but not grant, pardons—the British government had to grant them. Pardons were integral to the CONVICT SYSTEM where rewards and punishments were an important means of ensuring its working.

> **1794** As an exception to this rule, however, must be mentioned those people to whom unconditional emancipation had been held out at the expiration of a certain period, if then considered as deserving of his Majesty's mercy as at the time of making the promise. In the hope of this reward they continued to conduct themselves without incurring the slightest censure; and one of them, Samuel Burt, was deemed, through a conscientious and rigid discharge of his duty, to have merited the **pardon** he looked up to. Accordingly, on the last day of the month he was declared absolutely free. D. COLLINS *An Account of the English Colony in New South Wales* vol. 1 pp. 341–2

1850 Friday I was at Oatland, where I saw my name gazetted for a free pardon. I was joined by a comrade, Riley Whitney, who was also one of the eleven. ... Soon I was on my way, footing it with Whitney to Hobart Town. ... We arrived at the town, a distance of fifty miles, at eleven o'clock in the night, well tired with our day's travel. Early the next morning we called at the police office for our '**Pardons.**' We had to pass through another searching examination, to ascertain whether we corresponded with the description on record. W. GATES *Recollections of Life in Van Dieman's Land* p. 191

Parkhurst boy (also **Parkhurst lad**) a juvenile who, having served part of a sentence in Parkhurst prison on the Isle of Wight, was sent to Australia or New Zealand between 1842 and 1852.

In 1838 Parkhurst Prison became the first penal establishment set up for the reformation of young people. It was hoped that the colonies would accept these juveniles as apprentices. The boys chosen had spent at least two years at Parkhurst and were sent to Western Australia as 'Government Juvenile Immigrants' and were placed as apprentices for two to five years with a conditional pardon. The scheme ended in 1849, although some more were sent in 1851. A similar scheme existed in New Zealand in 1842. A number of Parkhurst boys were also sent to Van Diemen's Land but went as ordinary convicts, to Point Puer, the penal establishment for boys.

1844 SWAN RIVER—John Gavin, one of the **Parkhurst boys**, has been tried and found guilty at the Supreme Court of this colony for the murder of a youth named George Pollard, son of a respectable settler on the Murray, to whom this Gavin was apprenticed. He subsequently confessed his crime, and stated that it was at first his intention to have murdered Mrs. Pollard, but that he was fearful of being apprehended by the young man, and therefore took the opportunity of despatching him. He was executed and died, apparently, penitent. *Parramatta Chronicle* 22 June p. 3

1852 The worst class of men, in their piebald dress, were separated from those in pepper-and-salt, (who are for hire by private individuals;) and these again are separated from a more juvenile class, the **Parkhurst lads**. G.C. MUNDY *Our Antipodes* vol. 3 p. 226

Parramatta = PARRAMATTA CLOTH. [First recorded 1826.]

1827 The government gangs of convicts, also, marching backwards and forwards from their work in single military file, and the solitary ones straggling here and there, with their white woollen **Paramatta** frocks and trowsers, or grey or yellow jackets with duck overalls, (the different styles of dress denoting the oldness or newness of their arrival,) all daubed over with broad arrows,

P.B.'s, C.B.'s, and various numerals in black, white, and red; with perhaps the jail-gang straddling sulkily by in their jingling leg-chains,—tell a tale too plain to be misunderstood. P. CUNNINGHAM *Two Years in New South Wales* vol. 1 pp. 52–3

Parramatta cloth a coarse woollen cloth, originally manufactured by the inmates of the FEMALE FACTORY at Parramatta. [The settlement of Parramatta, 24 km west of Sydney, was established in 1788 by Governor Phillip when the settlement at Sydney Cove was in need of good agricultural land. It was then named Rose Hill. The first land grant in Australia was made there in 1789 to James Ruse, a convict who had served his sentence. In June 1791 the name of the settlement was changed to Parramatta, an Aboriginal word meaning either 'the place where eels lie down'.]

Parramatta cloth, often simply called PARRAMATTA, was the name of a special textile—a coarse woollen fabric—produced at the Parramatta female FACTORY. The factories employed women to do special work, and the cloth produced at the Parramatta female factory at Sydney from 1801 became an important part of early economic production. In 1826 the *Sydney Gazette* recorded that the retail price of Parramatta cloth was two shillings and sixpence per yard, compared to imported cotton muslin which sold for two shillings, threepence per yard. In 1827 the factory produced up to 522 yards of cloth per week. The cloth was made into labourers' outfits among its other uses.

> **1834** The inmates of the Factory are employed variously, according to their characters and stations in the establishment, but chiefly in the processes connected with the manufacture of a coarse woollen-cloth, called ***Parramatta cloth***, of which blankets and slop-clothing are made for the convict-servants of settlers throughout the territory. J.D. LANG *An Historical and Statistical Account of New South Wales* vol. 2 p. 52

pass a document authorising and regulating the movement of a convict. [Specific use of standard English *pass* 'a written permission'. First recorded in the convict context in 1796.]

Under the convict system, the term 'pass' referred to a document given to a convict or a TICKET OF LEAVE HOLDER, usually by an employer, overseer, or magistrate, that allowed them to move from one area to another for purposes such as work in another settlement or area, or to be out at night. A convict without such a pass might be liable to be arrested by local constables.

> **1809** [Enclosure of Hawkesbury Settlers' Address to Governor Bligh, Bligh to Viscount Castlereagh] We, the undersigned (who came Free into the Colony), impressed with the most lively sense of Gratitude, most respectfully acknowledge the blessings we experienced under your Firm, Upright, and Impartial

Administration; had your power been equal to your wishes, we have no doubt but you would have put a stop to that System of Monopoly, Extortion, and oppression long and severely felt by us and our Families, almost to the privation of every Comfort. ... You would have protected our Persons and Property by known laws, and encouraged Agriculture, which would have rendered us and our Families comfortable; we might then have slept in our Beds without the fear of our houses being assailed, our wives and daughters violated, and our Property plundered by Bands of lawless Ruffians wandering about with impunity for months at a time, protected by a **Pass** granted by a Convict Overseer. This, Sir, is strong language; but the Records of the Courts of Justice prove these enormous crimes to exist with impunity, and the Want of Discipline by escaping detection. *Historical Records of Australia* 1st series VII pp. 146–7

1822 The convicts assigned to settlers are not allowed to travel from one district to another without a **pass**, signed by a magistrate, and their names, as well as those of the settlers to whom they are assigned, are directed to be registered in a book kept by the chief constable of each district; and the changes that occur in their destination ought likewise to be noted there. A pass, signed by the master of a convict, is requisite to enable him to travel to any part of his own district on his master's business; but it is not now required, when he is sent to Sydney market, nor in any case is the pass directed to be shown to the chief constable of Sydney, or the principal superintendent there, but is addressed to all whom it may concern. J.T. BIGGE *Report of the Commissioner of Inquiry into the State of the Colony of New South Wales* p. 79

passed (of a convict) issued with a PASS.

1827 In the Lord Liverpool some prisoners, said to be runaways from Sydney, who found means to secrete themselves on board the Cutter Lambton on her last trip to Port Stephens, are forwarded in charge of a Constable to Sydney; on the arrival of the Lambton at Port Stephens, they (representing themselves as free) actually applied there for employment, but meeting a disappointment, they made for Newcastle, where they so far imposed on Dr. Brooks the Magistrate, as to obtain a pass to proceed to Sydney, from him; but some of the vigilant Constables were not to be deprived of their prey in this way, and Buler Hewson the *Izzy Chapman* of Newcastle, *dreaming* 'that all was not right,' seized upon the '*passed*' fugitives, and lodged them in custody, until upon subsequent enquiry it turned out that they were neither more nor less than runaways from the Government employ at Sydney—they are therefore forwarded to be disposed of there. *Sydney Monitor* 20 Sept. p. 655

passholder (in Van Diemen's Land) a convict who held a PROBATION PASS.
The system of probation passes, implemented under Governor Franklin from 1842 and prompted by Lord Stanley, Colonial Secretary, aimed to reduce the

number of prisoners on public support. Probation passes, like TICKETS OF LEAVE, enabled convicts to work for themselves for wages. Unemployment, however, especially in times of economic depression such as in 1844, meant a number of passholders were left idle and often turned to crime. This consequently led to resentment among the free settlers, which in turn led to the development of the ANTI-TRANSPORTATION movement.

1847 The average number of **passholders**, male and female, in service in Van Diemen's Land is 9,294; the maximum wages being £9 a-year. The average number of males and females in service holding a ticket of leave is 7,370; the wages £12 a-year. Z.P. POCOCK *Transportation and Convict Discipline in Van Diemen's Land* p. 4

1852 The demands of the settlers for laborers soon fell far short of the supply. The written contracts for the **passholders** in the first stages of service bound the master to pay over a portion of their wages to the crown: this course was troublesome. Thus few, except in the last stage of their service, were able to obtain employment at all; and the graduated scale of payment fell to the ground. The accumulation at the hiring depôts, sometimes to the number of 4,000, who could obtain no engagement, induced the governor to urge their useful employment in public works. J. WEST *The History of Tasmania* vol. 2 p. 309

passport = PASS. [This term was used less frequently than 'pass'. First recorded in 1796.]

1810 In Order as much as possible to prevent Prisoners and all other Persons of idle and profligate characters from imposing themselves on the Public as Free Men, as well as with a View to prevent such Persons, from injuring the peaceable and industrious Inhabitants by strolling idly about the Country, and committing Depredations upon them, His Excellency the GOVERNOR is pleased to direct, that in future no Person whatever (excepting the Officers Civil and Military, Gentlemen and Settlers, or Tradesmen who came out free from England), shall be permitted to Travel or Pass from one Settlement to another in this Colony, without being furnished with a regular written **Passport** from a Magistrate, or his Master if an indented Servant, if free by Servitude or Emancipation to produce his Certificate, and if permitted to be off the Stores to work on his own Account, to produce his Ticket of Leave. *Sydney Gazette* 18 Aug. p. 1

pebble a convict whose behaviour was incorrigible; a reprobate. [From the hardness of the stone pebble. In the 1848 citation (the earliest recorded) the 'pebbles' are former convicts from Tasmania, but they maintain their reputation as PENTONVILLAINS. The term, which is chiefly Australian, was later applied to any prisoner or person who was difficult to deal with.]

1848 [Geelong] A few days ago, a carpenter showed a note in one of the public houses in town which circumstance having been observed by three '**pebbles**,' who were watching him outside, they followed him until he got opposite the Church, when they attacked and attempted to rob him, but having a hand-saw with him he resisted and eventually put them to flight, after having wounded one of the ruffians in the side with the saw. The Pentonvillains are becoming a complete pest to Corio. *Port Phillip Herald* 29 June p. 2

1854 A LADY '**PEBBLE**'—A female passholder in respectable service was charged by her master with refusing to work. She pleaded not guilty, but she said she was starved: she had been at her place only since Friday, and had seen not one bit of butter, and very little meat, and the contrast was so great to what she had been accustomed to in her own dear country, Ireland, that she could not hold out any longer. Mr. Jones told her she had more to eat and drink in one day here than she had in a week in her own dear country, and sentenced her to fourteen days' solitary confinement, and to be returned to her service. 'To *That* service!' she indignantly exclaimed 'never!' Mr. Jones told her, if she did not go back, she would be made to do so 'Shall I' said she; 'I'll take three months first.' 'Perhaps,' said his worship, 'it may be double that period.' 'Well, then, I'll take six and be quite satisfied.' She was removed. *Guardian* (Hobart) 22 Feb. p. 3

penal colony = CONVICT COLONY. [In this and other combinations with *penal*, the word has its standard English sense 'having the nature or character of punishment; constituting punishment; inflicted as punishment'. The term is used elsewhere, but it has special significance in Australia where it describes various aspects of the CONVICT SYSTEM. *Penal colony* is first recorded in 1827.]

1843 We have been living here under the blackness of the shadow of being a **penal colony**; but if we take pains to represent to the nation at large things as they really are, the cloud will pass away; for rest assured, human nature will be admitted to be, as it truly is, the same all the world over: and let people calmly and fairly consider for themselves, the picture that is now represented to them, of the vast amount of vice, crime, and abject misery, at present existing in Great Britain, as compared with this place. *Sydney Morning Herald* 4 Sept. p. 2

1847 From the earliest times of the settlement there congregated on the steep ridge above the King's wharf all the worst characters of this **penal colony**—the felon, whose ill-directed punishment had only rendered him more obdurate, cunning, and slothful; the prostitute, who (if such a thing can be) had sunk yet lower; the *fence*, watching for a livelihood by plundering the plunderer. A. HARRIS *Settlers and Convicts* (1953) p. 7

penal establishment = CONVICT ESTABLISHMENT. [First recorded 1837.]

1837 Separated by Bass's Straits, and distant 120 miles to the south-east of New Holland, lies the Island of Van Dieman, whose extent nearly equals that of Ireland. From 1803, the period of its first settlement, to 1821, it continued to be a mere **penal establishment**. It is now a very important colony, under a distinct government, with a European population of 40,000 souls spread over its surface. W.B. ULLATHORNE *The Catholic Mission in Australasia* p. 8

penal gang = GANG. [First recorded 1827.]

1827 On arrival in Sydney, the police magistrate, accompanied by two others, should repair on board the ship; examine each individual separately, to verify the descriptive remarks; and according to the nature of his crime and previous character, sentence him to work a certain period, in single or double irons, in a **penal gang** employed in the distant interior of the colony upon road and bridge making, or clearing portions of land for prospective settlers. P. CUNNINGHAM *Two Years in New South Wales* vol. 2 pp. 297–8

1847 In the second stage, we find that old form of gregarious punishment, **penal gangs**, still retained, but under the new name of probation gangs. It must be well known to everyone, either theoretically or practically acquainted with the workings of the criminal mind, that to congregate two or three hundred criminals together, cannot tend to the strengthening of virtue, but must result in the corruption of the whole mass, and the annihilation of every latent virtue. J. ATKINSON *Penal Settlements and Their Evils* p. 15

penal settlement = CONVICT SETTLEMENT. [First recorded 1820.]

1836 'Penal settlements,' to which frequent allusion has been made, are the places to which criminals are sent after conviction, before a colonial court, of offences which degrade them even below the Botany Bay standard. The life-sentenced double convicts are usually sent to Norfolk Island. This island has no harbor, and the residents upon it are allowed no communication with the world, except such as is afforded by the arrival of new exiles. J.F. O'CONNELL *A Residence of Eleven Years in New Holland* p. 72

1839 We deny that Australia Felix is under the convict system, some few favored Sydney settlers have convict servants; but this is as FREE from being a PENAL **settlement** as the most Antipenal Adelaidian can wish. No convict population say we, and we rejoice in this respect at least, the Government does not intend to inflict such a CURSE UPON US. *Port Phillip Patriot* 20 Mar. p. 3

penal station = CONVICT STATION; PROBATION STATION. [First recorded 1825.]

1845 The object of this expedition was to visit the abandoned penal settlement of Macquarie Harbour on the western coast of Van Diemen's Land, with the view of ascertaining whether the capabilities of that place were such as to make it desirable to re-establish a **penal station** there for the reception of the doubly-convicted felons who were now for the first time to be sent to my charge from New South Wales and Norfolk Island. Macquarie Harbour had hitherto been accessible only by sea, and was of difficult entrance; the interruptions to communication with it were frequent, and were amongst the reasons which had caused the abandonment of the settlement by my predecessor, after much labour and expense had been bestowed on its formation. J. FRANKLIN *Narrative of some Passages in the History of Van Diemen's Land* p. 40

Penton = PENTONVILLE. [Abbreviation. First recorded 1847.]

1848 There has been a warrant out for some time against this Long for bolting from the service of Mr. Cunningham, and the police have rode at least 200 miles after him previous to this, but could not come up with him. The other fellow that escaped is a noted robber, and turns out to be a Van Diemonian; the present prisoner is a **Penton**. *Port Phillip Herald* 6 Jan. (Supplement)

Pentonvillain pejorative term for a PENTONVILLE. [First recorded 1844.]

The term Pentonvillain—a blend of PENTON and villain—was a derogatory term for the EXILES who came to Australia under a special scheme from 1847. See PENTONVILLE.

1844 Our readers must … be aware … that the oligarchy of the colony … have had the audacity to propose the conversion of this fair and fertile province into a den for the receptacle of British felons—the degrading of our free and untainted immigrants to a level with the crime-stained **Pentonvillains**, of whom the first sample came by the *Royal George*. *Melbourne Weekly Courier* 21 Dec. p. 2

1848 Verily if our Downing-street rulers will insist upon our receiving their **Pentonvillain** and other prison 'pets', they, or the Colonial Government must very soon be prepared to defray the expense of another gaol. *Port Phillip Herald* 25 May p. 2

Pentonvillainy the behaviour and activity of PENTONVILLAINS.

1848 Not a day, nay, scarcely an hour, elapses without furnishing the inhabitants of Melbourne with abundant reason for blessing our gallant delegate, Mr. Cornet Cunninghame, for the instrumentality he boasts of in directing the current of **Pentonvillainy** to his fair province. Scarcely an issue of this journal passes without the necessity of recording additional outrages committed by the Cornet's pets, and our 'domestic intelligence' to-day is no exception to this rule. ... On Friday night Messrs. Duncan and Thomson's stables were broken open and a valuable horse abstracted. The thief, a Pentonvillain, coolly went on the following morning to Mr. Wilson's livery stables in Elizabeth-street, where he hired a gig, gave a forged cheque in payment, and drove off by the Portland road. *Maitland Mercury* 13 May p. 4

Pentonville a person sentenced in Britain to transportation, but required first to serve eighteen months in Pentonville prison in London (or another reformatory prison) receiving moral and religious instruction and learning a trade, before being sent to Australia, especially to the Port Phillip District, on a conditional pardon. Often in combinations, as in **Pentonville exile**, **Pentonville man**, **Pentonville prisoner**, **Pentonville system**, etc. [First recorded 1845.]

Pentonville was a name given to the EXILES or prisoners who had served part of their sentence in Britain and were then sent to Australia on conditional pardons to work. The British prison of Pentonville was opened in London in 1842, and was a model prison aimed to reform prisoners through a SEPARATE SYSTEM. The Australian scheme was suggested in the 1840s, when the British government still wanted to transport prisoners but had to deal with considerable opposition in the colonies. The scheme of exiles was an attempt to send prisoners who were supposed to be at least partially reformed (the first group came from Pentonville prison and all those following were dubbed PENTONS, Pentonvilles or PENTONVILLAINS), and with some trade or skill, to supplement the labour force in Australia. The first group of Pentonvilles came on the *Royal George* and were sent to Port Phillip, a settlement that had refused to accept convicts. Many of the Pentonvilles or Pentonvillains were also sent to Van Diemen's Land. Considerable opposition from free emigrants to the scheme, both on the basis of not wanting labour competition or a convict 'taint', led to its demise. Many complained that the supposedly reformed Pentonvilles were in fact not reformed, and continued their criminal activities, thus lowering the moral tone of colonial society.

1845 The **Pentonville** men are decidedly the most hopeful set I have seen land here. A pleasing instance occurred, showing the temper of the men. A party of more than a score were proceeding from the depot, under the direction of a constable of this place. On their way, the latter informed them, that if they wished to have a glass, they might indulge themselves, as he would say nothing about it. They one and all replied, that it was their determination not to enter a public-house. The unprincipled constable, not content with this noble rebuff, observed that that need not prevent them from having a glass, for he would go into the house and procure it for them, which he accordingly did. Their integrity however remained firm, though thus severely put to the proof; not a man could be prevailed upon to taste! BACKHOUSE & TYLOR *Life and Labours of George Washington Walker* pp. 521–2

1847 Yesterday morning a Pentonvillain named Kinneard was brought before Mr. Heape and Alderman Condell, to answer breaches of the Master and Servant's Act. ... After an ample hearing of the case he was sentenced to two months imprisonment, and ordered on its expiration to return to his employment. Prisoner (leaving the court)—'Thank you, gentlemen, I shan't go back; I am quite satisfied to serve my time in gaol.' Alderman Condell—Very well, wait till you come before us again. We hear it vauntingly mentioned, that the **Pentonville** system is giving every satisfaction. Now, after it has had some time to work, experience is beginning to demonstrate the advantages resulting from the importation of this class of half-caste convicts. We are credibly informed that amongst the greatest ruffians in Melbourne a large proportion are Pentonvillains. *Port Phillip Herald* 25 Mar. p. 2

plant to hide (articles, animals, etc.), frequently in the earlier period used of stolen goods. [This originally FLASH term is first recorded in British English in the early seventeenth century. OED labels it: 'Orig. *Thieves' slang*; now esp. *Australian*'. First recorded in Australia in 1793.]

This term is frequently recorded during the convict period, and is especially associated by the writers with the criminal underworld.

1794 A theft was committed in the course of the month in one of the outhouses belonging to Government House, used as a regimental store-room; the articles stolen were fifteen shirts and seventeen pair of shoes. In searching among the rocks and bushes for this property, three white and two check shirts, one pair of trousers, and one pair of stockings, were found; but so damaged by the weather as to be entirely useless. These must have been **planted** (to use the thief's phrase) a considerable time; for every mark or trace which could lead to a discovery of the owner was entirely effaced. D. COLLINS *An Account of the English Colony in New South Wales* (1798) vol. 1 p. 396

1812 PLANT. To hide, or conceal any person or thing, is termed *planting* him, or it; and any thing hid is called, *the plant*, when alluded to in conversation; such article is said to be *in plant*; the place of concealment is sometimes called *the plant*, as, I know of a fine *plant*; that is, a secure hiding-place. J.H. VAUX *Memoirs* (1964) vol. 2 p. 258

1833 The prisoners have adopted the expression, 'to **plant**' a thing, to signify, to hide or conceal it, especially in regard to things stolen. J. BACKHOUSE *A Narrative of a Visit to the Australian Colonies* (1843) p. 169

pollutionist a person who supported the continuation of transportation, or the resumption of transportation. See ANTI-TRANSPORTATIONIST. [This pejorative term, not otherwise recorded in English, was used by anti-transportationists as rhetorical support for their argument that the colonies would be tainted or 'polluted' by the presence of convicts. First recorded 1847.]

1847 [At an Anti-transportation meeting, Melbourne] The principles agreed upon are embodied in the first five resolutions. The first of the five acknowledges the broad fact upon which the pro-convict party, or, as the *Argus* happily styles them, the '**Pollutionists**,' base the whole superstructure of their rickety cause,—the scarcity of labour, and the injury to property resulting therefrom.' But this evil, great and incontestible as it is, is wisely declared to be the least of the two between which the colonists have to choose; since the one offered as an alternative, 'the convict system,' is of so colossal a magnitude, and so fraught with peril to the moral and social well-being of society, that nothing but an inordinate love of money could induce any one to look upon it without horror and disgust. *Hobart Town Courier* 24 Apr. p. 4

principal superintendent of convicts the chief official in charge of convicts.

In New South Wales in 1829, Governor Darling set up an office of the principal superintendent of convicts to oversee the administration of all convicts in the colony. The office was in charge of all convict records, and dealt with all matters to do with convicts. If a convict applied for a pardon or ticket of leave, records were checked there; the office also took care of all mail to convicts and answered any general enquiries by the public to do with convicts. This office became a central part of the colonial bureaucracy. In Van Diemen's Land, the principal superintendent of convicts chiefly dealt with convict employment.

1837 General Darling, by an official notice, prohibited the convicts from directly addressing themselves, on any pretence, to the government, and confined them, in making their complaints, or other applications, to the course prescribed by law,—that is, to apply to the nearest bench of magistrates, by whom applications were forwarded to the **principal superintendent of convicts**; and in all instances of deviation from this course, the complaints were transmitted by the government to the masters of the convicts, who were obliged to make a report upon the allegations of the complainers. J. MUDIE *The Felonry of New South Wales* p. 189

1838 It is the duty of an officer, called the **principal superintendent of convicts**, to classify the newly-arrived convicts; the greater proportion of whom are distributed amongst the settlers as assigned servants; the remainder are either retained in the employment of the government, or some few of them are sent to the penal settlements. W. MOLESWORTH *Report from the Select Committee of the House of Commons on Transportation* p. 9

prison class = CONVICT CLASS. [In this and other combinations with *prison*, the word has its standard English sense of 'a place of confinement for those convicted of crimes'. In colonial Australia it is synonymous with CONVICT. *Prison class* is first recorded in 1849.]

1849 It was usual in former times to give well-behaved persons of the **prison class**, under such circumstances, a free grant of fifty or a hundred acres, together with twelve or eighteen months' ration from the public store to begin with; and the practice has left an attestation of its excellence, in the confirmed reformation and gradual advancement of the parties and their families, in at least four cases out of five. A. HARRIS *The Emigrant Family* (1967) p. 28

prisoner a convict. [The term *prisoner*, one who was confined by the government as punishment for a crime, was used in the same way as CONVICT, and is found in a number of combinations that describe aspects of the Australian convict system. The *Sydney Monitor* citation below indicates that the term 'prisoner' was seen as a more acceptable and respectable term than 'convict'. First recorded in the Australian convict context in 1800.]

1804 All **Prisoners** whatever, either Male or Female, having the GOVERNOR'S permission to be off the Stores, and holding Tickets of Leave, are to appear at the respective Settlements near where they are situated and employed, on Thursday next the 2nd of August, at 8 o'clock in the morning, carrying their old Certificates with them, which will be replaced by new ones to those who have the GOVERNOR'S permission to continue off the Stores. *Sydney Gazette* 20 July p. 1

1826 The decent term of ***Prisoner***, had been substituted by Macquarie, for the degrading one of *Convict*, as the latter designation had in its turn taken place of the old British appellation of *Felon*. *Sydney Monitor* 19 May p. 2

prisoner constable = CONVICT CONSTABLE. [First recorded 1834.]

1849 When I went to the cells at the gaols I was attended by a turnkey and a sentry, and sometimes by a PRISONER CONSTABLE. I never met with any material interruption by these men any further than that their presence *was* an interruption. Whenever I have requested them to withdraw, they have done it. T. ROGERS *Correspondence Relating to the Dismissal* p. 28

prisoner labour = CONVICT LABOUR. [First recorded 1828.]

1834 On the 17th, we rode, by way of the Hollow Tree, to the Coal River, and from thence, on the 18th, to the Eastern Marshes. The road between Jerusalem and this place, is undergoing improvement, by a long cut, in the side of a steep hill. It is formed by **prisoner labour**, and is a great accommodation, though it is yet only passable for horses, and requires some nerve to ride along it. J. BACKHOUSE *A Narrative of a Visit to the Australian Colonies* p. 345

prisoner labourer = CONVICT LABOURER. [First recorded 1828.]

1828 While on the wheat subject, we cannot help congratulating the Colony on the arrival of so many **prisoner labourers**, while so many more are shortly expected, who we doubt not, will be all assigned to the agriculturists as they may require them, which will not only be a relief to the Government, but enable the settlers to carry His Excellency's late recommendation, as to the raising of as much grain as possible, into effect. *Tasmanian* (Hobart) 15 Aug. p. 3

prisoner of the Crown = PRISONER; CONVICT. [First recorded 1822.]

1826 [A.C. Mummery to John Lakeland, Principal Superintendent of Convicts] The Proprietor [of the *Colonial Times*, Hobart] offered me £10.0.0 per Month—I acceeded to the proposition—and conducted the Journal for one Month. I now learn Mr Bent will be restored to Society on Friday next, and having been requested to write a strong article on a certain Topic, I know not whether by the Proprietors direct wish or not, but certainly with his knowledge—I have therefore *bona-fide declined any further connection with the Paper*, upon the following grounds—I will not belong to any sect, or party, either by keeping company, or resorting any where—or by writing or publishing any thing against the Authorities of the Colony for two palpable and ostensible reasons—

1st. because I am a **Prisoner of the Crown**, and consequently not entitled to the free use and liberty of Speech becoming one not under a Penal Bond.

2ndly. For the best of all possible reasons—since I really, and unfeignedly believe the present local Government are sincere in their intentions, and praiseworthy in their motives. E. FITZSYMONDS (ed.) *Mortmain: A Collection of Choice Petitions, Memorials and Letters of Protest and Request from the Convict Colony of Van Diemen's Land* (1977) p. 99

prisoner overseer = CONVICT OVERSEER. [First recorded 1829.]

1834 The employment of **prisoner overseers** in the Chain-gangs and Road-parties, is liable to many objections. It has been ascertained, that in many instances, their conduct toward the men placed under them, is very oppressive, especially, where they think they can extort money by oppressing some and favouring others; and that, in some cases, they act in collusion with prisoners who abscond; agreeing with them, that they shall give themselves up to certain constables, with whom, and the absconding parties, they divide the reward for their apprehension. J. BACKHOUSE *A Narrative of a Visit to the Australian Colonies* Appendix p. lxi

prisoner population = CONVICT POPULATION. [First recorded 1827.]

1827 At the same time that the Editor of the Times (ludicrously enough!) stiles himself the *man of the people*, and indiscriminately attacks all the measures of Government, he arrogates to himself the merit of having advised chain gangs, and other severe inflictions on the prisoners in this Colony; and not satisfied with all this, his uneasy mind seems not to be at rest, till he shall see the **prisoner population** bound down as slaves to their several masters; that is, they shall be taken entirely out of the hands of their natural protectors, the Government, and delivered over, with all the little property they may possess, into the hands of individuals. *Tasmanian* (Hobart) 18 Oct. p. 2

prisoner servant = ASSIGNED CONVICT. [First recorded 1807.]

1827 We heartily agree with our new contemporary, *the Gleaner*, in his remarks on the late capture of certain run-a-way cut-throats, by some of the **prisoner-servants** of the settlers on the South Creek. Along with him we ascribe *the exposure by these prisoners of their lives in the desperate conflict which they voluntarily entered into, to a nobler motive than the mere hope of having their names inserted in the Justice Books, until by a series of hairbreadth escapes, they might at least procure that unsecure bauble, a Ticket-of-Leave. Of which* ONE SAUCY *word to* ONE *gentleman before* ONE *stocking-weaver magistrate, will subject the brave rescuer of his master's life and property from the knife of the murderer and the fire brand of the incendiary, to be at any time deprived.* Sydney Monitor 20 Apr. p. 388

prisoner settler = CONVICT SETTLER. [First recorded 1832.]

1832 [Mr W. Dun to Governor Bourke] At the time the land was given to me Newcastle was a Penal Settlement, and in the District only three or four free settlers, several **prisoner Settlers**, and many Government Cedar parties, under so little control on a Sunday that, at the request of Major Morrisett the commandant at Newcastle, I collected the prisoner Settlers and these men, as well as many of the Cedar party on a Sunday about five miles from my residence and performed divine service to them. *Historical Records of Australia* 1st series XVI p. 713

prison labour = CONVICT LABOUR. [First recorded 1857]

1857 St James's church is a large oblong brick building, with tasteful entrances at each extremity of the north side, made of a durable kind of sandstone. The interior is comfortably fitted up and lighted with gas. It is ornamented on the east end by a tall spire. The church was built in governor Macquarrie's time, by **prison labour**. J. ASKEW *Voyages and Travels* p. 194

prison population = CONVICT POPULATION. [First recorded 1827.]

1827 The Attorney General opened the case in a brief but lucid manner. He ran over the law on the subject of libels, which gives public writers permission to discuss public measures with the utmost freedom, provided the discussion be fair and without malice. Malicious and libellous comments were dangerous in a colony like this, where the **prison population** was so great as compared with the free population. It was amusing to hear our writers talk of oppression, when they themselves were the persevering cause of the prosecutions now pending. *Sydney Monitor* 1 Oct. p. 679

prison ship = CONVICT SHIP. [First recorded 1824.]

1843 I beg to submit also, that such a measure as the multiplying of **prison ships** in our harbour, besides the enormous expense it would entail, would be attended with other evils of various descriptions, amongst which I will merely enumerate the injury done to the health of the women, already probably in some degree affected by a four or five months' voyage; the loathing and rest-lessness and discontent which such a position would engender in their minds, and which would make their confinement much more intensely felt when in view of the peopled and busy shore than on the solitary ocean; the temptations which would exist to enter into communication with the boats' crews which must go alongside the ships to carry supplies, requiring a great deal of vigilance to prevent; and the extreme difficulty on the other hand of procuring trust-worthy officers, even at a high remuneration, for any such onerous vocation. J. FRANKLIN *Confidential Despatch* p. 25

probation 1 = PROBATION SYSTEM

1855 Bushranging was very prevalent in Governor Arthur's time. The most noted robbers were Michael Howe and Brady. In 1834 the Black War, against the poor Aborigines, was proclaimed. Colonel Arthur was succeeded, in 1837, by the benevolent Sir John Franklin, the friend of education and religion. The old Assignment system of convictism was changed for that of **Probation** in 1840. J. BONWICK *Geography of Australia and New Zealand* p. 162

2 the condition of a person serving a sentence under the PROBATION SYSTEM; the period of probation; a stage in this.

1865 Autumn arrived, and in April, 1847, my first three years of '**probation**' in Australia being at an end, I received a pass making me eligible for employment upon my own account, and was removed to Hobart Town. J.F. MORTLOCK *Experiences of a Convict* p. 84

3 used attributively, to describe those who were serving their sentence under the PROBATION SYSTEM.

1844 Four **probation** lads, the very personification of impudence and knavery, were placed in the dock, charged by the district constable on duty with singing, shouting, and using bad language, while in the cell in Birdcage-walk. The ring-leader, a saucy fellow, declared on his honor and word that none of 'em opened

his mouth since they were put in the cell; indeed they had to complain of being
of being confined in an under cell, when there was plenty of room in an upper
one, which was more airy and agreeable. As the lads were so fond of singing and
shouting, his Worship sentenced each to receive twenty-five lashes before breakfast, the following morning; and the lads left the dock, complacently smiling.
Colonial Times (Hobart) 13 Feb.

probationary (of a convict) undergoing PROBATION. See PROBATION SYSTEM.
[First recorded 1840.]

> 1840 The immediate effects of the establishment of **Probationary** Gangs, and
> the consequent non-assignment of the Convicts on arrival, are already seriously
> felt. *Tasmanian Weekly Dispatch* (Hobart) 21 Aug. p. 4

probationer a person who is serving a sentence under the PROBATION SYSTEM.
[First recorded 1840.]

A convict or prisoner who served a sentence under the PROBATION SYSTEM was
sometimes called a 'probationer'. The probation system allowed convicts to move
through several stages, depending on their behaviour, so that they could ultimately earn their freedom and work for themselves. If convicts were well behaved
in their time in the PROBATION GANGS, they could obtain a PROBATION PASS and
then later a ticket-of-leave and possibly a conditional pardon.

> 1851 The first experiment tried was that of probation; the principal feature of
> which was to send the convicts as before to Van Diemen's Land, and, instead
> of parcelling them out to the settlers on their arrival, the men were retained in
> probation gangs, to undergo various periods of punishment, before they were
> allowed to be assigned. … The **probationers** were at first worked on the roads
> and the public works; then it was ordered that they should be educated, and
> catechists and schoolmasters were appointed for each station:—and ultimately
> the men were required to be treated kindly, and not like convicts suffering the
> retribution due to their crimes. The probationers instead, therefore, of work-
> ing, wasted their time, and stations where hundreds of men were congregated,
> have not effected five pounds' worth of public labour in as many months.
> H. MELVILLE *The Present State of Australia* pp. 135–6

probation gang a detachment of prisoners required to complete a term of
supervised labour on public works. [First recorded 1841.]

Probation gangs were an essential part of the probation system. After arrival in
Van Diemen's Land, prisoners were assigned to probation gangs. This was the first
step in the PROBATION system as a convict worked his way towards freedom. These
gangs were worked from PROBATION STATIONS in unsettled parts of the colony and
usually consisted of at first 250 to 300 convicts and later 300 to 400. They
worked on such projects as building roads and in agriculture. Their behaviour was

closely monitored and if they behaved well, they would be passed on to the next stage of the system. The convicts were placed in three classes, depending on the treatment they were to receive.

1843 [Lord Stanley to Lieutenant-Governor Sir John Franklin] The second stage of punishment is that of the **Probation Gangs**. These Gangs will be assembled in Van Diemen's Land. They will be composed first of Convicts who have passed through the period of detention at Norfolk Island, and secondly of Convicts sentenced to transportation for a less term than life, who may be indicated by the Secretary of State for the Home Department as proper to be placed in this class. The Probation Gangs will be employed in the service of the Government, and, with rare exceptions, in the unsettled Districts of the Colony. No Convict placed in the Probation Gang will pass less than one, or more than two years there, except in case of misconduct. ... The Probation Gangs will be employed in hard labour. But the labour of all should not be equally hard. Every Gang should be broken into two or three Divisions distinguished from each other by such mitigations of toil or other petty indulgencies as may be compatible with the condition of Criminals suffering the punishment of their offences. By transference of the men from one of these Divisions to the other, an effective system of rewards and penalties might be established. *Historical Records of Australia* 1st series XXII p. 518

probationism = PROBATION SYSTEM. [First recorded 1844.]

Probationism was ideally supposed to be a better way to handle convicts and help improve the colony of Van Diemen's Land. In practice, it failed in several ways. Economic problems meant that those who gained their TICKET OF LEAVE could not find employment and thus might turn to crime to support themselves. The PROBATION STATIONS were expensive to maintain and the numbers of convicts in the PROBATION GANGS were too large for adequate supervision.

1856 Convictism, according to most old settlers, was attended with fewer evils when in the early days, and before the hated period of **Probationism**. Ten years before the introduction of Sodom infamy, Dr. Ross, of Hobart Town, had a vision of such a crushing aggregation of sin, as to fill his mind with horror, though he believed no Christian Government would ever sanction 'such a Gehenna,' which would drive free settlers away from 'the horror and the disgrace.' J. BONWICK *The Bushrangers: illustrating the early days of Van Diemen's Land* p. 7

probation party = PROBATION GANG. [First recorded 1841.]

1843 An officer entitled Comptroller of Convicts; to be appointed to the charge of the **probation parties**, and at his suggestion alone are relaxations to be granted to any member of them. The estimated number in those gangs will be about 8000. *Colonial Observer* (Sydney) 17 June p. 1103

probation pass a document issued to a convict who had served his time on the PROBATION GANG, authorising the holder to work for himself in private employment and earn wages. The pass was a step towards a conditional or absolute PARDON. See also PROBATION SYSTEM. [First recorded 1843.]

> **1843** [Lord Stanley to Lieutenant-Governor Sir John Franklin] After a Convict shall have passed through the Probation Gang, he will next proceed to the third stage of punishment and become the Holder of a **Probation Pass**. But no Convict may enter on this stage except on two conditions. Of these, the first is the obtaining from the Comptroller of Convicts a Certificate of general good conduct, ... and secondly the having fully served in the Probation Gang during the whole of the period for which the Convict had been placed there. The essential distinction between the 3rd Stage and those which preceded it will be that the holder of a Probation Pass may, with the consent of the Government, engage in any private service for wages. *Historical Records of Australia* 1st series XXII p. 519

probation passholder the holder of a PROBATION PASS. See also PROBATION SYSTEM. [First recorded 1844.]

A probation passholder was a convict who was granted and held a PROBATION PASS. Such a convict could work for himself in private employment and earn wages. One of the major failures of the probation system was that such convicts could not obtain employment due to economic depression and thus were more likely to turn to criminal activity to survive. This undermined the entire purpose of the system.

> **1844** In order to afford every facility to the hiring of **probation passholders**, two principal hiring depôts will be formed—one on the south side of the island at Bridge water, and one on the north side at Perth; and at one or other of these depôts person desirous of engaging the services of probation passholders will make application, either personally, or by their agents. With the same view, men on being allowed to become passholders will remain ten days at the probation gang station, from which they are about to emerge, before proceeding to join the nearest of the foregoing depôts, thus affording an opportunity to the settlers resident in the neighbourhood to hire them. At the expiration of ten days, should they not have been hired, they will proceed to the nearest hiring depôt. *Colonial Times* (Hobart) 9 Jan. p. 4

probation station an establishment for the accommodation of prisoners serving in PROBATION GANGS. See also PROBATION SYSTEM. [First recorded 1842.]

Probation stations were set up as part of the probation system instituted in Van Diemen's Land. They were mostly set up in unsettled areas where convicts in probation gangs were assigned to various works such as agricultural labour and building roads. Examples of probation stations included Flinders Bay, established in 1841 for timber clearing, and Saltwater River, established in the same year as an agricultural station.

> **1851** The probation discipline as first established, would not work well, and the local authorities were ashamed of the system; so the probation gangs of the settled districts were broken up, and the principal station was established at Maria Island; this island is situated near Oyster Bay on the eastern coast, it is about a couple of miles from Middle Island, and thence two miles to Sand-spit Point: a good swimmer could therefore easily cross the narrow channel through which small vessels occasionally pass to and fro to the upper settlement near Waterloo Point. The **probation stations** being thus placed out of sight, no longer afford amusement to the inhabitants, and the 'jolly probationers' as the colonists term them, are now cooped up on the island, and taught all manner of things good and bad. H. MELVILLE *The Present State of Australia* p. 137

probation system a system for the management of convicts, introduced in Tasmania after the abolition of ASSIGNMENT in 1839: under the system a convict, whose conduct continued to be satisfactory, progressed through stages, as confinement, supervised public labour, paid employment, etc., to a pardon. Also in abbreviated form **probation**. [Transferred use of *probation* in the sense 'a testing or trial of a person's conduct'. First recorded in a convict context in 1840. This precedes the US (1878) and British use of the term in criminal jurisdictions.]

In Van Diemen's Land, following the Molesworth Committee Report of 1838, it was decided that a more serious deterrent needed to be put in place than the assignment system and thus the probation system was introduced from 1839. The basis of the system was that convicts would serve a fixed period in labour gangs, followed by stages of gradual amelioration of their sentence with the attainment of ultimate freedom if their behaviour warranted it. The system was not implemented uniformly, and ultimately collapsed due to economic problems.

> **1848** The largest edifices raised by private capital are the banks and the hotels; and the number and extent of the public buildings are surprising, considering the age of the settlement. All of these may be said to have been erected solely by convict labour, previous to the introduction of the **probation system**: at present, public works are almost at a stand-still, for want of money to pay the convicts employed, as it is the policy of the probation system not to exact labour without remuneration. J.C. BYRNE *Twelve Years' Wanderings in the British Colonies* vol. 2 p. 25

public gang a party of convicts detailed to perform PUBLIC LABOUR. [First recorded 1796.]

1796   Toward the latter end of the month two men from each officer were ordered to join the **public gangs**, it being found wholly impracticable to erect without more assistance any of the buildings which had now become indispensably necessary. Storehouses were much wanted; the barracks were yet unfinished; houses were to be built for the assistant-surgeons, those which had been erected soon after our arrival being now no longer tenable. D. COLLINS *An Account of the English Colony in New South Wales* (1798) vol. 1 p. 485

public labour work undertaken by convicts on projects that benefited the government and the community. [First recorded 1792.]

Public labour was vital to the economic success of the early Australian colonies. Until free migrants came to the colonies in any significant numbers, convicts working at public labour provided the colonies' infrastructure that was the basis for the future Australia. They built roads and bridges, government buildings such as the Hyde Park barracks, and cleared the BUSH for settlement. See also CONVICT LABOUR.

1792   [Governor Phillip to Right Hon. Henry Dundas]   In Norfolk Island their provisions will last for a longer time. You will, sir, naturally suppose that I anxiously look for the arrival of those ships by which we expect a further supply of provisions, and I am very sorry to be under the necessity of adverting to the observation I have so often made, that the colony, having been almost constantly on a reduced rations, is a great check on the **public labour**, as well as the cause of many very unpleasant circumstances. Men who are inclined to be discontented find an ample source, and the convicts an unanswerable excuse, when pressed to labour. *Historical Records of Australia* 1st series I p. 372

1832   Now, professing as you do, that yours is the Journal of the People, how comes it that you have taken no notice of this projected application of the **Public labour**, at a time when so many parts of the Colony are without roads on which carts can travel with safety? *Colonist* (Hobart) 5 Oct. p. 3

public servant a convict assigned to PUBLIC LABOUR or work for the government. [This term is first recorded in 1797, as a euphemistic term for CONVICT. By 1812 it was being used to describe a non-convict member of the public service (the Australian equivalent of the British and US 'civil service').]

1797   [Governor Hunter to the Duke of Portland]   Many who were here for life settled without any conditional emancipation or deed, and some who had several years to serve the public had been permitted to call themselves settlers. Such of those as were good and industrious characters, I was unwilling to recall to public work, after having labour'd hard to establish themselves on a farm; others of less worth our necessitys oblig'd me to order in and work for the public. Thus you will discover, my Lord, how impossible it was for me to do anything on Government account for want of **public servants**. *Historical Records of Australia* 1st series II p. 18

1799 A number of the public labouring servants of the crown having lately absconded from their duty, for the purpose either of living by robbery in the woods, or of getting away in some of the ships now about to sail, that none of those concerned in the concealing them might plead ignorance, public notice was given 'that any officer or man belonging to the above ships, who should be known to have countenanced or assisted the convicts above alluded to in making their escape, would be taken out of the ship, and punished with the utmost severity of the law. … Such of the above **public servants** as might have taken to concealments on shore for the purpose of avoiding their work, or making their escape from the colony, if they did not return within a week to their respective stations, might, upon discovery, expect the most exemplary punishment; but they would be pardoned for the present attempt if they returned immediately.' D. COLLINS *An Account of the English Colony in New South Wales* vol. 2 p. 266

public store = STORE. [First recorded 1790.]

1802 [Order Regulating the Ration] To prevent the scarcity felt last year, the following weekly ration will be issued until further orders: To all males victualled from the **public stores**—Wheat, 9 lb.; maize, 3lb. shelled, or 4½lb. in cob; pork, 2 lb. 10 oz.; sugar, 6 oz. Women and children in proportion. The addition of 3 oz. of sugar will be continued until a full ration of meat or grain can be issued. *Historical Records of Australia* 1st series III pp. 519–20

public work 1 = PUBLIC LABOUR. [First recorded 1789.]

1789 Six men were to cut the timber down on an acre of ground in one week: six men to clear away and turn up an acre of ground fit for receiving seed, in twenty-eight days: two sawyers to saw one hundred feet of sawing each day. At these tasks the convicts would have an opportunity of saving time to themselves; and, as that time was to be employed in clearing gardens and ground to cultivate for their own use, what was thus saved from the **public work** would not be lost to society; although it was to be feared that some would pass their time in idleness. J. HUNTER *Transactions at Port Jackson* pp. 344–5

2 (usually as **public works**) a project or construction undertaken as PUBLIC LABOUR. [First recorded 1801.]

Public works included bridge and road building, the clearing of land and also agriculture on government-owned STATIONS.

1801 It required near Seventy thousand bricks to complete the building of one barrack, and twenty thousand tiles to cover it in—to furnish bricks for these barracks and other buildings, three gangs were constantly at work, which comprised three overseers and eighty convicts. ... The Provisioning and Clothing all these people must be very considerable, and will be found to amount to an enormous sum when the expenses of the **public works** erected in this colony come to be conducted. G. BARRINGTON *A Sequel to Barrington's Voyage* p. 27

1834 We have been given to understand, that the Government have refused to lend the men from the **Public Works** to assist in getting in the harvest; and should such be the case, it is really highly reprehensible; but as we do not know it for a fact, we are unwilling to believe it can be true, and therefore merely mention the circumstance, in order that it may induce the Government to do their duty to the agricultural interests of the Colony, in accordance with the custom of the mother country, and from the manifest expediency and propriety of the measure. *Colonist* (Hobart) 21 Jan. p. 3

punishment gang a detachment or group of convicts who had been assigned to difficult work and/or strong disciplinary measures as a form of punishment. [First recorded 1832.]

1838 [Lord Glenelg to Sir John Franklin] All Convicts, before being assigned, should be coerced in gangs under the immediate control of the local Govt., these Gangs to be kept separate from what are now considered the '**punishment Gangs**' consisting of Criminals twice convicted. *Historical Records of Australia* 1st series XIX p. 469

R

ration a fixed allowance of provisions, especially food, provided for CONVICTS, government officials, and (at times) FREE SETTLERS. [First recorded in the Australian convict context in 1802.]

In the colonies, those convicts who were in government care were fed on rations supplied by the government through the Commissary. Supplies were obtained either from Britain or off-shore, or purchased within the colonies. The ration system was open to abuse, particularly by stores' supervisors, and food riots by convicts were relatively common. The convict diet was generally good, but distribution of rations was sometimes unreliable and inequitable. The withholding of rations was sometimes used as a form of punishment.

> **1835** Under Colonel Sorell the imports of the Colony were merely necessaries of life; and the exports, the Commissariat expenditure, and the capital of fresh emigrants, entirely paid for every thing—truly the trade was exceedingly confined, but what could be expected from a young Colony? As might be imagined, a market so limited in its supply, fluctuated to an amazing extent: at times certain descriptions of British manufactured goods would sell at far less than their cost price, at other times a most extraordinary profit would be realized—but this is the case in all markets so situated; and as the trade of the place encreased according to the population, so did these fluctuations become less frequent, and less sudden. The Commissariat then took wheat into the stores at a certain fixed price of 10*s.* the bushel, and each settler had a right to turn into the stores so much wheat, according to the number of acres he had in cultivation. The Government were then always purchasers, and **rations** were allowed to free emigrants for six months after their arrival; rations also were allowed to all Government Officers, and convicts in the employ of the Authorities and settlers. H. MELVILLE *The History of Van Diemen's Land* p. 6

1841 [William Buckley to John Montague, Colonial Secretary] The humble Petition of William Buckley respectfully sheweth that the said William Buckley whom your honor was pleased to appoint as Gatekeeper &c to the Nursery in Liverpool Street and which situation Petitioner has held for three years during which time he has been married humbly solicits your Honour would be pleased to allow **Rations** to be issued to his wife and child on account of the smallness of his pay as well as for the numerous duties which petitioner has to perform. E. FITZSYMONDS (ed.) *Mortmain: A Collection of Choice Petitions, Memorials and Letters of Protest and Request from the Convict Colony of Van Diemen's Land* (1977) p. 24

re-transport to commit a convict guilty of a further offence to a PENAL SETTLE-MENT, especially one at which a more severe form of punishment was imposed. [First recorded 1791.]

Secondary transportation to a penal settlement was the most dreaded sentence after execution, and could be ordered after summary trial by two or more magistrates. A number of convicts committed further crimes after arriving in the colonies and were sent to such places of SECONDARY punishment such as Norfolk Island, Port Macquarie, and Port Arthur.

1838 For crimes of greater magnitude convicts are re-transported. The penal settlements of New South Wales are Norfolk Island and Moreton Bay; at the former, the number of convicts in 1837 were about 1,200; in the same year the number at Moreton Bay did not exceed 300 ... Moreton Bay is likewise a place of punishment for convict females, who are **re-transported** for offences committed in the colony. W. MOLESWORTH *Report from the Select Committee of the House of Commons on Transportation* p. 16

1839 The incorrigible offenders are **re-transported** to a penal settlement, away from the settled districts, named Port Arthur. As visitors are not allowed admission upon this settlement, we are unable to give the details of the discipline exercised there. By its effects, however, upon the minds and conduct of those unfortunate beings who have suffered from its rigours, we may judge it to be tremendous. The place seems to be a terrestrial purgatory. The men are often driven to the commission of suicide,—many to that of murder, in order, as they have afterwards declared, to be brought to Hobart Town and hanged. J. DIXON *The Conditions and Capabilities of Van Diemen's Land* p. 47

road In the phrase **(up)on** (or **to**) **the roads** (of a convict) engaged in forced labour on the roads. [First recorded 1837.]

A convict might be sentenced to serve time working in a ROAD GANG, which meant that he was forced to labour on building or repairing roads. This work was important to the development of the early colonies.

1847 Now convicts, though they do not mind a few months **on the roads**, are decidedly averse to Port Arthur. And this would afford me a prospect of being able to exercise some authority over him [a convict servant], and as he would receive kind treatment in my service, if he would accept of it, I should not despair of being able to keep him till he obtained a third class pass, which they all rather desire, as it not only entitles them to receive the whole of their wages; but by an extended liberality on the part of the officers of the Government, those eligible for service are often permitted to roam about in search of employ. Z.P. POCOCK *Transportation and Convict Discipline* p. 11

road gang a working party of convicts assigned to building and repairing roads. [First recorded 1819.]

Road gangs often consisted of convicts in government care who had been sentenced to the road gang as a minor punishment. The building and repairing of roads was one of the major public works that convicts undertook.

1834 In the **road gang** it has (since Governor Darling left the Colony) become a common practice to let the men *hire themselves out to the settlers*. No less than from twenty to thirty men, inmates of a road-gang in the Hunter District, were lately let or hired out by the overseer to the settlers, at the rate of ten shillings a week; for which the overseer received his share of the spoil. Thus, men in the road-gangs become fed and clothed better than those assigned to the settlers. And hence it is, that at the present moment, road-gangs are not only like the ironed-gangs, *no terror to misbehaved men,* but they operate as a premium for offences; they are the ultimate reward, as it were, of the more audacious, who for the temporary inconvenience of a very light pair of fetters on his legs in an ironed-gang, without work, will endure that inconvenience in order to terminate his well-concerted intrigues in the pleasures of a *road*-party. J. MUDIE *Vindication of James Mudie and John Larnach* p. xviii

road party = ROAD GANG [First recorded 1822.]

1838 Large parties of convicts, called **road-parties**, are employed in making roads in New South Wales and Van Diemen's Land; these parties consist mostly of convicts who have been returned to Government by their masters as being unfit for service, and of convicts who, having been convicted of some offence in the colony, have been sent, on the expiration of their sentence, to work for a certain period on the roads before they were re-assigned. W. MOLESWORTH *Report from the Select Committee of the House of Commons on Transportation* p. 13

1838 Every one of those witnesses spoke in the strongest terms of the disorders, crimes, and demoralization which were occasioned in the colony of New

South Wales by the **road-parties**. Composed entirely of criminals, some of them of the very worst character (all of them ultimately degraded and demoralized by associating together), these parties were dispersed over a wide extent of country, under a most incomplete and inefficient system of superintendence, with overseers, most of whom had been convicts, and in many cases with convicts for the deputy overseers, to whose sole charge the road-parties were sometimes left for many days. Prisoners in the road-parties were sometimes in league with the convict servants of the neighbouring settlers, upon whose property they committed every description of depredation, the fruits of which were consumed in intoxication and other debauchery. W. MOLESWORTH *Report from the Select Committee of the House of Commons on Transportation* p. 14

runaway a convict who escaped from official custody or from assigned service. [First recorded 1790.]

The terms ABSCONDER, ABSENTEE, and BOLTER were other common terms for runaway convicts. The number of runaways and their propensity for crime led to the introduction of the Bushranging Act of 1830, which allowed for the arrest of anyone suspected of being a runaway, with such persons having to prove that they were not by the production of a PASS or CERTIFICATE.

1818 [Governor Macquarie to Earl Bathurst] This last Ship, having touched at the Cape of Good Hope, received on board there, and brought back to this Colony, Sixteen *Runaway Male Convicts* from Port Jackson, who had contrived Means thro' the Connivance of the Sailors, to Stow Away and Secrete themselves on board … It is hardly possible to find these **Runaways**, when the Sailors are in league with them and Connive at their Concealment on board, few Ships leaving this Port without Carrying off some Convicts of both Sexes. *Historical Records of Australia* 1st series IX p. 79

S

scourger = FLOGGER. [First recorded in an Australian convict context in 1827.]

1848 Our party consisted of four policemen, well mounted and armed, a carpenter, bullock-driver, and *scourger*—in all seven. The carpenter was taken for the purpose of erecting a hut and stabling; the bullock-driver for conducting a team of six bullocks and a dray, laden with ammunition and stores; and the latter personage for the enviable and honourable service of flagellating such poor miserable wretches as might, through misconduct and the decree of the commissioner, be subjected to corporal punishment. Of course, none but prisoners of the Crown were exposed to such a degradation. C. COZENS *Adventures of a Guardsman* pp. 123–4

scrag to hang on the gallows. [This FLASH term is first recorded in England in 1756, and the verb derives from the noun *scrag* in the sense 'neck'. It is first recorded in Australia in 1801.]

This word is typical of the general underworld slang that was present in the early colonies, and is well represented in the early Australian written records. See FLASH.

1801 In the second year of settlement, it was reported that a man was found murdered in one of the coves, a short distance from the settlement; a general muster of the convicts thereupon took place, but no person was absent except Caesar, a black fellow, who had absconded a few days before. … in his intellects he was not far removed from the brute creation; his appetite was so ravenous that he could devour the full ration of three days in one; to pamper this appetite he was compelled to steal from others;—and this he did at every opportunity, without even caring for the consequences; indeed he was so indifferent about being punished with death, that he used to declare if they should **scrag** him he would quiz them all, and show some gig at the *nubbing-cheat*, before he was turned off. G. BARRINGTON *A Sequel to Barrington's Voyage to New South Wales* p. 52

1844 Maher ... informed Howell, in an ominous and prophetic tone, that ere eight days were past, some who were in the Gaol would be 'lagged' but he feared none would be **scragged**, although there were some who ought to be. *Parramatta Chronicle* 29 June p. 2

secondary pertaining to a criminal offence committed after arrival in Australia (a secondary offence) or the punishment for this (a secondary punishment). Especially in the combination SECONDARY PUNISHMENT. [First recorded 1824.]

Convicts who committed a crime in the colonies would be tried before a magistrate who might sentence them to hard labour or time in a penal settlement. Until the mid-1820s, sentences were rarely lengthened, only made more severe. After the New South Wales Act of 1823, however, those who were given secondary punishments, especially those who were RE-TRANSPORTED, often had to serve a new length of time in addition to their original sentence.

1824 George's Town contains five or six hundred inhabitants, consisting, with very few exceptions, of prisoners in the immediate employ of Government, and the persons in office over them. As it is a place of **secondary** banishment, and possesses a factory for women, the people are for the most part of the worst description of convicts. It is generally hoped, that the head quarters will be removed to Launceston, even though the factory should remain where it is. Too much expense has been incurred in George's Town, to permit the Government entirely to abandon it. E. CURR *Account of the Colony of Van Diemen's Land* pp. 46–7

1851 The commonality of the people are learning that the horrors of convictism have little to do with transportation, and that it is only *secondary convictions*, or offences committed in the colony, that entail any kind of punishment, and that the crime then must be of a grave description, that will lead the way to the penal stations. H. MELVILLE *The Present State of Australia* pp. 180–1

secondary punishment punishment for criminal offences committed by a convict after arrival in Australia. [First recorded 1832.]

1835 With respect to a **secondary punishment** of serving in ironed-gangs, I have witnessed their effects for the last twenty years, and consider that progressive improvements have been made in their lodging, victualling, clothing, and general comforts; but until lately no improvement in their industry, and none, even now, in their moral conduct. This consequence I mainly attribute to the want of classification of criminals; hitherto, the gangs have been too numerous (all eating, sleeping, and working together), without any distinction or encouragement for improved industry or conduct. Hence the youth or novice in crime is at once initiated into all the habits of vice and demoralization, by the more depraved ruling bullies of the gang, who inculcate upon his mind scheming, laziness, and indolence, so as to kill time by doing the least possible work. *Colonist* (Sydney) 30 July p. 243

second-convicted = DOUBLE-CONVICTED. [First recorded 1840.]

1849 By calling the prisoner Knight '*the school-assistant*,' Captain Blachford meant to infer that I was only a sort of school-master to the convicts on his station; and hence he persisted in always calling the monitor of the evening school my '*assistant*,' which was intended to be a contemptuous mode of designation towards me. I have also to remark in the next place, that in finding fault with my conduct as chaplain, and sending me a verbal order by a **second convicted** prisoner, he acted in defiance of all that was courteous, and contravened a positive law of the island. T. ROGERS *Correspondence Relating to the Dismissal* p. 49

second-sentence(d) = DOUBLE-CONVICTED. [First recorded 1827.]

1827 Coal is sold by government at the pit-mouth for 5s. per ton, and at Sydney for 20s. per ton, the freight thereto being 15s. The Newcastle mine has been hitherto worked by the *second-sentence* men, sent down for punishment, and by their means about four thousand tons are annually dug up and disposed of, amounting in value at the pit's mouth to 1000*l.* and at Sydney to 4000 guineas. P. CUNNINGHAM *Two Years in New South Wales* vol. 2 p. 3

separate designating aspects of the CONVICT SYSTEM that employed the idea of keeping prisoners separate. [Used elsewhere in a prison context, but chiefly Australian. First recorded in Australia in 1839.]

In the Australian convict context the term referred primarily to the separate prison or system, first designed in Britain and adopted in Australia. Until 1832 in Britain there were usually three or more prisoners to a cell, and there were no distinctions made about kind of prisoners—for example, people awaiting trial could be imprisoned in the same cell as long-term sentenced inmates. A first step in reform was the construction of prisons that had separate cell blocks radiating out from a central control area, so that prisoners could be separated into these cell blocks according to the kind of crime committed. The next development was a separate cell system, where each prisoner was accommodated in a separate cell. This allowed them to be isolated from one another and an emphasis was placed on reforming such prisoners. Surveillance of prisoners was designed to be greater under such a system. A prison designed on these principles was called a 'separate prison' or 'model prison', and the first to be completed, in 1842, was at Pentonville in London. In 1847 it was decided that a similar prison would be constructed in Van Diemen's Land at Port Arthur, and this was completed over the next few years. Prisoners were to be kept in separate cells and to have a minimum of interaction with each other so as to prevent criminal contamination and conspiracy, and to allow the prisoner to reflect on his crimes and repent.

> **1845** The men whose expectations were raised that they would find ready employment at good wages on arriving here, are, in considerable numbers, breaking stones upon the highway, an employment which thou art aware is here associated with the lowest degradation and punishment. Perhaps this may be better than allowing them remain in idleness. Those interested in the existence of the **Separate** System, as carried into effect at the Pentonville Prison and consummated here, must not be disappointed if it does not realize all their anticipations. BACKHOUSE & TYLOR *Life and Labours of George Washington Walker* (1862) p. 522

> **1852** We visited an admirable edifice nearly finished at vast expense for the prosecution of the solitary and silent system. There are long galleries of '**separate** apartments,' as they are delicately termed; court-yards where the prisoners are brought out one by one to take their exercise under the eye of a constable; and a chapel so fitted up that each man will—like a prebend or a horse, have a stall for himself, so constructed that he can see no one but the parson and the constables. The prisoners not in solitary confinement are marched to church, and have large pews or rather pens for their accommodation. G.C. MUNDY *Our Antipodes* vol. 3 p. 215

servant = ASSIGNED CONVICT. [First recorded in the convict context in 1802.]

A servant, or person employed in the household or private service of another, was likely to be a CONVICT SERVANT or ASSIGNED SERVANT in colonial Australia. Thus 'servant' was often a shortened form of these two designations. Servants in colonial Australia were employed in either government or private service and were subject to similar treatment as British servants.

> **1812** The Governor received me very graciously, allotted me a neat brick-house in the vicinity of the office, and a government-man, victualled from the King's-stores, as a **servant**. J.H. VAUX *Memoirs* (1964) vol. 1 pp. 178–9

servant of the Crown, a euphemism for CONVICT (one who works for the government). [First recorded 1788.]

> **1834** Those sent into private families are without any mark of disgrace, but are apparently the same as hired servants in England; they are fed and clothed, but receive no wages. It is said they never forgive a person who accidentally calls them 'convicts;' they denominate themselves '**servants of the crown**,' and settlers invariably do the same. J. ROBERTS *Two Years at Sea* pp. 125–6

service the state of (a convict's) being in the employ of a private individual or of government. [First recorded 1832.]

Convicts were generally either in private service, which meant they were ASSIGNED to a private master or household, or in the employ of government (also known as being in SERVICE OF GOVERNMENT). Convicts in private service were similar to servants in Britain in terms of the law, but could be flogged or subjected to other punishments (assigned by a magistrate) for misbehaving.

> **1843** Having pointed out to your Lordship how very far it is from the truth that the holders of tickets of leave are as a class better-conducted than assigned servants, or employed by a better class of people, I would beg leave to suggest that some degree of restriction should be enforced by law upon their disposal of themselves in private **service**, even though it should be deemed right to give them more liberty in this respect than they had in the preceding stage; for it seems very unreasonable, and lamentable, that the very service which now, as an assigned servant, the female prisoner is not allowed to enter, as being thoroughly disreputable, should be the very first which she rushes into when she has become her own mistress. J. FRANKLIN *Confidential Despatch* p. 46

service of government (of a convict) the state of being in the employ of the colonial government as opposed to private ASSIGNMENT.

> **1850** *Julia Chard*, now *Danby*, t.l., per *Sovereign*, was charged by constable Simpson with misconduct in being away from her authorised place of residence since December last. She pleaded guilty, and the prosecutor stated that she had been living in a house of ill-fame. The woman was discharged to the **service of Government**, because she did not attend the last general muster. *Irish Exile* (Hobart) 29 June p. 6

servitude the period of time a person served as a convict. [Specific use of standard English *servitude* 'absence of personal freedom'. First recorded in the Australian convict context in 1787.]

> **1787** [Governor Phillip's Instructions] And whereas we have by our Commission, bearing date [2nd April] 1787, given and granted upon you full power and authority to emancipate and discharge from their **servitude** any of the convicts under your superintendence who shall, from their good conduct and a disposition to industry, be deserving of favour: It is our will and pleasure that in every such case you do issue your warrant to the Surveyor of Lands to make surveys of and mark out in lots such lands upon the said territory as may be necessary for their use; and when that shall be done, that you do pass grants thereof with all convenient speed to any of the said convicts so emancipated. *Historical Records of New South Wales* vol. 1 part II p. 90

1852 To erect the barriers of caste around so small a section, and to exclude emancipists from the common intercourse of social life, was a task no Governor could then accomplish, without danger. The changes which followed Macquarie's administration, especially the growth of a free population, enabled his successors to effect what, in 1817 to 1820, had been attempted in vain. The opposition encountered by Macquarie, and which he resented with the ardour of his character, enabled his enemies to represent him as the patron of criminals. He was said to look upon their offences in the light of misfortunes, which they were to repair in the country of their exile, rather than to atone by the severities of toil and privation; and that they were taught to look upon no title to property, as so just as that which had been derived by passing from crime to conviction; from thence to **servitude**, emancipation, and grant. J. WEST *The History of Tasmania* vol. 2 pp. 151–2

settler's man a convict assigned to a settler. [First recorded 1804.]

A settler's man was a convict assigned to the service of a settler. Settlers in Australia employed convicts to do work on their properties such as agricultural work and caring for sheep and cattle.

1804 At half past eleven o'clock on Sunday night, an express was received by HIS EXCELLENCY, from Captain ABBOT, Commanding Officer at Parramatta, with intelligence that the Prisoners at Public Labour at Castle Hill, and the **Settlers men**, were in a state of Insurrection, and had already committed many daring Outrages: Sydney was instantaneously alarmed, the Military and Inhabitants were under Arms, and the Captain, Officers, Marines, and Ships Company of His Majesty's Ship Calcutta came on shore, in Ten minutes after the alarm was given, and by the GOVERNOR'S Orders all Horses throughout the Town were held in requisition. *Sydney Gazette* 11 Mar. p. 2

seven (also **seven year** or **seven years'**) used to designate a convict who had a seven-year sentence of imprisonment. [First recorded 1827.]

Seven years was the most common sentence, with about half of those transported to the Australian colonies having such a sentence. A person with such a sentence was also known as a SEVENER.

1829 A **seven years'** convict, both as regards the future welfare of the colonies and the state of society at home is, I conceive, the best prisoner that can be sent out; he is in general young, and his crime, as his term of imprisonment implies, of course not very heinous. H. WIDOWSON *Present State of Van Diemen's Land* p. 63

1833 That, the number of years, for a **seven**, fourteen, or life convict, to serve in the Gangs, before he can get his ticket-of-leave, to be mentioned, and the

ticket-of-leave always to be granted, except the man should have conducted
'himself incorrectly, but his additional period to serve, to be defined. Thus,
seven years men, if sent at all, three years in the Gangs, and the remainder of
their sentence to have tickets-of-leave on good conduct; to be mustered weekly
if living in Town; and monthly, if in the Country; paying to the Government
by annual instalments, the expenses their Country has been put to, by their
crimes. T. BANNISTER *A Letter on Colonial Labour* p. 12

sevener a convict sentenced to a term of SEVEN years, the most common sentence given to the transported convicts.

> **1847** *Thomas Simpson.*—Larceny. Seven years transportation.
> [After this man left the dock, the Pentonville convict Devlin, who appeared to
> be so much affected a few minutes before, as to shed tears, burst into a fit of
> laughing, and giving a low 'flash' whistle, exclaimed to a fellow 'exile,' 'halloo!
> there's an old bloke of a "**seven'ner**" for you.'] *Port Phillip Herald* 3 Aug. p. 3

short-sentence(d) (of a convict) sentenced to a short term of imprisonment,
usually of seven years. [First recorded 1835.]

> **1851** The British Government finding a difficulty in disposing of their con-
> victs, have lately forwarded some portion of the prisoner population to West-
> ern Australia, and the introduction even of convict labour, cannot be otherwise
> than beneficial to a community so impoverished as the Swan has been for want
> of labourers. It is nevertheless sincerely to be hoped that the home authorities
> will not force upon the settlers the educated 'Exiles,' but that the system of
> assignment formerly carried out so successfully in New South Wales and Van
> Diemen's Land may be adopted; nor must the colony be inundated with con-
> victs as Van Diemen's Land has been, but only a sufficient number of **short
> sentenced** men should be sent there. H. MELVILLE *The Present State of
> Australia* p. 51

single iron one fetter. [First recorded 1802.]
A single iron was placed around the ankle of a convict as a form of punishment, and to prevent convicts working on labour gangs from absconding. A single
iron was a less severe punishment than a DOUBLE iron.

> **1804** On Friday eleven servants of the Crown, employed as smiths in the
> Government Work-shop, were complained of before HIS EXCELLENCY by their
> superintendant, for insolence and repeated refusal to comply with his direc-
> tions. Two were selected from among the number, and as principal aggressors
> ordered to work in irons in the gaol gang; the others to return to their former
> work: but as a punishment to labour in a **single iron** every evening until dusk.
> *Sydney Gazette* 23 Dec. p. 3

skilly a thin, watery porridge, gruel or soup, fed to the convicts as part of their RATIONS. [This abbreviated form of *skilligalee* (itself a fanciful formation) is first recorded in Britain in 1839 in the context of the prison hulks, and later in prisons and workhouses. The earliest record of *skilligalee* is from J.H. Vaux (see FLASH): 'Tolerable flour, of which the cook composed a certain food for breakfast, known among sailors by the name of skilligolee, being in plain English, paste'. First recorded in the Australian convict context in 1842.]

> **1846** The daily rations allowed to the prisoners is, for breakfast and supper a pint of **skilly** and six ounces of coarse bread; for dinner, twelve ounces of fresh meat and eight of salt, one half pound of vegetables made into soup, and a pound of bread. The meat is always of the poorest quality, and as it passes through many dishonest hands, but a small portion of it reaches the men. I have no hesitation in asserting that at least one half of the crimes committed by the prisoners, and for which they are so severely punished, may be attributed to the insufficiency of their rations. A craving appetite brings many a poor fellow to the triangles, and I am perhaps justified in adding, the gallows. L.W. MILLER *Notes of an Exile to Van Dieman's Land* p. 284

slops garments and blankets made cheaply from poor material and distributed to convicts. [From standard English *slops* in the sense 'ready-made clothing and other furnishings supplied to seamen from the ship's stores; hence, ready-made, cheap, or inferior garments generally'. First recorded in the Australian convict context in 1798.]

Convicts in prisons and government service were given this cheap clothing (similar to British working-class clothing) as uniforms. Once convicts were 'off the STORES' they could buy clothes for themselves. Supply of clothing to the colonies, especially in the first years, was often patchy and inadequate. Men were generally issued with short jackets, trousers, shirts, and tall crowned hats; women with jackets, petticoats, skirts, kerchiefs, caps and hats.

> **1798** They [the watchmen] were required to detain and give information to the nearest guardhouse of any soldier or seaman who should be found straggling after the taptoo had been beat. They were to use their utmost endeavours to trace out offenders on receiving accounts of any depredation; and in addition to their night duty, they were directed to take cognizance of such convicts as gamed, or sold and bartered their **slops** or provisions, and report them for punishment. D. COLLINS *An Account of the English Colony of New South Wales* vol. 1 p. 78

> **1822** The superintendence of the government convicts in New South Wales is generally considered to be vested in the person of William Hutchinson, who has filled the situation of principal superintendent of convicts at Sydney since the 9th of April 1814. The previous condition of this individual is described in

the evidence of Mr. Harris. During the period in which he served as a convict at Sydney, he had charge of a small gang of convicts employed about the town; but having been accused of being accessary to the theft of a bale of **slops** from the king's stores, that were found in his possession, he was tried and sent to Norfolk Island, where he conducted himself well as superintendent of convicts, and was recommended by Lieutenant-colonel Foveaux to Governor Macquarrie on his arrival. J.T. BIGGE *Report of the Commissioner of Inquiry into the State of the Colony of New South Wales* p. 52

social system a system of convict management formulated by Alexander Maconochie (1787–1860) and partially adopted as an experiment on Norfolk Island. [First recorded 1839.]

Maconochie believed that existing penal methods were debasing and thus devised a flexible incentive scheme for rehabilitating convicts, which allowed them rewards for good behaviour that might ultimately lead to freedom. He believed cruel and degrading punishments and conditions were wrong. His 1837 *Report on the State of Prison Discipline in Van Diemen's Land* influenced the Molesworth Committee's 1838 recommendations. He was then appointed superintendent at Norfolk Island in 1840 to put his ideas into practice. His experiment failed, partly because he was not given enough time to test them and also because of numerous outbreaks of trouble on the island. He was recalled in 1844 and his system written off as a failure.

1838 BUT IT IS A SOCIAL SYSTEM; and in this light, as distinguished from a *Separate* one,—and still more from the present, which is an intensely *selfish* and demoralizing one, I confidently maintain that it is founded on better principles. It is more in harmony with human nature than either of them,—more powerful in its machinery, —and more calculated, accordingly, to produce a lasting effect on those subjected to it. It is also higher in its aims. It desires to *influence*, not merely to *coerce*; to influence *whole classes* also, not merely *individuals*;—to give to each well-intentioned criminal the support and sympathy *of his fellows* in a *virtuous* career, not merely to deter him from following bad examples, or to seclude him from their (supposed) noxious influence;—to prepare him thus for society, in society, not to sequester, and unfit him for it;—and to nourish his good resolutions by a systematic *esprit de corps* in his class, not to sentence him to the most painful and difficult of all possible tasks, the steady resistance of the impulses which, in existing circumstances, his companions are alone calculated to convey to him? A. MACONOCHIE *Thoughts on Convict Management* p. 71

1840 We understand that Sir George Gipps fully enters into all Captain Maconochie's views of the **Social System**, and that he has introduced it on a small scale on the roads round Sydney, where all the men who get their tickets suspended for slight offences, are working out their probation in small social system parties, without overseers. There is great reason to hope that the head quarters of the 'Social System' will be ultimately brought to Port Arthur, and that Norfolk Island will be an auxiliary establishment as an hospital for *incorrigibles*. This will be the making of Hobart Town, for it is calculated that there will be always 10,000 probation men at the head quarters, and that there will be from 2,000 to 3,000 discharged every year when the system is fully in operation. Captain Maconochie and his family proceed by the *Lagton*, via Sydney, for Norfolk Island, where it is expected he will only remain for a short time before shifting his flag to Port Arthur. *True Colonist* (Hobart) 3 Jan. p. 7

special = GENTLEMAN CONVICT. [First recorded 1832.]

1832 The gentlemen convicts, who are denominated **specials**, were in the habit of being sent to a depot at Wellington, and I believe, that at no time did the number of these exceed one hundred. When I visited that place, there but 40, out of whom, I had reason to believe, there were several who, at no period, had any title to be considered as gentlemen; and although there were amongst these several who had been officers of the army and navy, few, if any of them, could be said to have received a liberal education. J. HENDERSON *Observations on the Colonies of New South Wales and Van Diemen's Land* pp. 9–10

station an outpost of the colonial government, usually an establishment for convicts employed on public works. [Specific use of *station* 'a place where soldiers are garrisoned; a military post'. The first *stations* in Australia were for convicts. But by the 1820s the term was used in the compound *home station* to mean 'the principal residence on a large stock-raising property, together with the associated buildings and establishment (yards, accommodation for employees, etc.)', and by the 1840s it was used in the sense 'an extensive sheep or cattle raising establishment'. First recorded in the convict context in 1816.]

Stations were often located in isolated areas where convicts did such work as clearing the wilderness. Sometimes convicts were sent to such isolated stations as punishment. An example of a punishment station was Coal Mines Station at Plunkett Point in Van Diemen's Land, a punishment station for Port Arthur. Stations were also an important feature of the probation system, in which convicts were required to spend time working at PROBATION STATIONS, as part of their reformation.

1822 Since the improvement of the roads and bridges was undertaken by Major Druitt, the chief engineer, in the year 1819, several gangs of convicts, amounting in the month of November 1819 to 362, under the superintendence of overseers, have been employed in this service. The gangs vary from 30 to 60 each; and as their work proceeds, they remove their huts, which are always constructed of the branches and bark of the eucalyptus, from one **station** to another. This operation is attended with very little difficulty and no expense.

J.T. Bigge *Report of the Commissioner of Inquiry into the State of the Colony of New South Wales* p. 26

1854 Few scenes are more magnificent than those opening each moment to your view, coasting along Frederick-Henry Bay; and the stranger immediately exclaims, 'What a paradise this might be, were all those romantic looking hills and undulating lands inhabited!' But, alas! save at the **stations**, built alone for the punishment of crime, no human dwelling meets the eye; and, while thousands crowd our overgrown cities in the Old World, and street upon street is filled with the abodes of poverty and destitution, sweeter land than ever the sun shone upon now lies a neglected waste. H.B. Stoney *A Year in Tasmania* p. 37

stepper = TREADMILL. [Used elsewhere but first recorded in Australia in 1832.]

1832 Frank Howard, having moistened his clay the previous evening until he was unable to walk, was sentenced to try 'the **stepper**' for ten days. *Sydney Herald* 23 Jan. p. 2

stockade a structure in which convict gangs working in outlying districts were accommodated. [Transferred use of standard English *stockade* 'a military fortification'. First recorded in the convict context in 1832.]

In the convict colonies, a stockade usually consisted of a staked fence, surrounding a number of convict facilities, including the men's and hospital huts. Some of the convict stockades were re-usable or mobile.

1834 [Governor Bourke to Lord Stanley] One Cook and one Mess Man will be allowed to each **Stockade**, who will be assisted by a delegate chosen in rotation daily from among the Prisoners in Irons. *Historical Records of Australia* 1st series XVII p. 339

1850 Now all my hopes of gaining permanent liberty were blasted; I felt as the tiger does when he is snared; my situation was then worse than any in which I had previously been; my heart sunk within me, and I groaned while I remained passive to the power of those who had got me once more within their grasp. I was that day and night at the police office, and the next morning taken before a soldier officer, of the name of Willison, and by him sentenced to fifty lashes, with orders to be sent to a **Stockade** station; I think eighteen in number were all handcuffed. As I was leaving the court house, the soldier past by with ten shillings in his hand, that he had received for my apprehension and conviction; what he thought I cannot tell, but what I felt I do know. C.A. King *Life of Charles Adolphus King* p. 26

store (often in plural **stores**) the stock of provisions, clothing, and other necessities for the inhabitants of the colonies; the building that housed them. [First recorded 1789.]

The government stores were necessary for survival, particularly in the early, difficult days of settlement. They provided not only convicts but also the various government personnel and some settlers with provisions. Convicts who were supported by the government stores were known to be **on the stores**; those able to support themselves (for example, on a ticket of leave, or on ASSIGNED SERVICE) were **off the stores**. Those off the stores were free to dress and eat as they pleased. In times of economic difficulty, however, the stores helped to sustain convicts and settlers alike. The stores were essential in the development of the colonial economy and local industry. See also KING'S STORES.

> **1829** When a prisoner is in future to be assigned to a Settler, he will receive a complete suit of slop clothing from the Public **Stores**, for which his master must pay, on delivery, the cost-price and charges of importation. The rate of a suit is, for the present, fixed at £1 10s. By this mode, it is hoped to obviate the dissatisfaction which has been frequently expressed at receiving servants from the Government insufficiently clothed. *Tasmanian Almanack* pp. 70–1

Also in the phrase **off the store(s)** [First recorded 1792.]

> **1832** [Governor Bourke to Lord Goderich] The condition of the holder of a Ticket of Leave or Exemption is usually this: He is first of all *taken **off the Stores***, as it is technically called, or relieved from the power of a Master by whom he was clothed and fed, and is authorized within a certain specified district to pursue any honest avocation for his livelihood. *Historical Records of Australia* 1st series XVI p. 805

Also in the phrase **on the store(s)** [First recorded 1801.]

> **1813** [Governor Macquarie to Earl Bathurst] Your Lordship does not direct any other Indulgences to be given to Mr. Lord, besides his Grant of Land. I have however taken upon myself the Responsibility of putting himself and his Family **on the Store** for Eighteen Months, and have assigned to him Six Government Men, as Laborers, who are also to be Clothed and Victualled at the Expence of the Crown for the same Period of Time. *Historical Records of Australia* 1st series VII pp. 725–6

superintendent of convicts an official who supervised overseers and convicts, and was a kind of chief overseer. [First recorded 1790.]

> **1822** The **Superintendent of convicts** is thus perfectly apprized of every thing requisite for directing a just and satisfactory assignment of the prisoners; and as, when once they are placed in his hands, no other authority interposes, much good or evil is to be expected from his management. Mr Hutchinson, the person now exercising that office at Sydney, was himself formerly a convict; and from his various means of obtaining intelligence, well may he be supposed,—so

far as the ample jurisdiction he exercises can extend,—to possess information universally correct regarding the circumstances of every family: he is therefore fully competent to determine what description of convict is best suited for any particular service: too often, however, does caprice, if not motives more unworthy, appear to influence him in the performance of this important duty. T. REID *Two Voyages to New South Wales and Van Diemen's Land* p. 252

swag a thief's plunder or booty. [The OED gives this definition and adds that the term is used generally to mean 'a quantity of money or goods unlawfully acquired, gains dishonestly made'. While this is a FLASH term, the OED's earliest evidence is from Australia in 1812.]

This flash term was obviously used by the convicts in its underworld sense, but by the middle of the nineteenth century it had developed its distinctive Australian sense: 'the collection of possessions and daily necessities carried by a person travelling on foot, often in the bush; especially the blanket-wrapped roll carried by an itinerant worker'. This sense of *swag*, and other terms such as *swagman*, owe their existence to the underground slang that was transported to Australia with the convicts.

> **1812** SWAG: a bundle, parcel, or package; as a *swag* of *snow, &c. The swag*, is a term used in speaking of any booty you have lately obtained, be it of what kind it may, except money, as Where did you *lumber the swag*? that is, where did you deposit the stolen property? To carry *the swag* is to be the bearer of the stolen goods to a place of safety. *A swag* of any thing, signifies emphatically a great deal. To have *knap'd* a good *swag*, is to have got a good booty. J.H. VAUX *Memoirs* (1964) vol. 2 p. 272.

swell mob a group of professional criminals. [The OED defines *swell mob* (earliest citation 1836) as a 'class of pickpockets who assumed the dress and manners of respectable people in order to escape detection'. There is slightly earlier evidence in Australia, where a poem published in 1832 alludes to pickpockets, but uses *swell mob* to mean the more general criminal class. This is typical of most of the Australian evidence, where it tends to mean 'professional' criminals (thieves, forgers, etc).]

> **1832** Not many months from that same day
>   Did I remain with Dad;
>   Who would not let me have my way,
>   'Cause why, he said 'twas bad;
>   But from the hour I saw that fight
>   Somehow a notion ran
>   Within my breast that in dad's spite
>   I'd be a SWELL-MOB man. *Hill's Life* 16 Nov.

1837 A common labourer, or industrious mechanic, whom want of work and distress may have driven into the temporary commission of crime, is as liable and as likely to be transported, as the most expert thief and experienced depredator in London. Every convict ship takes out to the colony men of the above description, as well as desperate and practised burglars, habitual and experienced receivers of stolen goods, artful and designing swindlers, skilful forgers, robbers of banks and mail coaches, and a sprinkling of all sorts of the villains denominated the ***swell mob***. J. MUDIE *The Felonry of New South Wales* pp. 177–8

T

task work a set piece of work assigned to a convict for completion; piece-work. [First recorded 1789.]

Task work was common in Britain for skilled workers, and since it gave these workers the freedom to complete work at their own rate, it was a sign of status and independence. It formed an important part of the early convict system. Soon after establishing the colonies, it was realised that it was more effective to assign convicts to task work than to set regulation working hours. Convicts were thus given task work, and upon completion, they could enjoy their 'own time' or could work for themselves for extra money or goods. However, the citation below suggests that sometimes a more restrictive system of task work was implemented, to increase both productivity and control over the convicts. Task work continued as an important part of organising labour on government farms.

> **1822** The variety of work carried on at Sydney is described by Major Druitt in his evidence, and it appears that **task work** is allotted to every convict, where such an arrangement is practicable. Since the appointment of that officer in the year 1819, the quantity of task work has been increased to the nail-makers, brick-makers, stone-cutters and sawyers, and it has been an object with him to raise it, as nearly as he could, to the extent that an able bodied man can perform in a day, and within the hour appointed for the cessation of government work, and this plan has, in some species of labour, been found to be practicable; but it is adopted more for the purpose of securing and ascertaining that a certain quantity of labour is performed, than of stimulating the quicker performance of it by the hope of reward; for although the task may be performed before the appointed hour, the workman is not allowed to retire, either to the barrack or to his own home, but remains in the lumber yard till the expiration of the hours of work, and if the allotted task be not accomplished in that time,

the chief engineer has the power of ordering the defaulter to work on Saturdays after ten o'clock. J.T. BIGGE *Report of the Commissioner of Inquiry into the State of the Colony of New South Wales* p. 29

ticket = TICKET OF LEAVE. [First recorded 1819.]

1838 [Sir George Gipps to Lord Glenelg] Since Convict labor has become so exceedingly valuable as it now is, it is a matter of very frequent complaint that Masters prevent their servants getting Tickets of Leave from an unwillingness to lose their labor; and that they even cause (in some cases) their men to be punished, for the sake of retaining their services, it being known to your Lordship that each punishment, which an assigned servant receives, puts him back a year in getting his **Ticket**. *Historical Records of Australia* 1st series XIX p. 604

ticketer = TICKET OF LEAVE MAN or TICKET OF LEAVE WOMAN. [First recorded 1844.]

1844 David Ockworthy, T.L., was charged by D.C. Smith (*parvus*), with refusing to tell who he was when taken in charge at 12 o'clock the night before. He was sent for two months on the roads, his Worship observing that there was rather too much of this sort of work now carrying on amongst the **ticketers**. *Colonial Times* (Hobart) 2 Nov. p. 3

ticket holder = TICKET OF LEAVE HOLDER. [First recorded 1845.]

1845 A man in the employ of Mr. Jerman, at Fitzgerald's Swamp, being awoke about midnight, on the 20th, by a very loud noise among the sheep pens, got up, thinking that the native dogs had taken a fancy to a little fresh mutton, but on going out, discovered that the dog was one on two legs, who was coolly driving off some hundreds of sheep. His master being immediately called, started in pursuit with him. After the man who, on finding that he was observed, had bolted; and they succeeded in capturing him, he turned out to be a **ticket-holder** named Connell, lately been liberated from custody, on a charge of murder, owing to the evidence against him being defective. *Parramatta Chronicle* 31 May p. 4

1852 The memorandum of the chief police magistrate, beside briefly describing the practice of former times, recommended important changes for the future. Instead of assignment from the ships, he suggested that all prisoners should be placed on the public works, for a period to be fixed by the judges. He proposed a new distribution of time penalties: thus instead of seven, fourteen years, and life, to recognise by law a more minute and proportionate subdivision. In assignment, he recommended wages, rateable at the discretion of the government; afterwards a *first-class* ticket-of-leave, with a permission to choose employers; and a *second class*, to include most of the privileges of freedom, voidable only by a court of quarter sessions for specified offences. The conditional pardon he deemed it necessary to defer a longer time than usual; since, when released from surveillance and responsibility, **ticket-holders** often relapsed into the vices from which they had previously emerged. J. WEST *The History of Tasmania* vol. 2 p. 268

ticket man = TICKET OF LEAVE MAN. [First recorded 1827.]

1827 For our own parts, provided such convict servants be in future assigned to persons indifferently, and permitted to be employed in Sydney, that is to say, are assigned on some equitable plan, and not given to the creatures of the Government only—not to the civil and military officers only—then we should, on a broad principle, highly approve of the prisoners being for the most part sent up the country. All the effects of such a measure will be good. It will tend to raise the price of ticket and free labour in the towns, and the possessors of ticket and free service being mostly married men, good wages will enable them to bring up their families with the greater decency. **Ticket-men** up the country have a poor life of it under the present regulations. Their tickets and their persons will be much safer under our Sydney magistrates, than they would under the country ones. *Sydney Monitor* 23 Mar. p. 356

ticket of exemption (in full **ticket of exemption from Government Labour** or **Service**) a permit issued to a convict allowing residence with a spouse. [First recorded 1830.]

A ticket of exemption was a type of ticket or pass that differed from a TICKET OF LEAVE. With a ticket of exemption an individual was not allowed to employ him or herself, or to acquire property. It simply allowed a convict to reside with a person named on the ticket, usually a spouse or family member. Thus women were the most likely to receive such tickets. The holder of such a ticket was required to attend muster and church. The main purpose of this type of ticket was to save the government from responsibility, especially financial, for them.

1836 Convicts are discharged from the factory by three methods—tickets of leave at the expiration of half their time of sentence, **tickets of exemption** upon the arrival of their husbands in the colony, and tickets of exemption upon the application of a suitor, who must marry, forthwith, the damsel whose liberty he seeks. Sailors who have conceived a penchant for lady passengers on the voyage out, and are also, upon their arrival in the country, so in love with it as to wish to remain; and *legitimate* settlers who have served out their sentences and taken grants of land, are usually the applicants for wives at the factory. J.F. O'CONNELL *A Residence of Eleven Years in New Holland* pp. 47–8

ticket of leave 1 a permit or document that allowed a convict to live and work as a private individual within a stipulated area until the expiration or remission of sentence. [First recorded 1801.]

Such tickets were an important incentive for good behaviour. Tickets of leave were granted for good behaviour and also as part of an attempt to reduce the number of convicts being supported by government. Tickets were only issued to convicts after payment of a fee to the clerk who prepared it. Once convicts had their tickets they were free to work as they pleased, although they were still convicts in legal terms. After the receipt of a ticket and after having held one for a certain period of time, a ticket of leave holder could apply for a PARDON. Ticket of leave holders could not move to another district without permission, and movement between districts required a PASSPORT; the ticket of leave could also be revoked for bad behaviour. The ticket of leave or PASS system, introduced in New South Wales by Governor King, was integral to the convict system, and those granted a ticket of leave formed an important part of the colonial labour force and economy.

1813 [Governor Macquarie to Earl Bathurst] **Tickets of Leave** give no further Advantage or Privilege to the Holders of them, than that of Exemption from Public Labour; a Man, having a Ticket of Leave, is at liberty to work for himself and is no longer Victualled at the Expence of the Crown. They are mustered every Sunday and Obliged to Attend Church with the other Convicts, which retains them Still under the Eye and Observation of the Superintendants of Convicts. Tickets of Leave have generally been given by me to Men, who have been for many Years working for Government, or Assigned to Settlers, as Servants. Their having a Wife and Family to support forms another Strong Claim for this Indulgence being Conferred on them. Some few Convicts, who have been in the Line of Gentlemen before their Condemnation, and who bring very High Recommendations from Home, I have been induced to give Tickets of Leave to immediately on their Arrival. *Historical Records of Australia* 1st series VII p. 779

1859 By the regulations now in force, prisoners under sentences of less than three years are restored to freedom, if they are attentive and industrious at work, and their general conduct in confinement is irreproachable, when they have completed two thirds of their sentences; prisoners under longer sentences receive **tickets of leave**, if well conducted, when they have served one half of their sentences; these tickets of leave enable them to reside and work for their own advantage in any district in the colony they may select; but places them under the surveillance of the police, to whom they are required to report their residences. If they continue to conduct themselves properly, they are restored to freedom when they have served for a period equal to one third of the time they originally served in the gang. W. FAIRFAX *Handbook to Australasia* p. 61

2 a convict who held a ticket of leave. Such convicts were not legally free, and if they behaved badly or broke the law, their ticket might be revoked. This threat of revocation was an incentive for convicts to behave well.

1826   The Clerk of the Bench in writing down the evidence, does not write *the words of the witnesses*, but *his own words*; and which latter, are *not always a correct explanation* of the words of the witnesses. Besides what right has Mr. Fulton, who is the proxy for the Judge in taking down the notes; to go to Kaine's house *as a Police Officer*, and, by the whole tenour of his behaviour, *identify himself with her Accuser*, seeing he is allowed to set down *the evidence by which she is to be judged?* The other witness against Kaine, Howarth, was reminded by the Magistrate, previous to his deposition, '*that he was a **ticket-of-leave**;*' by which she complains the man would perhaps feel excited to swear something different to what he would have sworn, if he had not so been reminded. *Sydney Monitor* 1 Sept. p. 123

ticket of leave class the group of the colonial population who held tickets of leave. [First recorded 1851.]

1851   Those possessing the indulgence [of a ticket of leave], are obliged to muster occasionally, but otherwise they enjoy the same privileges as the free inhabitants—they enter into business, and very many of them are traders and shop-keepers. They are not allowed to hold landed property; so that in many respects the **ticket of leave class** possess about the same privileges in the colony, as the Jews now do in Great Britain. When the ticket of leave owner has retained his indulgence for the stipulated time, under the modern system, he obtains his conditional pardon, and becomes free of the Australasian settlements, he then can hold land, and is in every respect free, on condition that he does not return to Great Britain.   H. Melville *The Present State of Australia* p. 139

ticket of leave constable a police officer who had a TICKET OF LEAVE. [First recorded 1837.]

1842   Police Magistrates in general appear to have a strong sympathy with the dregs of the constabulary. 'This fellow feeling makes them wondrous kind,' and leads them to a belief in their own and each other's infallibility. Magistrates are too frequently the mere tools of their own petty officers; this arises from sheer indolence, and a **ticket-of-leave constable** may, if he take the trouble, virtually become the ACTING police magistrate. *Geelong Advertiser* 7 Mar. p. 2

ticket of leave convict a convict who held a TICKET OF LEAVE. [First recorded 1849.]

1857   We arrived at Newcastle soon after eight o'clock, where we remained a few minutes to land and take in passengers, after which we started for Sydney. After rounding the Nobbies a strong southerly breeze rose, and in about half-an-hour a heaving sea was tumbling us about at a tremendous rate. Mother

Smith and her husband both turned sick, and made a serious uproar between them. ... There was a young man, a **ticket-of-leave convict** from Morton Bay, who was in a dreadful state of alarm about going down; and his wife, a pretty young woman, with an infant in her arms, was clinging to him for support. J. ASKEW *A Voyage to Australia and New Zealand* pp. 250–1

ticket of leave holder a person who held a TICKET OF LEAVE. [First recorded 1835.]

1846 [Sir Charles Fitz Roy to Right Hon. W.E. Gladstone] An application (of which I have the honor to transmit a Copy herewith) having been recently submitted to me, requesting free passages to be granted to the Wife and children of Bryan Veech, a **Ticket of leave holder** under this Government. I feel it my duty to bring under your notice the great hardship of the decision of Her Majesty's Government ... to the discontinuance of free passages for the Wives and families of Convicts to this Colony, on account of its being no longer a place of Transportation, and the encreased expenditure that would be thereby incurred. *Historical Records of Australia* 1st series XXV p. 190

ticket of leave man a male convict who held a TICKET OF LEAVE. [First recorded 1807.]

1838 Ticket-of-leave men find no difficulty in obtaining work at high wages; and having acquired experience in the colony, they are frequently preferred to lately-arrived emigrants. They fill many situations of trust in both colonies; such, for instance, as constables in the police, overseers of road-parties, and chain-gangs; the better educated have been employed as superintendents of estates, as clerks to bankers, to lawyers, and to shopkeepers, and even as tutors in private families; some have married free women, are in prosperous circumstances, and have even become wealthy. W. MOLESWORTH *Report from the Select Committee of the House of Commons on Transportation* p. 18

ticket of leave muster a routine assembly of all those with tickets of leave to ascertain their whereabouts. [First recorded 1837.]

1848 The annual **ticket-of-leave muster** has also taken place, but the gentry holding that indulgence are by no means punctual in reporting themselves to the magistrates; their periodical visits to the village, however, are not marked by drunkenness or irregularity, as in former years—but their musters now pass off in the most orderly manner. *Sydney Morning Herald* 14 Jan. p. 2

ticket of leaver a convict who held a TICKET OF LEAVE. [First recorded 1852.]

1852 The aggressions of the savage are followed by acts of reprisal on the part of the white man. The overseer, the stockman, and the shepherd of the distant pasturing station may be hireling convicts—emancipist, expiree, or **ticket-of-leavers**—not models of virtue and forbearance. G.C. MUNDY *Our Antipodes* vol. 1 p. 228

ticket of leave servant a convict servant who held a TICKET OF LEAVE. [First recorded 1829.]

1829 The next description of servant is the one which is free by servitude; and who has the modesty to ask 10s., 15s., and even 20s. a-week wages, in addition to his board and lodging; and on receiving a reproval for any acts of drunkenness or disturbance in your house, it is no unusual thing to be told that he is as free as you are; a species of audacity that frequently terminates in his leaving your employment during harvest, or some other equally important period. Nor are you much better off with **ticket-of-leave servants**, who will ask the same wages as the free man; but with this difference, that you have a check upon them in the case of misconduct, a representation of which to the proper authorities, will deprive them of their ticket, and they are again reduced to the situation of convict servants, of whom I will proceed to speak. H. WIDOWSON *The Present State of Van Diemen's Land* p. 53

ticket of leave woman a female convict who held a TICKET OF LEAVE. [First recorded 1820.]

1846 The great mass, however, of the women in the factories are composed of those who are returned thither for crimes and misdemeanours in assigned service, or of **ticket-of-leave women** under punishment. There is undoubtedly a reluctance in respectable families to take the women from the factories; they prefer having the newcomers from the ships. J. FRANKLIN *Confidential Despatch* p. 14

ticket woman = TICKET OF LEAVE WOMAN. [First recorded 1847.]

1847 The immortal bard has told us that 'a rose by any other name would smell as sweet,' but a recent case, heard before Mr. Macdowell, shows that even Shakespeare's genius is sometimes in error. A **ticket woman**, flashily dressed, having a dash of 'romance' in her composition, and who stated her name was *Miss* Wilhelmina Lavinia Lucretia, (something else, our reporter did not catch,) was charged with having been found in the paddock on the previous evening, rather too much 'how come you so,' and was uttering (as the policeman said) strange 'jabberish,' at a very untimeous period of the night. *Britannia* (Hobart) 17 June p. 2

town gang a party of convicts assigned to hard labour on public works in a town. [First recorded 1796.]

1796 The carpenters continued erecting the temporary shed for provisions; the **town gang** was employed delivering the storeships; and at Toongabbe some women were employed in making hay, intended to be put on board the king's ships for the cattle to be purchased at the Cape for the colony. D. COLLINS *An Account of the English Colony at New South Wales* (1798) vol. 1 p. 485

1804 The inhabitants of Sydney are desired to send Assistance to the Superintendant who has the direction of the repairs wanting to the Public Roads leading towards Parramatta, as specified in a former Order, the Government **Town Gangs** being now at work thereon. *Sydney Gazette* 2 Sept. p. 1

transport 1 *noun* a person who was under sentence of TRANSPORTATION. [The term is first recorded in the context of the transportation of convicts to America in 1767. It is first recorded in an Australian context in 1803, and in Australia the term often serves as a euphemism for 'convict'.]

1803 On Wednesday 10 prisoners who were capitally convicted at the last Criminal Court, were respited by His Excellency, on condition of their becoming **Transports** for Life. *Sydney Gazette* 10 Apr. p. 3

2 *verb* to deport (a person sentenced in Britain or Ireland) to a penal colony in Australia. [Specific use of *transport* in the sense 'to carry away or convey into banishment, as a criminal or slave' (OED), first recorded in 1666 in the context of sending convicts to the American colonies. First recorded in the Australian convict context in 1788.]

1801 In the autumn of 1794 warrants of emancipation passed the great seal of the settlement, in behalf of Robert Sidaway, who received an unconditional pardon, in consideration of his diligence, good conduct, and strict integrity in his employment for several years, as the public baker of the settlement; and William Leach, who was permitted to quit the country, provided he did not return to England till the term of his transportation was expired. Eight were permitted to list in the New South Wales Corps, and James Harris, James Ruffler, and Richard Partridge, who were all **transported** for life, received a pardon, or (according to their own term) were made free on the ground, which enabled them to become settlers, as were also William Joyce, Benjamin Carver, and William Waring. G. BARRINGTON *A Sequel to Barrington's Voyage to New South Wales* pp. 61–2

transportable (of a criminal offence) attracting a sentence of transportation to a penal colony in Australia. [First recorded in 1769 in the context of sending convicts to America. First recorded in the Australian convict context in 1833.]

A transportable offence was a criminal offence that was likely to attract a sentence of transportation as punishment. This offence might be committed in the home country, but it might also be a crime committed in the colonies for which a sentence of transportation to a PENAL SETTLEMENT or place of SECONDARY punishment was given.

1833 [Governor Bourke to Right Hon. E.G. Stanley] I do not think that limiting by Act of Parliament the Eligibility of the Candidate in the same way that it is limited in Canada and Newfoundland, namely to Persons who had never been convicted of Felony or any **transportable** Offence, would be received with an ill-grace by the generality of the Colonists, nor even by the better thinking part of the Emancipists, few of whom stand in that relative position to the Electors as to be likely to be returned even if eligible to become Members of the Legislative Council. *Historical Records of Australia* 1st series XVII p. 306

1846 [Right Hon. W.E. Gladstone to Sir Charles Fitz Roy] He observes that the fact of having arrived in the Colony, under a Sentence of Transportation, fixes on a man in New S. Wales a character, of which, in after life, he never can entirely divest himself. Though he become perfectly free by the expiration of his Sentence or by virtue of a Pardon from the Crown, he is liable to be punished for subsequent offences in a manner, in which a man, who came free to the Colony or was born in it, cannot be punished; that is to say, he may be worked in Irons, and, if he commit **transportable** offence, he is transported to a penal Settlement (either Norfolk Island, or Tasman's Peninsula) instead of being sent to what is called a Probation Gang in Van D. Land. *Historical Records of Australia* 1st series XXV p. 57

transportation 1 The deportation of a person sentenced in Britain or Ireland to a penal colony in Australia. [First recorded in 1669 in the context of sending already convicted felons to the American colonies. First recorded in the Australian convict context in 1789.]

By the eighteenth century, transportation was an established punishment in British law, as Britain continued to transport its prisoners to the American colonies. For serious crimes, execution or transportation was the usual punishment, with transportation originating as a measure of executive clemency for those who were to be executed. It was an act of banishing or exiling the unwanted from the country, and largely ensuring that they would not return. The idea of transportation was well entrenched in British penal practice. Thus, after the American Revolution, hulks moored in rivers and ports were used to house prisoners until transportation to Australia began in 1788.

1838 The punishment of **Transportation** is founded on that of exile, both of which are unknown to common law. Exile, according to the best authorities, was introduced, as a punishment, by the Legislature in the 39th year of Elizabeth;

and the first time that Transportation was mentioned was in an Act of 18 Chas. I, c. 3, which empowered the judges to exile for life the moss-troopers of Cumberland and Northumberland, to any of his Majesty's possessions in America. The punishment, authorized by this Act, is somewhat different from the one now termed Transportation, inasmuch as the latter consists not only of exile to a particular place, but of compulsory labour there. W. MOLESWORTH *Report from the Select Committee of the House of Commons on Transportation* p. 7

2 The committal to a penal settlement of a person sentenced in Australia. [First recorded 1799.]

This was also known as a SECONDARY sentence and was one of the most dreaded punishments, the most severe short of execution.

> **1836** Still another method of arresting runaways is, to disguise soldiers, and send them, in such squads as not to alarm suspicion, into the interior. It is however dangerous service. Bushrangers who have plundered a house, or a market cart, are burglars or highway robbers, and of course liable, upon conviction to death. Murder of their pursuers can subject them to no worse punishment, and may procure their escape. The sale or gift of arms or ammunition to a bushranger is punishable by **transportation** to a penal settlement, or other heavy penalty; yet the fugitives provide themselves in some way with arms, and encounters with them are by no means trifles, after they have been absent long enough to become desperate.   J.F. O'CONNELL *A Residence of Eleven Years in New Holland* pp. 66–7

transportationist a person who favoured the continuance of the convict system. [First recorded 1847.]

A person who supported the system of transportation, especially the continuing influx of prisoners as a subsidised labour force, was known as a transportationist. Just how effective the system of transportation was and how good a deterrent it was were issues heavily debated in the colonies and in Britain. See also ANTI-TRANSPORTATIONIST—who tended to label transportationists with the more pejorative POLLUTIONIST.

> **1850** The great, the only argument, of the **transportationists** is, that convicts make cheap servants. This we deny, but we care very little about what may be called the *commercial* aspect of the system. That is to say, our abhorrence of convictism would not be in the slightest degree abated if its advocates could prove to demonstration that it would be the means of making the colony the richest community on earth. Riches obtained at the expense of morals are not a blessing, but a curse. *Sydney Morning Herald* 27 Sept.

> **1852** The petition asked for representative government, the abolition of transportation, and the importation of 12,000 free immigrants at the expense of

Great Britain; and it recommended the removal of the men to the colony of North Australia, or wherever they might be required. Meetings were held by different classes in several districts of the colony. In the most populous the feeling decidedly favoured abolition. Not the least important of the series were held in Launceston. ... A few **transportationists** induced a respectable shopkeeper to propose thirty-nine reasons for the continuance of transportation, but the warmth of his elocution and the frequent repetition of 'because' in an Aberdeen accent, dissolved his party in laughter. The good humoured logician acquiesced in the voice of the assembly and abandoned the cause of transportation for ever. J. WEST *The History of Tasmania* vol. 1 pp. 280–1

transportation question transportation as an issue of public debate in Australia. [First recorded 1847.]

Transportation as a system of punishment was a topic of great debate in the colonies, especially in the 1830s and 1840s. There were many opponents of the system with various arguments against it. These arguments ranged from resentment towards the cheapness of convict labour undermining the value of free labour, to moral arguments about the corrupting effects of the system on colonial society.

1852 Amongst other events which occurred between 1846 and 1850 were the attempt to re-introduce convicts into Australia, the consequent formation of the anti-convict league, the long struggle to obtain steam communication, and the passing of the Act of Parliament which separates Port Phillip, under the name of Victoria, from New South Wales, and gave representative assemblies to the three colonies of New South Wales, Victoria, and South Australia. On the **transportation question**, the Home Government was defeated, and suffered to retain only Van Diemen's Land as a settlement to which felons might be transported. *Four Colonies of Australia* p. 16

transportation system the system of transporting British prisoners to the Australian colonies as a form of punishment and reform. [First recorded 1825.]

1825 The evils and expense of the **transportation-system** would certainly be lessened, by placing the convicts more in the service of farming and grazing settlers, out of the reach of the temptations and evil communications of great towns, the establishment of which was too much the policy of the late governor. The solitary life of a shepherd, or a stockman, would gradually soften the heart of the most hardened convict; but instead of this, Governor Macquarie's system was to keep them congregated in barracks, and employed at a ration of a pound and a half of meat, and the same quantity of flour, *per diem*, upon showy public buildings, many of them works of mere supererogation. Of wretches possessed of no better means of reformation than these, it could not be expected that industrious colonists should ever be made. B. FIELD *Geographical Memoirs on New South Wales* p. 458

transported deported as a convict to a penal colony in Australia. [First recorded 1822.]

Large numbers of British and Irish prisoners were transported to the Australian penal colonies. New South Wales received transported prisoners from 1788 until transportation's official end in 1840. Van Diemen's Land was established as a place of transportation in 1803 and continued to receive convicts until 1852, with 67,000 convicts transported. The last site to which transported convicts were sent was the Swan River Colony in Western Australia established in 1850 and with transportation ending in 1868. A total of 9668 convicts were transported there.

> **1836** Beside the **transported** population, there are growing generations of Anglo-Australians, but, to do them justice, they keep wonderfully clear of the infection of guilt, though there must be its quantum of crime to every people. The girls are in special interesting; early mature, early old, and borrowing from their new and antipodal birth-place a simplicity and artlessness the reverse of the studied manners of older countries. J.F. O'CONNELL *A Residence of Eleven Years in New Holland* p. 100

transported convict a convict transported to an Australian penal colony. [First recorded 1824.]

> **1847** Until the year 1804, all our **transported convicts** were sent to New South Wales; in that year, Van Diemen's Land was first used by the British Government as a penal settlement, to relieve New South Wales from a portion of the convicts transported from Great Britain. Since the year 1840, New South Wales has received no fresh convicts; the whole number having been sent to Van Diemen's Land. J. ATKINSON *Penal Settlements and Their Evils* p. 9

transported felon = TRANSPORTED CONVICT. [First recorded 1840.]

> **1840** [Sir George Gipps to Lord John Russell] The views, developed by Captn. Maconochie in this Paper, are scarcely I fear consistent with those of Her Majesty's Government ... inasmuch as it would seem to be the intention of Government that every **transported Felon** should, during the period of at least two years, receive no indulgence whatever. *Historical Records of Australia* 1st series XX p. 527

transported offender = TRANSPORTED CONVICT. [First recorded 1829.]

> **1835** The Law of England—framed, or at least sanctioned by the Representatives of the nation, when it awarded a certain punishment to different offences—provided also, that on suffering that punishment, or obtaining the King's pardon, the offender became restored to all his original rights as a British subject, and restored to that place in society to which his own conduct

might entitle him; and the free emigrant population of the Colony readily concurred in the principle. Not so Mr. STEPHEN and Colonel ARTHUR'S nominee Legislators. By their enactment, a man who has been at any time a **transported offender**, is never to be permitted to regain his place in society; his back is to be for ever subject to the infernal lash. ... Here we find the Legislature separate them from the rest of the free community after they have regained their freedom, degrade them into a sort of *pariah* caste, and fix upon them what is worse than an indelible brand, and which death alone can efface. It is clear that they have no more right to inflict this degradation on the men who have regained their freedom, than upon those who never lost it. *The True Colonist* (Hobart) 21 Aug. p. 168

trap an officer of the law, especially a police officer. [OED records this as slang for 'One whose business it is to "trap" or catch offenders; a thief-taker; a detective or policeman; a sheriff's officer' (earliest evidence 1705), but points out that in this sense it is now Australian. In any case, most of the nineteenth-century evidence is Australian. This is an example of FLASH language that spread into more general Australian English.]

> **1832** *Prisoner to his Master*. You lousy old dog you, I'll serve you out; didn't I keep the *traps* out of your house when they were all around it? Didn't I save you from going to gaol? *Hill's Life* (Sydney) 13 Aug. p. 2

> **1846** VILLAINOUS TRAPS—The Sydney unboiled received a rap on the knuckles from Captain Innes on Monday, and a check has thereby been given to an infamous system of perjury. Every prisoner of the Crown who has lately been charged as a runaway, although he may have been but an hour or two absent from his work, the temptation of the 10s. sweetens down the oath, but a trifle of that sort is now-aday so common both in Sydney and elsewhere, as to be a matter of no surprise. *Sydney Star* 27 Mar. p. 1

treadmill a system of large wheels upon which a number of men climbed for certain periods of time as punishment. [First recorded in Britain in 1822, and in Australia in 1825.]

The treadmill, also known as a STEPPER, was a form of punishment developed in Britain and adopted in the colonies. While in Britain it had no purpose other than to punish those sentenced to it, in the Australian colonies treadmills were watermill-type wheels on which men climbed, and were generally used to grind grain into flour. In 1822 the first treadmills were built at the Carters' Barracks and were based on a design by William Cubitt, civil engineer of Ipswich, England.

> **1825** One of the larky boys, John Wilson, prisoner of the crown, was charged last Monday with having furiously driven a chaise in the streets of Sydney, to the great danger of the passengers and moreover, with wantonly and cruelly

beating the horse he was driving in the said chaise and himself in a great state of intoxication. This stepper-out was sentenced by His Honour to like-wise step it out for ten days at the **tread-mills**, newly erected at Carter's Barracks. We are pleased to observe that these discipline mills which are productive of obvious utility in grinding corn, will be the means of curbing such thoughtless behaviour as that mentioned above. The punishment consists of *perpetual climbing* without being able to *idle away a single moment*. ... The tread-mill much resembles a water-wheel. It consists of long horizontal steps and it is moved round by prisoners *treading* on the steps successively; a rail is extended at the top of the wheel, from end to end, by which the treaders support themselves. G.C. INGLETON *True Patriots All: or news from Early Australia—as told in a collection of broadsides* (1952) p. 102

1838 The **treadmill** is contiguous [to the Carters' Barracks], but is under distinct superintendence. It has one wheel, for eighteen men, and another, for ten; and when the mill is not at work, the men are kept running round a circle, in the yard. There are now about eighty men, under sentence to this punishment. J. BACKHOUSE *A Narrative of a Visit to the Australian Colonies* p. 455

triangle a tripod upon which convicts were bound and then FLOGGED. [The OED points out that this term has a military origin, and referred to 'a tripod, originally formed of three halberds stuck in the ground and joined at the top, to which soldiers were ... bound to be flogged'. First recorded in the Australian convict context in 1829.]

The Cunningham citation suggests that the term 'triangle' may have been transferred to refer to anything upon which a convict might be tied for a whipping.

1827 You may hear people even now, in gossiping over old adventures, relate their tales of shooting parrots, to make pies of, in the middle of our main street—then a crowded wood;—of felling and stumping trees on spots where our best houses stand; or of losing themselves in the thick brush then surrounding our Australian capital; while the *veteran convict* will point out to the *rogue of yesterday* the tree, still green and flourishing near the house of the naval officer, dedicated in older times to the office of a **triangle**, under whose many boughs many thousand lashes have been inflicted upon well-deserving backs. P. CUNNINGHAM *Two Years in New South Wales* pp. 70–1

1850 Four men, (at all times,) were kept at this place [prisoners' barracks], for the purpose of flogging, twenty-five lashes being given by a right handed man, and twenty-five by a left-handed—four men to administer one hundred lashes,—a bucket of water stood under the **triangles**, to revive the fainting spirits of the bleeding man or boy;—upon the fifth day all turned out to work upon the road leading to south Head. C.A. KING *Life of Charles Adolphus King* p. 15

turn in to return (an assigned convict) to official custody. [First recorded 1830.]

1831   Since the very necessary regulations introduced by Government, of making persons pay twenty shillings each for assigned servants they receive from the ships, the Police Office is not so troubled as usual with servants who used to be **turned in** at the caprice of the master, when they could be got without any expense, but now they seem determined to have their twenty shillings worth out of them.   *Sydney Morning Herald* 1 Aug. p. 4

V

Vandemonia a name for Tasmania, especially as a penal colony. [First recorded 1838.]

'Vandemonia' was a shortened form of Van Diemen's Land—it played both on the name of the colony, and on *demon*, a pejorative term for the convicts of the colony. Van Diemen's Land was the name given to the island by Abel Tasman in 1642 in honour of Antonio Van Diemen (1593–1645), governor of the Dutch East Indies. The island was settled in 1803 and became a separate colony from New South Wales in 1825. The colony's name was changed to Tasmania in 1853, after a strong push by the ANTI-TRANSPORTATION movement, whose members wanted to erase the taint of convictism suggested by names such as Vandemonia being applied to the colony.

> **1838** Without exertion from the people (who are the true rulers) nothing can thrive. I am confident, with an enthusiastic spirit on THEIR part, for the advancement of Literature and the Fine Arts, Tasmania would gradually ascend from the degradation in which she is at present plunged. She is now like a lovely rose-tree, rent asunder by the violent gust of Faction and party feeling; her bloom is fading with an untimely frost, and her branches are torn by the tempest of discord. Why is it thus? Was **Vandemonia** formed but to propagate the convict's foul breath? or was she meant to afford a peaceable abode for the industrious emigrant—a place such as that where the Poet painted Gertrude and her lover? Surely yes! and the time may YET come, when we may look up, smiling in sunshine, and our little Isle may be proclaimed once more the Queen of the South Seas. *Cornwall Chronicle* (Launceston) 15 Sept. p. 1

Vandemonian a convict who had served a sentence in Tasmania or who had escaped from a prison in Tasmania. See VANDEMONIA. [First recorded in the convict sense in 1847.]

'Vandemonian' emerged in the 1830s as a term for a person born in or a resident of Van Diemen's Land, and was initially a neutral word. However, it gradually acquired pejorative connotations because of the island's convict history, and it came to be used as a derogatory term for a Tasmanian convict. The convicts of Van Diemen's Land were heavily criticised for their unruly and wild behaviour. Those Vandemonians who were sent to Port Phillip in 1836 as a labour force were resented by the free settlers. General resentment towards the presence of convicts led to the rise of the ANTI-TRANSPORTATION movement. When many Vandemonians went to Victoria in the 1850s after gold was discovered (most were conditionally pardoned, but some were escapees), they were blamed for the increasing crime rate. In 1852 a Convicts Prevention Act was passed, which excluded from Victoria all holders of conditional pardons from Van Diemen's Land; the Act was never rigourously enforced but it might have deterred a number of ex-convicts from going there. The Act represented, however, the strong anti-convict sentiment present amongst free settlers.

1847 The **Van Diemonians** are, it appears, resolved to go to work at last, as no less than two gross robberies, accompanied by violence, were committed in the town of Melbourne on the night of Friday last. About half past eleven o'clock a bushman lodging at Mr. John Holley's, Little Flinders-street, was returning home when he was waylaid by three ruffians, who knocked him down and robbed him of a cheque for £16 and £4 in cash. About the same hour another man was subjected to almost similar treatment, in Bourke-street, near the Bazaar, but he was fleeced of only £2. *Port Phillip Herald* 12 Jan. p. 2

1857 The mining population of Ballarat, at the period of my arrival, was small in comparison to its amount when I left it, about a year and a half subsequently; perhaps it amounted in all to about ten thousand, but afforded me quite sufficient occupation in my magisterial capacity. Drunkenness, and crimes arising from its baneful effects, such as wounds and frequent homicides, were but too common; horse-stealing was an everyday occurrence; and as the diggers formed the carcase upon which the old convicts, or **Vandemonian** vultures, gathered together in their different wanderings, every description of villainy was rife at Ballarat; and no London police-office could exhibit a greater variety of crime than appeared sometimes upon our charge-sheet. J. D'EWES *China, Australia and the Pacific Islands* pp. 38–9

Vandy = VANDEMONIAN. [First recorded 1858.]

1858 'Who told you that, Tacks,' said Gimlers, turning sharply on his mate; 'whoever did, told lies; you always believe lies, Tacks'. Tacks, abashed at this attack, ventured, in a low tone, to mutter something about strangers, and 'sticking up,' and '**Vandies**'. 'A. Pendragon' (G. Isaacs) *Queen of the South* p. 80

W

watch-house a building in which suspected lawbreakers were held under temporary arrest. [First recorded in Australia in 1810.]

A term originating in Britain, a watch-house was a station for night watchmen (see NIGHT WATCH) in which they might receive and detain in custody until morning any disorderly or unruly persons brought in. In the Australian colonies, those brought in might be convicts or free persons, but convicts or ex-convicts would have made up the largest number of detainees.

> **1843** I have also caused **watch-houses** to be erected at convenient distances on the main road to Launceston and in other places, in which women as well as male prisoners who are on the march are confined by night, and thus the great evils to which women were exposed formerly in travelling under the escort of constables to or from the factories are in some degrees remedied. J. FRANKLIN *Confidential Despatch* pp. 23–4

white book see BLACK BOOK.

woods used in phrases with various verbs of motion, especially **to take to the woods**, where (of a convict) it means 'to escape from custody into the bush or unsettled areas of the colony'. See also ABSCONDING, BUSH. [First recorded 1788.]

> **1790** The criminal court was twice assembled during this month. At the first a soldier was tried for a felony, but acquitted. At the second William Harris and Edward Wildblood were tried for entering a hut at Parramatta, in which was only one man, and that a sick person, whom they knocked down, and then robbed the hut. They were clearly convicted of the offence, and, being most daring and flagrant offenders, were executed at Rose Hill, near the hut which they had robbed. These people had given a great deal of trouble before they committed the offence for which they suffered. At the latter end of the last

month they **took to the woods**, having more than once or twice robbed their companions at Rose Hill. As they were well known, the watch soon brought them in to the settlement at Sydney. D. COLLINS *An Account of the English Colony of New South Wales* (1798) vol. 1 p. 139

1801 The Irish Convicts, who had **taken to the woods** were soon apprehended; they confessed that they had formed a plan to rob the mill house, the governor's and several others, and that they were to be visited from time to time in their concealment, by their associates in the town, who were to supply them with provisions, and such information as was necessary for their safety, they also acknowledged that the attack on Randal's house was committed by them and their associates. G. BARRINGTON *A Sequel to Barrington's Voyage to New South Wales* p. 21

work in chains (or **irons**) **1** (of a convict) to wear fetters while engaged in hard labour. [First recorded 1790.]
Convicts were assigned to work in such CHAIN GANGS as a form of punishment. See also IRONS.

1790 The governor's garden had been the object of frequent depradation; scarcely a night passed that it was not robbed, notwithstanding that many received vegetables from it by his excellency's order. Two convicts had been taken up, who confessed that within the space of a month they had robbed it seven or eight times, and that they had killed a hog belonging to an officer. These were the people who were ordered by the justices to **work in irons**. D. COLLINS *An Account of the English Colony of New South Wales* (1798) vol. 1 p. 111

1849 The total consequence, meantime, of this crazy system, and of its maintenance by the most harsh and irritating administration of the law embodying it, was that hundreds of the convicts were driven to desperation. After they had been starved and scourged out of their senses on farms, and had become, through the very tyranny exercised upon them, eyesores to master or overseer, they were next transferred, if they failed to take to the bush at once, to the gangs **working in** or out of **irons** on the roads. At these places they were gradually made completely fit for the pandemoniums of the penal settlements. A. HARRIS *The Emigrant Family* (1967) p. 189

2 to cause (a convict) to labour in fetters. [First recorded 1807.]

1840 In the course of a short time, the footman grows careless, is found occasionally drunk, fills the house, in the absence of his master, with bad language—little things are missed, then things of more importance—a flogging follows, and then the tread-mill. He there finds a number of reckless companions, who teach him that he is entitled to remunerate his own services. He returns a hypocrite, and a conscientious thief. His master hesitates on further punishment, knowing he may fare still worse with a new servant, until, no longer endurable, the man is sent to an iron-gang, to **be worked in chains** for three months. W. ULLATHORNE *The Catholic Mission in Australia* p. 20

working gang a party of convicts assigned to work on a particular job or to undertake certain types of labour, often as a form of punishment. [First recorded 1790.]

Members of a working gang were in the employ of government and did work vital to building the infrastructure of the colonies, such as constructing bridges and roads.

1790 The **working gangs** being now so much reduced by the late embarkation, the hoy was employed in bringing the timber necessary for this building from the coves where it was cut down and deposited for that purpose. D. COLLINS *An Account of the English Colony of New South Wales* (1798) vol. 1 p. 101

1838 We went about two miles into the bush, to visit some **working gangs**, with whom we had a religious interview: they were seated, as has been usual on such occasion, on logs of wood, or on the ground, in a sheltered place; and we were kindly provided with a wheelbarrow, leaned against the tree, and covered with a sack, as a seat. In our visits to these men, we have generally read a chapter from the Holy Scriptures, then made a pause, and subsequently, given expression to such impressions as were made upon our minds, either in testimony or in prayer. J. BACKHOUSE *A Narrative of a Visit to the Australian Colonies* p. 275

Y

yellow frigate a HULK used for the accommodation of convicts. [First recorded 1859.]

1859 Tales of adventure now began to flow fast, and amongst them was narrated an anecdote of the notorious Melville, better known as the 'captain,' who received a sentence of nearly thirty-two years for stealing a number of horses, or as a prisoner in a chain-gang once compendiously phrased it, on being asked what brought him there, 'for stealing only a piece of rope,' exclaimed his interrogator, 'oh, sir, but there was a horse at the end of it, you must know!' But to return to Melville. After he had been for some time in fine, airy lodgings in the '**yellow frigates**,' as the hulks are called from their being painted yellow, he fancied he should like to get out; and he tried twice very hard to effect this. The first time he pretended to be suddenly inspired with very religious feelings, and wished to see the chaplain; and on the worthy gentleman coming into the cell to see this sinner, he politely requested his reverence to change clothes with him. The chaplain refused, gave the alarm, and Melville's religious feelings and the chaplain vanished together! W. BURROWS *Adventures of a Mounted Trooper* p. 127

yellow jacket a convict. [First recorded 1843.]

[From the colour of their clothing, especially the yellow-coloured jacket they wore. See CANARY.]

1843 I took up the tripod with one hand, and with my bag of dollars on my other shoulder, I walked on, but it was a weary job, and before I had gone a couple of mile I was quite knocked up. I sat down again by the road-side, and I was so tired that I was almost tempted to leave the dollars where they were, or to bury them in the bush. While I was looking about for a convenient place, I saw a lot of people coming along the road, and I soon perceived it was a road-gang of **yellow-jackets** going to work. I was terribly troubled at this, for I thought they might be tempted to make an attack upon me, so I clapped my bag into the tripod again, and sat down upon it, careless-like, till they should pass by. C. ROWCROFT *Tales of the Colonies* (1858) p. 386